This work presents the methodology and results of an international research project on second language acquisition by adult immigrants. This project went beyond other studies in at least three respects: in the number of languages studied simultaneously; in the organisation of co-ordinated longitudinal studies in different linguistic environments; and in the type and range of linguistic phenomena investigated. It placed the study of second languages and inter-ethnic discourse on a firm empirical footing.

Volume I explains and evaluates the research design adopted for the project. Volume II summarises the cross-linguistic results, under two main headings: native/non-native speaker interaction, and language production. Together they present the reader with a complete research procedure, and in doing so, make explicit the links between research questions, methodology and results.

Adult language acquisition: cross-linguistic perspectives

Volume I

Field methods

The **European Science Foundation** is an association of its fifty-nine member research councils, academies and institutions devoted to basic scientific research in twenty-one countries. The ESF brings European scientists together to work on topics of common concern, to co-ordinate the use of expensive facilities, and to discover and define new endeavours that will benefit from a co-operative approach.

The scientific work sponsored by ESF includes basic research in the natural sciences, the medical and biosciences, the humanities and the social sciences.

The ESF links scholarship and research supported by its members and adds value by co-operation across national frontiers. Through its function as a co-ordinator, and also by holding workshops and conferences and by enabling researchers to visit and study in laboratories throughout Europe, the ESF works for the advancement of European science.

This publication arises from the work of the ESF Programme on Second Language Acquisition by Adult Immigrants.

Adult language acquisition: cross-linguistic perspectives

Volume I
Field methods

Edited by
CLIVE PERDUE

Written by members of the European Science Foundation project on adult language acquisition

Published by the Press Syndicate of the University of Cambridge
The Pitt Building, Trumpington Street, Cambridge CB2 1RP
40 West 20th Street, New York, NY 10011-4211, USA
10 Stamford Road, Oakleigh, Melbourne 3166, Australia

First published 1993

Printed in Great Britain at the University Press, Cambridge

A catalogue record for this book is available from the British Library

Library of Congress cataloguing in publication data

Adult language acquisition: cross-linguistic perspectives/edited by Clive Perdue:
written by members of the European Science Foundation project on adult language
acquisition.
  v. cm.
  Includes bibliographical references and index.
  Contents: v. 1. Field methods.
  ISBN 0 521 41708 2 (v. 1)
  1. Second language acquisition. 2. Immigrants-Europe-Language.
I. Perdue, Clive. II. European Science Foundation.
P118.2.S44   1993
401'.93-dc20 92-35757 CIP

ISBN 0 521 41708 2 hardback

S A

C'est pour
       Lara

Contents

Preface

These volumes present the results of a large research project which investigated adult language acquisition, *Second Language Acquisition by Adult Immigrants*. The project set out to study the structure and success of the acquisition process in adult learners, and to discover the explanatory factors behind these phenomena. It also aimed to place the study of second languages and inter-ethnic discourse on a firm empirical footing. To achieve these aims, it undertook a co-ordinated study of ten different linguistic cases of second language acquisition in five industrialised European countries: France, Germany, Great Britain, The Netherlands and Sweden.

The research design made it possible to make systematic cross-linguistic statements from a pairwise comparison of the acquisition of one target language (TL) by speakers of different mother tongues (or 'source languages': SL), as well as the the acquisition of different TLs by different speakers of one SL. The organisation by language of the project is as follows:

Target languages

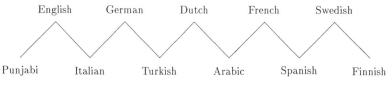

Source languages

The bulk of the data analysed in the project's different research areas (see below) comes from longitudinal case studies of four learners from each language pairing: four Italian learners of English, four Italian learners of German, four Turkish learners of German, and so on. Short biographies of these learners can be found in Appendix B of Volume I. These learners were contacted as soon as possible after their arrival in the respective target country, and their progress was monitored over two and a half years by the expedient of regular, tape-recorded or video-recorded encounters, at four- to six-week intervals. During these encounters, they participated in a whole range of data collection techniques designed to elicit data relevant for the different research areas. In order to assess any possible effect of such systematic observation of the acquisition process of these learners, data were collected and compared from a matched group of learners of Dutch, French and Swedish using similar techniques, but on three occasions only, at the beginning, middle and end of the longitudinal study. Results from this 'control study' are reported in Volume I.

Six areas of research were chosen, in order to reflect the complex linguistic tasks such learners face in an environment where, initially, they interact with native speakers of an unknown language in situations where they have to make themselves understood. These areas are: *Ways of achieving understanding, Feedback in adult language acquisition, Reference to space, Reference to time*, and two aspects of the learners' problem of arranging words: *Word formation processes*, and *Utterance structure*. The results from these studies form Volume II of this work.

As far as second language studies are concerned, this project goes beyond previous research in the number of languages – both source and target – which are simultaneously studied, in the organisation of co-ordinated, longitudinal studies in these different linguistic environments, and in the range and type of linguistic phenomena investigated. Six research teams from the Universities of Brabant, Göteborg, Heidelberg, Paris, Provence, and the Polytechnic of West London were involved. (These teams are given in Appendix A of Volume I.) The question of comparability in such a large-scale undertaking was taken very seriously in initial planning, and a year was spent in piloting all aspects of the research methodology. This work resulted in the writing of a 'Field Manual', whose main purpose was to provide a comprehensive guide to the aims and methods of the project for participating researchers. The interest shown in this manual by researchers not involved in the project resulted in its subsequent publication, *Second Language Acquisition by Adult Immigrants: A Field Manual*, Ed. C. Perdue, Newbury House, Rowley, Mass. 1984. One of the functions of Volume I of the present work is to provide a critical evaluation of the project's research design as it was set out in the Field Manual, in order both to introduce advanced students to these problems, and to inform future research.

After piloting, the main project started in 1982, and lasted until 1988. The first three years were spent collecting data and doing pilot analyses, while the second period was devoted to the systematic transcription and analysis of the data, and writing the final research reports. The main body of the data has since been stored on the computer in the form of a data archive, which is described in chapter 7 of Volume I. The data archive is a public facility, and these volumes also serve to invite any reader interested in doing research on spoken (first and second) language use, or in using longitudinal studies as a basis for language training programmes, to avail him- or herself of these data.

Many hands built this project up from a gleam in Willem Levelt's eye, to six lengthy final reports and a data archive which includes copies of all published work based on data collected during its course. Authors of the individual chapters of these volumes are given in the appropriate places, and their affiliations may be found in Appendix A (chapters without such specification were written by the editor). The editor wishes to emphasise the stimulating, sometimes conflictual, but always rewarding years of working together which lie behind these volumes, which should be seen as the product of teamwork. During the editing process, some individuals took the trouble to read and comment on different chapters, and the help of Angelika Becker, Mary Carroll, Roeland van Hout, Eric Kellerman and Wolfgang Klein is gratefully acknowledged. All remaining imperfections and inaccuracies are of course to be laid at the editor's door.

Acknowledgements

These volumes are the outcome of an enterprise which came into be-ing eleven years ago thanks to the unstinting efforts of Sir John Lyons, and Professor Willem Levelt, of the Humanities and Social Sciences Committees of the European Science Foundation (Strasbourg). It was an additional activity of the European Science Foundation, and the Max-Planck-Institut für Psycholinguistik (Nijmegen) provided the central co-ordination. Ten member organisations of the ESF con-tributed financially to the project. They are: the National Fund for Scientific Research (Belgium), the Academy of Finland, the National Centre for Scientific Research (France), the Max Planck Society (Ger-many), the Netherlands Organisation for the Advancement of Pure Research, the Norwegian Research Council for Science and the Hu-manities, the Humanities and Social Sciences Research Council (Swe-den), the Swiss National Science Foundation and the Economic and Social Research Council (United Kingdom). Moreover, the Dutch, French, German, Norwegian and Swiss organisations just mentioned generously gave extra funds to allow the data archive, the *European Science Foundation's Second Language Data Bank*, to become opera-tional. The project also benefitted from the help and support of the ESF's secretaries for the Social Sciences.

A Steering Committee of outside specialists appointed by the ESF (see Appendix A) gave freely of their expertise, and were kind enough to give detailed comments on the six final research reports before they were submitted in 1988. The staff of the Max-Planck-Institut für Psycholinguistik have given generously of their time, energy and – seemingly unlimited – good-natured cheerfulness throughout the project. Special thanks are due to Sylvia Aal for the painstaking preparation of this manuscript.

The contribution of the project's researchers who are not authors of chapters in these volumes should not go unacknowledged, as their role in this piece of collaborative research was just as important.

Thanks are due, above all, to the learners introduced in chapter

3 of Volume I, who allowed us to observe their language and life in a strange country over a period of nearly three years. The research presented here would obviously not have been possible without their co-operation, which is acknowledged with immense gratitude.

A short note on presentation

Authors' names whose work is cited in Volume I as belonging to the ESF project's bibliography, that is, published work stored in the data archive, are prefixed with *ESF*. Work by authors not so prefixed may be found in the *References* section.

The transcription conventions of the data archive are given in detail in Appendix C of Volume I. They have been somewhat simplified in the body of the text in order to improve the legibility of examples. The following conventions may be noted: + represents a short pause, and / a self-correction; sequences in another language than the TL are enclosed in * *, sequences in broad phonetic transcription are within [ ], and ' ' enclose English glosses of the examples. The glosses are intended to give the reader an idea of the meaning of the example, and are not intended as a grammatical analysis.

The abbreviations 'source/target country', for 'country where the source/target language was/is learned' are used, since some other possible expressions, such as 'mother country' or 'host country' have connotations which do not always correspond to the experiences of the learners studied here. Finally, the generic learner is sometimes a 'he', sometimes a 'she', depending upon whether the hands behind the pen of a particular chapter are predominantly male or female.

1 Aims of the ESF project

1.1 Three questions

This project examines the second language acquisition of adults who arrived to settle in industrialised European countries for economic or political reasons. In as far as such learners manage to acquire the language of the country of immigration, they do so largely through everyday interaction with their new language environment rather than through formal tuition. This language acquisition takes place in a context characterised by social, educational and linguistic problems. The project set out to study some of the latter, in the hope and conviction that a better understanding of these would eventually contribute to a better understanding of social and educational issues.

So far as social issues are concerned, the cases of acquisition studied are representative of the linguistically most important immigrant communities of Western Europe in the 1980s (communities which are moreover often numerically more important than regionally-based autochtonal minority language communities). They typify the problems of dealing with a linguistic environment on unequal terms. The study of such asymmetrical discourse, where the non-native learner has to deal with the socially dominant language and its representatives, can be seen as a contribution to the study of inter-ethnic communication (and misunderstandings), and of the links between language, social position and disadvantage.

As for educational issues, a possible definition of language pedagogy would be that it is an attempt to intervene in a naturally occurring process in order to make this process more efficient. From this point of view, the project should be seen as another in a series of studies (see chapter 2 for an appraisal) which describe and explain the acquisition process in an everyday social setting, so that pedagogical intervention may be better informed.

The project concentrates on linguistic issues: it investigates three general and inter-related questions about second language acquisition by adult immigrants, set out in its Field Manual as follows:

I.   the factors on which acquisition depends;
II. the general structure of second language acquisition with re-
     spect to

    a. the order in which elements of the language are acquired
     and
    b. the speed and success of the acquisition process;

III. the characteristics of communication between native and non-
     native speakers of a language. (ESF:Perdue 1984:3)

These volumes have a double purpose: to explain how the project set
about investigating the above questions, and to present the answers
it was able to formulate. In Volume I, the approach we take to
the study of adult second language acquisition (ALA) is explained:
why we studied the discourse activity of individual learners over time
(chapter 5) and the criteria motivating our choice of learner (chapter
3); what aspects of this activity were studied (chapter 4) and the
techniques we used (chapter 6); why comparative studies of learners
of different languages were undertaken (chapter 5). Volume II gives,
in condensed form, the cross-linguistic results of the six main research
areas of the project, grouped under two headings: native/non-native
speaker interaction, and language production. These results were
originally submitted to the ESF in the form of research reports.

We thus present the reader with a complete research procedure,
and in doing so, try to make the links between research questions,
methodology and results as explicit as possible. The reader should
then have the means to assess the potential of such a procedure for
him- or herself. This introductory chapter will be devoted to a discussion of the three initial aims of the project in turn; the discussion also
introduces the research areas, and serves as a menu for subsequent
chapters. An effort will be made throughout Volume I to evaluate
the initial aims of the project in terms of what it was possible to
achieve, so that readers may draw their own lessons for future research. In this respect, Volume I serves as an updated Field Manual,
as promised in the preface of the original in 1984.

1.2   The *learner variety* approach

The approach taken by the project corresponds closely to what is
most often called the 'interlanguage' approach (Selinker 1972), which

can be traced back to Corder (1967, see also 1971). It is characterised by two basic assumptions (differences in emphasis exist between authors) which are that:

- the internal organisation of an interlanguage (or *learner variety*) at a given time is essentially systematic, and
- the transition from one variety to the next over time is essentially systematic.

Neither of the assumptions is trivial. Neither supposes that this systematicity directly corresponds either to that of the learner's mother tongue or to that of the language to be learned. Moreover, neither precludes a certain amount of variation, which may or may not be amenable to explanation. The goal of the approach is primarily to reveal, describe and explain the 'horizontal' and 'vertical' systematicity of learner varieties *in their own right* (rather than to view them as impoverished or distorted versions of the target language). The fully-fledged target language may then be considered to be the final learner variety in which the organising principles and their interaction have attained their fullest complexity.

The project investigated this double systematicity by reconstructing from audio- and video-recordings of different types of native/learner interactions (see chapter 6), aspects of the learner's activities of production and comprehension (question III of 1.1), by tracing the evolution of these activities (question II), and by seeking to identify the factors determining the evolution observed (question I).

What is proposed in the different empirical chapters of Volume II is therefore a *reconstruction* of how relatively simple linguistic systems (that is, learner varieties) are used in communication, and of the ways in which this use modifies the system (usually prompting its complexification). Such modification occurs as learners find ways to encode (or better to encode) their communicative needs. Adults typically do not attain the 'final' learner variety of native mastery of the TL system, while nevertheless achieving a level of competence which allows them to understand and to make themselves understood in the second language (this point will be taken up in paragraph 4 below). Hence the often-made observation that the production of such learners is both relatively simple and regularly structured.

In studying this selective progress by the learner, we may be gaining important insights into the relative complexity of sub-systems of the TL itself, thanks to the learner's own analysis of the communicative possibilities of the TL input. More generally, the interplay between form and function in learner varieties is more transparent than in fully-fledged languages, and may provide a *window* on the interacting constraints on all linguistic systems in use. We will try to demonstrate that there is a limited set of interacting organisational principles which operate in learner varieties, and that the kind of interaction observed and the way it evolves can be explained by identifiable factors. The approach to ALA outlined here should therefore cast some light on the structure and functioning of linguistic systems in general.

1.3   Question I: Determining factors

For heuristic purposes, the factors potentially determining the acquisition process were divided into three broad groups in the Field Manual (p. 9):

(a) *The cognitive/perceptual disposition of the adult speaker.* This biologically given disposition is subsequently influenced by learning experience, and in particular by first language acquisition, during which the learner comes to master the specific expressive devices of the language, the semantic and cognitive categories that underlie them, and the ways they are to be used appropriately in communication (see paragraph 1.5 below). Thus it was expected that the first, or 'source' language (SL) would provide an initial linguistic and conceptual framework for the learner in his analysis of the new 'target' language (TL). Cross-linguistic influence, both in the contrastive, and in the psycholinguistic sense (Kellerman and Sharwood-Smith 1986), is traditionally held to be a major factor in ALA, and is, in principle, fully amenable to investigation.

(b) *Propensity factors* comprising the learner's communicative needs, attitudes to the TL and its speakers, and motivation to acquire the TL. Learning a second language represents a considerable cognitive effort, and it was supposed that the process would continue until some balance is reached between cognitive effort and communicative needs. These factors are not fully controllable, nor necessarily amenable to linguistic investigation, thus a choice has to be made as to what can be investigated. As will be seen, our investigation was restricted, on the whole, to the learner's need to find means to express certain essential concepts which are grammaticalised in languages.

(c) *Exposure to the language.* Two sets of inter-related factors were proposed: the first was the type and quantity of the TL with which the learner comes into contact (the 'input'); the second concerned the learner's interaction, as a social being speaking a foreign and dominant language, with native speakers of that language (the 'right to speak'). While it is, in principle, possible to control the TL input fully (in some classroom settings, for example), this is clearly not the case for an adult living in daily contact with TL speakers, where such contact has an effect on his attitudes towards them, and hence, perhaps, on his motivation to learn. Choices also have to be made here as to what may be investigated.

Such was the division proposed. Notice that it is a tripartite, not a bipartite division. The assumption was that it is not sufficient, in attempting to explain ALA, to study the interaction of a learner's cognitive-linguistic disposition and TL input; it is also necessary to explain *why* the learner would apply this disposition to new linguistic material.

As far as *cognitive/perceptual* factors are concerned, ALA studies contribute specifically to our understanding of how languages operate and are acquired, because cognitive and linguistic development are disentangled: during the acquisition of his first language, the learner has come to understand the concepts which underlie it – what modality is, agency, causality, deixis, definiteness, quantification, aspect, hearsay, etc. The learning task is then to scrutinise the new input for linguistic means to encode such concepts, at least in the early stages.

Furthermore, because the major intervening factor to be accounted for – the learner's source language – can, in principle, be controlled for, it should be possible to identify in the process (or processes) of acquiring a second language those phenomena which are specific to a particular language (or culture), and those which recur over different language pairings, allowing general statements about ALA. Although it is not the only way of attaining this goal, an investigation which compares the acquisition of many TLs by speakers of many SLs, seemed nevertheless to be an efficient way of doing so during the planning stages of the project, and still seems to be. We studied the acquisition of five TLs (Dutch, English, French, German, Swedish), by speakers of six SLs (Arabic, Finnish, Italian, Punjabi, Spanish, Turkish).

The reasoning behind this design was that if the analysis of these cases of acquisition could be made comparable, then it would be possible to make much more general statements than those available at the time. Evidence for the vertical systematicity of learner varieties (question II), for example, took the form of acquisition orders (see chapter 2); it was possible to give acquisition orders for *each* of the TLs studied. What was not available were statements generalisable to *all* of the languages studied, modified by SL-TL particularities. Some importance was given to this cross-linguistic dimension of the research design of the project, both in the language pairings (see chapter 5) and therefore in the selection of informants (see chapter 3).

Concerning *propensity factors*, it was hypothesised as a first approximation, that in his daily life, the adult immigrant acquires what is most urgently needed, in the sense that he will systematically scrutinise the TL input for the means to express those concepts which are essential to understanding and being understood. His analysis of the input therefore obeys a *communicative logic* which it is necessary to identify, and which is reflected in his own production; hence the characterisation (in paragraph 1.2 above) of the production of such learners as regularly structured, although relatively simple in relation to fully-fledged languages. This notion of communicative need is amenable to linguistic investigation, whereas other propensity factors, such as the learner's attitudes to the TL and its speakers, lend themselves less readily to such an investigation.

This brings us on to *exposure to the TL*. The environment in which learning takes place is, by definition, linguistically asymmetrical, which has the immediate consequence for the learner that he is trying to understand and make himself understood with a code that is, in many respects, different from that of his interlocutor, and this drastically increases the potential for mutual misunderstanding. It is therefore necessary to supplement the analysis of comprehension purely from the learner's point of view by also closely studying how understanding is jointly achieved in real-time discourse activity. One contemporary hypothesis was that the regularity and relative simplicity of such learner varieties are determined not only by the analytic heuristics of the learner, but also by the use of 'foreigner talk' by native TL speakers towards adult immigrants, thus denying them access to the fully-fledged code (Clyne 1984:91). Problems of exposure to the TL are further discussed in chapter 3.1.

How can the notion of 'communicative need' be operationalised for different learners with different attitudes and motivations, living in different countries? How can one define what is communicatively 'urgent'? One may assume that the absolute priorities an adult immigrant faces are (i) to recognise and re-use words to denote relevant entities, attributes, actions, etc. in the social environment and then (ii) to find means for relating these words to each other and to the context of their use (Andersen's 1984:79, 'relational meanings'). It is extremely difficult to operationalise the study of (i). Although one may attempt to measure the richness and variety of a learner's vocabulary in specific tasks over time, it is quite another problem to assess his actual vocabulary and its exact relation to the social environment.[1] The acquisition of means to express relational concepts (ii) is less bound to particular personal circumstances and motivations; for example, a capacity to refer to the relevant entities and to contextualise them for the interlocutor in time and space is crucial to successful spoken interaction whatever the external circumstances. It may be assumed that an adult language learner is capable of performing (producing and understanding) such communicative tasks in his first language. Hence, we may gain some insight into the vertical systematicity of the acquisition process as well as into the horizontal organisation of learner varieties by looking at the way such tasks are accomplished at various stages of the acquisition process.

However, the interplay between such basic operations as reference, or setting in time and space, and their grammatical encoding in individual languages is complex. Languages have very different means of expressing a given operation, so that, although it may be hypothesised that the adult initially seeks to find new, not to say novel ways of encoding the concepts he has from his SL, he may still learn to express new distinctions during the course of the acquisition process (see von Stutterheim 1986, for the expression of Turkish temporal concepts in learner German). However, the adult learner's attempts at such communicative tasks provide an initial basis for comparative cross-linguistic analysis, as we shall see below.

These preliminary considerations led to a research design (see chapters 3 and 5) where a number of specific communicative tasks were analysed in different discourse settings, and where *cross-linguistic influence* was systematically controlled for.

---

[1] At least, the project's attempts in this direction were certainly not crowned with success (see chapter 5.1).

1.4   Question II: Order of acquisition, speed and success

A salient characteristic of untutored adult learners is that they achieve very different degrees of language mastery. Few, it seems, achieve native-like proficiency. Some stop (or, to use Selinker's, 1972, term, 'fossilise'[2]) at a very elementary level. Others come between the two extremes. These large differences in success naturally raise the following questions:

> Are we researching a unitary process, or different processes showing real structural differences? In either case, what are the factors that are responsible for the very different tempos and end-points of acquisition that are observed?

These questions can be reformulated from the point of view of the end-product:

> Are the different fossilised varieties the outcome of different acquisition processes, or do they present different stages in one acquisition process which, due to factors which we wish to understand, comes to an early halt in some cases, whilst reaching a higher level in other cases?

Many studies have been made in order to understand the reasons for the differential success of adult language learners; some are discussed in chapters 2 and 3 in relation to the criteria adopted for selecting informants for this project. Suffice it to say here that the above questions make clear the link between the first and second research aims of the project (describe the individual acquisition process and identify the factors determining it) and point to the necessity of undertaking *longitudinal studies* (studies of the same individuals over time) from as near as possible to the onset of this process and until the end-point is reached.

When the project started, there were very few longitudinal studies published (see chapter 2), thus most developmental statements were extrapolations from cross-sectional studies (studies of different learners at different stages of proficiency). It was important, in an attempt to characterise the factors motivating individual development and provoking fossilisation, to gauge the relative success of a learner variety *in use, over time.* By following the development of the same

---

[2]Selinker's term has now become generally used. Selinker and Lamendella (1979) distinguish between stabilised and fossilised varieties, a distinction which can be ignored for present purposes.

individuals over time, it is at least, in principle, possible to answer the questions formulated above. We now go on to discuss the context of untutored adult language acquisition.

1.5 Question III: Language in use

Adult immigrants find themselves in the seemingly paradoxical position of having to learn the language in order to communicate, and of having to communicate, often in difficult circumstances, in order to learn the language. In practice, however, their mastery of a first language instantly allows them to draw on a rich repertoire of non-verbal and discursive skills for conveying and inferring meaning which are not (or are only partially) bound to their source language. These skills are those which allow the learner to use the SL repertoire appropriately in verbal interaction, allowing him for example to check for differences in background knowledge and for communicative success. In TL communication, they allow him to maximise the efficiency of a restricted repertoire of lexical items and grammatical rules.[3] Analysis then starts by putting oneself 'in the learner's shoes', and trying to understand what his communicative intent was, or what he understood, in a given context at a given time. It is in this sense that the approach was said, in paragraph 1.2 above, to be a *reconstruction* of selected aspects of the learner's activities of production and comprehension.

This approach can be illustrated by just one example from the project's pilot study. A learner of German had to give an instruction to a TL-speaker to put an ashtray into a bag. He said:

(1) *aschenbecher + tasche*

(1) contains no mention of the addressee, no verb and no determination of the objects denoted. But the instruction was successful because from the point of view of non-verbal skills, both speech partners knew that the utterance was an instruction, and that ashtrays can go into bags. The ashtray and the bag were unambiguously identifiable in the speech situation and separated at the time of utterance. From the point of view of discourse skills, the word order of (1) is iconic:

---

[3]These skills include so-called 'communication strategies'. As Kellerman (1991: 144) demonstrates, 'such strategies are part and parcel of normal native speaker communicative life' and 'constitute a ready-made resource to be exploited in the second language'. The use of such strategies emerges particularly clearly in learner data precisely because the learner's linguistic repertoire is limited.

reference is first made to the entity to be moved before the entity designating its position at goal. Order of mention is used to mark the semantic relations of *theme* (the entity to be situated) and *relatum* (the entity in relation to which it is situated, see Volume II:I.4) precisely because both are identifiable in situation (ESF:Carroll 1990). Had the theme not been identifiable, because one of a set, hidden, or not previously mentioned, then it would have been necessary to localise it through an identifiable relatum. Hence, the hypothetical utterance:

(1')   *da + aschenbecher*

would be interpreted in situation to mean that in the place referred to by *da* ('there'), there is an ashtray . From the point of view of object reference, the denoting of the ashtray in a shared communicative context, by a simple noun in the topic (1) or the focus (1') component of the utterance (see Volume II:I.1), carries here the functional load of the TL definite (1) or indefinite (1') article. In (1), there is no reference to time, as the act of giving an instruction implies a time after this act. Reference to the action and the exact spatial configuration at goal are left implicit; they are inferrable once theme and relatum have been defined in the speech situation (cf. the *canonical location* of Volume II:I.4).

The type of successful reliance on situation and context illustrated by this simple example has as a consequence that the analyst's understanding of untutored language acquisition will be incomplete unless he studies how the learner's variety is put to use in *interaction* at a given time, i.e., how a restricted repertoire of lexical items and grammatical rules is applied, and how the repertoire interacts with more general communicative skills, and how and why this *interaction* of rules and skills changes over time. These considerations clearly justified studying the first two questions of the project discussed above in the context of (III): language in use.

There are two uses of the term 'interaction' in the previous paragraph: as an abstract space where the partially covert cognitive process of building up a new repertoire takes place in 'interaction' both with the already established native system and with exposure to aspects of the target system through a concrete activity called 'linguistic interaction'.[4] Hence there is a double constraint, both initially

---

[4]In contexts where this ambiguity may prove confusing, we shall on occasion call this latter 'interaction', 'discourse activity', and reserve the term 'interaction' for the covert process of elaboration of a learner variety.

and over time, on the acquisition process: as Giacobbe puts it, the process is determined by:

> the limits of the (learner) system already in place on the one hand, and the requirements of the discourse activity on the other. The construction of the system thus depends on the discourse activity, and conversely, the history of the construction of the system governs potential success in discourse activity and the means developed to achieve it.[5] (ESF:1989:14-15)

Understanding acquisition can thus be seen as understanding the interplay between these two 'interactive spaces'. The learner communicates in order to learn, and vice versa, but the process is constrained both by communicative needs and by the potentialities of the repertoire that he has.

The organisation of a learner's variety at a given time is thus doubly constrained: extrinsically and intrinsically (see chapter 2.1 for these terms). It is *extrinsically* constrained by the type and quantity of TL input that has become available for analysis, in and by discourse activity. If Clyne's 'foreigner talk' hypothesis were correct (see paragraph 1.3 above), many of the explicit relational means of the TL would simply be unavailable for the learner, which is a further reason for studying the acquisition process through language in use. It is *intrinsically* constrained in that the learner cannot deal with all aspects of the TL input, just as he cannot transfer all his linguistic knowledge (rules, or, as we shall see, even words) until the system in construction is 'ready' for them. Each successive learner variety has its specific constraints, which in turn constrain the direction in which it can develop. For example, if the organisation of the SL comprises a subject, and subject-verb agreement, then this knowledge is of no practical use for the analysis of the TL (as we shall see) until the learner has been able to differentiate verbs from other categories in the input and has acquired some means to mark the relationship between the verb and its arguments.

The learner's activity of system construction may be assumed to provoke variable behaviour. The hypotheses which he formulates and tests leave traces in discourse activity such as self-editing, partial understanding, lack of understanding, and a 'selective deafness' to

---

[5]'les limites du système déjà construit d'une part, les exigences de la situation d'interaction langagière de l'autre. La construction du système est ainsi dépendante de la situation d'interaction; et réciproquement, les possibilités de réussite et les modalités développées pour le faire, dépendent de la façon dont le système fut construit.'

pedagogic attempts on the part of the TL speaker. This variability, which has received little attention in ALA cross-sectional studies, was at least partially controlled for in the project (see chapter 5), thanks to its longitudinal design.

1.6   Summary: aims and research areas

The approach taken in this project involves a reconstruction of how a learner deals with selected communicative tasks in spoken discourse activity. These tasks are spelled out in chapter 4: they are defined in relation to recurrent aspects of discourse activity which need to be comparable across learners and languages, and over time, if firm generalisations are to be made. Hence the need for comparative, cross-linguistic, longitudinal analyses.

The research areas chosen for study reflect the above perspective in that they are tasks the type of learner we are studying *has to* find the means to achieve:

- whatever his social circumstances, his primary exposure to the language is through discourse activity, basically in everyday contacts with native speakers. He will need to give himself the wherewithal to understand the new language from participation in such communication, by taking turns in a conversation, using the TL-interlocutor as a resource, and indicating non-understanding. Hatch and her students (see Hatch 1980 and the references there) were among the first to study how dialogic discourse is structured and acquisition proceeds in ALA. Hatch points to the double task facing the learner in 'communicating by learning':

  > The adult learner must do two things: (1) solicit enough ...to figure out the topic, the probable questions being asked on the topic...and at the same time (2) keep the partner in the conversation. (Hatch 1980:187)

- in making himself understood, he will need to arrange the TL items he has in larger units: phrases, utterances, stretches of discourse. These units need to be situated, on different levels, in relation to the here-and-now of the speech situation, and spatial, temporal and other relationships need to be drawn between them.

Such tasks are simply listed here, and obviously need much more precise specification. They are discussed in greater detail in chapter 4, and fully described in Volume II, which is divided into two parts: production, and interaction. They characterise a type of cross-linguistic study of learner varieties where the potentially generalisable phenomena involve how the learner attempts communicative tasks which are recurrent in spoken discourse activity, whether or not these attempts are 'idiosyncratic' (Corder 1971) in relation to TL grammars.

The relationship between learner varieties and the TL grammar is not straightforward. The suggestion was made in 1.2 above, that learners' idiosyncracies are best understood neither as distortions of some aspect of the TL, nor as the TL with bits 'missing'. If the learner variety is systematic, as we have supposed in 1.2, it follows that the words and constructions which form this systematicity cannot be put into one-to-one correspondence with the 'equivalent' words or constructions of a different system: the TL system. They have their own functional logic. As von Stutterheim and Klein put it:

> A structural analysis will overlook or cannot cope with the majority of those cases where learners have built up a system of their own by using L2 structures with meaning or function other than those of the L2. (1987:193)

It is obviously unrevealing to reconstruct the learner's 'communicative intention' in example (1) as (the German equivalent of): 'You put the ashtray into the bag' and then analyse (1) as containing the 'object' and 'goal' complement of the 'implicit', or 'deleted' verb *put*. But the nearer a learner's production appears to be to the TL, the more tempting it becomes to imagine a 'corresponding' TL version and use the analytic categories relevant to the latter version to analyse the former. The 'closeness fallacy' (ESF:Klein and Perdue 1989) is insidious and ubiquitous, and leads inevitably to false dichotomies such as 'error/non-error'. This is why it is necessary to capture the systematicity of the learner's variety *in its own right*, in the quest for analytic categories relevant for the description of hitherto unexplored linguistic systems, and the way they function.

This we will proceed to do in Volume II, after examining the problem in somewhat more detail in chapter 4 of this volume. First, though, we compare our aims and approach to those of related work in ALA (chapter 2), and explain (chapter 3) how these aims, informed by the lessons of previous work, led to the selection of the informants.

2 Previous longitudinal studies

2.1 Introduction

Systematic research into ALA began barely twenty years ago, but the period has seen an explosion of theoretical and empirical studies of the phenomenon. The purpose of this chapter is not to provide a critical survey of all published work. Excellent general introductions exist which fulfill this function, for example, Klein (1984/6/9), Ellis (1985), McLaughlin (1987) and Larsen-Freeman and Long (1991). Rather, a limited number of studies will be presented which are relevant to the ESF project, in order to assess their methodology, findings, and the explanations for these findings. 'Relevant' means either that a study influenced the original thinking on the project, or that a study gave itself comparable research areas, or both. The emphasis will be on the (few) published longitudinal studies of acquisition in a social setting, or cross-sectional studies which make developmental predictions about ALA in a social setting. Space precludes any discussion of non-empirical work on ALA, on ALA in a classroom setting, and on the discourse activity of the bilingual speaker in inter-ethnic communication.

Three major projects and one thesis on untutored second language acquisition by adult immigrants had been completed by the piloting stage of the ESF project:

- on the acquisition of TL-German, the *Heidelberger Forschungsprojekt 'Pidgin Deutsch'* (henceforth 'HPD'; see Klein and Dittmar 1979) conducted a cross-sectional study with a population of forty-eight Spanish and Italian workers, and *Zweitspracherwerb italienischer und spanischer Arbeiter* (ZISA) conducted a cross-sectional study with forty-five Italian, Spanish and Portugese workers (Clahsen, Meisel and Pienemann 1983), as well as a longitudinal study with twelve learners (see Clahsen 1984, 1987; Meisel 1987). Work in the Netherlands by Jansen and Lalleman (1980a, b), Jansen *et al.* (1981), Lalleman (1983) and Belder *et al.* (1980)

adopt aspects of HPD's methodology. ZISA's framework has been applied to other types of acquisition (Pienemann 1984, Pienemann *et al.* 1988; Nicholas 1984, 1987). Meisel (1991) provides a recent evaluation of ZISA's results. Jordens (1988) is a major critical discussion of the acquisition of Dutch and German syntax, based on the previous studies.

– on the acquisition of English: Cazden, Cancino, Rosansky and Schumann (1975) conducted a ten-month longitudinal study (henceforth the 'Harvard study') with six native speakers of Spanish: two children, two adolescents and two adults. Schumann's (1978) study of one of the adults, and subsequent work by Hilles (1986, 1991) on this corpus are summarised below. Huebner's twelve month longitudinal study of an adult Hmong speaker was published in 1983, during the early stages of the ESF project. Sato (1990) gives detailed comparisons between Huebner's study and her own. Despite the age of her informants (pre-adolescence), Sato's work will be discussed for this reason, and also because a major part of her study – on the marking of past time reference – overlaps with the study of temporality of the ESF project.

The vast majority of the work published by the planning stage of the project thus concerned the acquisition of English and German, with some studies of Dutch. Outside the project's piloting work, there was little or no comparable work on the untutored acquisition of Swedish or French,[1] and above all, no cross-linguistic studies.

The areas of linguistic research at this period were overwhelmingly concerned with morphology and syntax (however, ZISA also dealt with general aspects of ALA such as foreigner talk and pidginisation, for example Meisel 1980, and ZISA and HPD produced smaller studies on the lexicon). Indeed, the data from the major projects are still actively fuelling current syntactic debates – in particular as regards two phenomena which are of interest for the first chapters of Volume II: the 'null-subject' and related grammatical phenomena (Rizzi 1982), and the acquisition of word order (these two phenomena being themselves related in the most researched linguistic cases of acquisition, the acquisition of English or German by speakers of null-subject Romance languages).

As we mentioned in chapter 1, explanations are sought in ALA studies not only for the order in which items are acquired relative to each other, but also for the overall tempo of the acquisition process, in par-

---

[1]Noyau (1986) examines the varieties of two long resident Spanish immigrants at two points in time. These informants were advanced learners.

ticular its slowing down and stopping. We will organise this chapter around Py's (1982:9) distinction between 'extrinsic' and 'intrinsic' explanations, as it reflects to a large extent, the chronology of this research: from extrinsic (psycho-sociological, socio-biographical) explanations to intrinsic explanations, be they couched in processing, grammatical or functional terms. We will discuss each type of explanation in turn.

2.2   Extrinsic explanations

Extrinsic analyses attempt to characterise the developmental stages attained by learners, to identify the factors which have determined this overall attainment, and the ways in which these factors interact.

As development in the German (and Dutch) studies is mainly described in terms of mastery of different aspects of sentence syntax, it may be helpful for some readers to look at the short account of Dutch and German word order in chapter 5.2, before the discussion of the results of these studies. The account is obviously simplified, but is nevertheless adequate for most of the acquisitional results.

Heidelberger Forschungsprojekt 'Pidgindeutsch'
The HPD study attempts to relate certain measurable factors – 'bias factors' such as linguistic origin, age, previous schooling, professional qualification, sex; and 'environmental' factors such as contacts with Germans at work or in leisure time, abode, duration of stay – with their subjects' linguistic performance, measured from a corpus of 100 sentences per subject by an index of frequently used rules derived from a variety grammar (see Klein and Dittmar 1979, chapter 3).

The bundles of rules which most clearly reflect inter-individual variation, constituting an individual's 'syntactic profile', are: presence versus absence of the sentence subject; presence versus absence of the verb; verbal auxiliaries and complements; degree of pronominalisation; complexity of the noun phrase and the type of determiner; type of adverbial phrase/clause. HPD draw developmental implications from their study, with the caveat that cross-sectional studies do not allow stronger statements than 'certain regularities *are usually acquired* in a linguistically definable order' (Klein and Dittmar 1979:125. Italics theirs).

The developmental extrapolations are these: subjects and verbs are supplied more and more frequently, these latter tending to be accompanied first by a modal verb, then by an auxiliary (but never both, as would be possible in the TL). The internal structure of the adverbial phrase complexifies, and there is a slight decrease in its use by the most advanced learners, which is explained by the concomitant increase in use of auxiliary and modal verbs to mark the temporal and modal contextualisation of the sentence, hitherto supplied by initial adverbials. Within the noun phrase, simple nouns (proper names or bare common nouns) are attested before (third person) pronouns. For lexical NPs, first of all the bare noun is used; then there is a two-item stage where numerals, quantifiers and, later, articles accompany the noun; thirdly, adjectives accompany nouns, and finally, three-item combinations occur. This latter group of findings is broadly replicated in a study of the NP development of Turkish learners of Dutch by Belder *et al.* (1980). For pronominalisation, there is a clear tendency, more closely studied by Klein and Rieck (1982), to replace zero by pronouns. This development is limited to supplying third person subject pronouns (the first and second person *ich* and *du* are used right from the beginning), and oblique (object, possessive) cases represent a serious learning problem. Klein and Rieck hypothesise that learners build a 'basic system' consisting of the first and second person pronouns, plus a single, all-purpose third person form, and an oblique form for the speaker (*bei mir*), this system being motivated by the requirements of the discourse activity (conversation).

HPD relate these tendencies, albeit with limited success, to word order, and in particular to the place of the verb in the sentence. Analysis is restricted to sentences with overt verbs and subjects, as the variability in the other sentences is too great: 'it has not been possible to describe these variations in a systematic manner' (Klein and Dittmar 1979:151). For the lowest groups, interpretation becomes difficult given the very small number of occurrences; only 13 out of 600 sentences in the lowest proficiency group have both verb and subject. Overall, the verb most often occupies the second position of the sentence; the most frequent exceptions concern sentences where the verb is in third position, preceded by both subject and a contextualising adverbial (see above, the decrease in use of this latter). Sentences which clearly contain a verb in final position (i.e., sentences with at least the constituents $X - V_{fin} - Y - V_{inf}$, where X or Y is the subject, and both X and Y are filled, see chapter 5.2) are rare overall, and non-existent in the early stages. Sentence-final particles (the 'separable prefixes' of ZISA's stage 3 below) are generally very rare.

Subsequent work by Klein (1981) and Dittmar (1984) concentrated 'in a systematic manner' on the analysis of the very early stages of acquisition, in terms of 'theme-rheme structure' (Klein), or of development from Givón's (1979) 'pragmatic' to 'syntactic mode' of expression (Dittmar). In this type of account, subject-predicate structure takes over from an initial topic-comment structure, and the initial form-meaning relationships become less transparent as more morphosyntactic markings are acquired. Dittmar illustrates this pragmatic mode of organisation by the learners' use in the elementary stages of contextualising adverbials of time and modality, as opposed to modal verbs and verb inflexion. Such a description will be further discussed in chapter 4.2.

As for the determining factors they investigated, HPD's results indicated that length of stay in the target community played some role during the first two years. After two years, this factor is overruled by others: the higher a learner was rated on the syntactic index, the more likely he/she was to have been aged twenty-two years or less at immigration, to have contacts with Germans at work and, more importantly, during leisure time, to have attended school and to have a formal professional qualification. HPD chose not to consider *propensity factors* such as learners' motivation and attitudes as the possible measurement criteria were questionable.

Zweitspracherwerb italienischer und spanischer Arbeiter
ZISA attempt to account not only for the degree of overall development, but also the variation that is observed between learners who can by certain criteria be deemed to be at the same stage of language development. An implicationally related series of developmental stages is defined, based on the re-ordering of words from a hypothesised underlying canonical order – subject-verb-object (svo) – from which their learners start: this developmental sequence is given in 2.3 below.

All learners (with a Romance SL acquiring German) go through some or all of these stages. However *environmental factors*, such as the social setting, acting on *propensity factors* (different learner-types characterised by their 'segregative versus integrative orientation') determine which strategies of acquisition and use a given learner will favour: elaborative simplification (in order to develop the acquired system further) or restrictive simplification (in order to facilitate the use of the system acquired). Simplification is regularly manifested by the *deletion* of items. The socio-psychological factors thus determine not only the degree of overall mastery of the TL, as with HPD, but also certain characteristics of the transitional stages: 'systematic variation within the developmental stages depends on combinations of extra-linguistic factors, such as motivation and contact' (Clahsen 1984:236).

The Harvard study

The Harvard study also identified, for TL-English, a developmental sequence concerning the auxiliary in declarative and interrogative, affirmative and negative sentences. For the auxiliary, an order of appearance was calculated. *Is* (copula), *can* and *do* were the first three to appear in all learners' production, although *do* never reached criterion for Schumann's informant Alberto. 'Criterion' refers to the morpheme order technique of calculating the appropriate appearance of a morpheme in a TL-obligatory context for that morpheme (Brown's 1973, criterion of 90 per cent suppliance for three successive samples where there are five or more obligatory contexts in each, is the most frequently applied). The appearance of these auxiliaries is reflected in the other developments: 'yes/no' and 'wh-' questions initially have no subject-auxiliary inversion, inversion appears selectively, starting with *is*. The order of acquisition for negation is, firstly, pre-verbal *no* and unanalysed *dont*, then aux+neg constructions appear initially with *is/can*; finally, *do* is analysed (*don't, doesn't, didn't*).

Alberto's development (Schumann 1978) had fossilised by the end of the longitudinal study – that is, after fourteen months in the United States – and his production shared surface features with pidgin languages. He never went beyond the first stages of the development described above; moreover, he marked neither the possessive nor the regular past, and his use of progressive *-ing* was erratic (his use of the regular plural, however, almost reached criterion). This early fossilisation was explained by an interaction of *propensity and environmental factors*. The socio-psychological distance of a learner from the TL and its speakers is determined by social factors such as the size and cohesion of the SL community in the target country, its relationship of dominance, non-dominance or subordination to the TL community, and these communities' attitudes to each other; and by psychological factors such as resolution or not of culture and language shock, stress, integrative versus instrumental motivation for TL acquisition, ego permeability. The constellation of these factors in the case of Schumann's subject defined his psycho-sociological distance from English as great. This distance accounts for this learner's restriction of his TL use to Smith's (1972) 'communicative function' of language, in situations exclusively involving the transmission of referential, denotative information, which in turn accounts for early fossilisation at a low level of language proficiency. Dittmar (1984, see above) also appeals to the passage from the 'communicative function' to the 'integrative and expressive functions' proposed by Smith, in explaining the passage from the pragmatic to the syntactic mode:

> ...the 'integrative function' (interaction type: person qua social identity – person qua person) and the 'expressive function' (interaction type: person qua person – person qua person) would be the exclusive reserve of expanded language varieties with sufficient stylistic flexibility. (Dittmar, *ibid.*:246)

Summary

These (relatively) early studies described sequences of morpho-syntactic development towards one TL ('acquisition orders'). They can be said to have isolated and tested empirically a number of factors which may determine the overall TL mastery achieved by different learners and, to a certain extent, the inter-relationship of these factors. The factors researched by these projects which are also relevant for the planning of the ESF project will be further discussed in chapter 3. Briefly, they are:

- *cognitive/perceptual factors* of age and educational background. SL influence is also relevant. It was investigated in these early studies, but not systematically, as we shall see in more detail below (2.4);
- *propensity factors* including the role of motivation and attitudes to the TL and its speakers, in determining the end-point of acquisition, or specific types of synchronic, inter-subject variation. The study of communicative need is also relevant. In the studies reviewed, it was conducted at the general, inter-group level of satisfying the 'communicative function' of language, or of 'leisure time activities with Germans';
- *exposure to the TL*. This factor was principally studied from a quantitative point of view. A telling example of this is Meisel's (1980) study of pidginisation and foreigner talk, which provides de-contextualised lists of recurrent features of foreigner talk across languages and contact situations, while noting that the frequency of use of such talk to learners is generally overestimated.

What these studies did not achieve, with one important exception discussed below, was an explanation of *why* development proceeds, and *why* the characteristics of a developmental sequence are as they are. In the end, the explanations of the developmental sequences described above take the form of correlations between bundles of rules defining a level of language achievement, and bundles of extralinguistic factors. Achievement is *essentially* determined by social factors (HPD), or socio-psychological factors (ZISA, Schumann).

The problem then is that these extrinsic (socio-biographical, socio-psychological) factors are not the place to look in order to explain what determines the detailed characteristics of the course of the acquisition process. While it is of fundamental importance to identify the extra-linguistic factors determining the end-point of the process, doing so only provides a partial answer to the second research question of the ESF project, *order of acquisition, speed and success*. That is, it is impossible to see how these extrinsic factors promote acquisition step by step. The quantification of *exposure to the TL*, for example, cannot specify the way in which relevant linguistic input is provided for the motivated learner at a given time. And the quantification of *motivation*, accordingly, will not explain why some specific item or rule was, at that time, perceived as relevant by the learner. What is needed is a move from the study of the relationship between the type and quantity of TL input and overall proficiency, to a more qualitative study of the input. Schumann's and Dittmar's appeal to the 'communicative' and other functions of language lacks any consideration of the dynamics of the relevant interactions which could explain the use of the linguistic features actually observed. What is involved here is the question of how acquisition is achieved *in discourse activity*. This move reflects the elaboration of the third broad question posed by the ESF project, *language in use*, in relation to its second question, *order of acquisition* (see chapter 1.4-5).

In the following paragraph, we discuss some proposed intrinsic explanations for this type of question, which involve *cognitive/perceptual factors* such as cross-linguistic influence and processing strategies, and will also look at a more detailed, qualitative type of analysis of a learner's exposure to the TL.

2.3 Intrinsic explanations

Source language influence
Source language influence could not systematically be investigated in the three major studies described above because they observed

either speakers of one Romance language (Spanish) acquiring one TL, English, or speakers of related source (Romance) languages acquiring one TL, German. Hence, no *tertium comparationis* was available, for example the acquisition of the TL in question by speakers of a different, unrelated SL. Hence the inconclusive nature of appeals to SL influence. Schumann, for example, notes the surprisingly correct use of the English plural by Alberto, and appeals to the positive influence of the SL to explain this plural marking. Such an appeal is open to dispute, however. Is Alberto's relative success due to his perception of the similarity of plural marking in Spanish and English? or is he experiencing the same intrinsic difficulties of English as child L1 acquirers, who supply the plural before the possessive?

The available SL-TL configurations do however explain the subsequent interest in null-subjects, and generative accounts of word order in verb-second languages. The data provide a rich testing ground for these phenomena.

One series of studies whose design did allow the systematic investigation of SL influence, albeit from a cross-sectional perspective, was Jansen and Lalleman (1980a,b), Jansen *et al.* (1981), and Lalleman (1983). Using a similar methodology to HPD's (cross-sectional, with proficiency level determined by a syntactic index, from a corpus of 100 utterances per learner), these researchers compared word order phenomena in the production of eight Turkish and eight Moroccan learners of Dutch.

Jansen *et al.* observe (see rules I and III of chapter 5.2) that the lexical part of the verb may 'alternate', occurring in second or final position in Dutch main clauses, and in final position in subordinate clauses. Furthermore Dutch (and German) allows pre- and postposition alternations for respectively location: *op de weg/in de kamer* ('on the road/in the room'); and direction *de weg op/de kamer in* ('up the street/into the room'). Turkish is typologically a verb-final language with postpositions, whereas colloquial Moroccan is verb-second with prepositions. The predictions are then that these learners will analyse the Dutch input for – and find – the typological possibilities of their respective SL, and overgeneralise these possibilities.

So few subordinate clauses were found in the corpus that verb placement analysis had to focus on main . Overall, the Turks use verb-final position significantly more than the Moroccans, and the higher they were rated on the syntactic index, the fewer verb-final structures they used. The SL was therefore held to guide initial processing strategies for word order. On the other hand, both groups of learners preferred prepositions from the outset. The difference between the groups of learners was most noticeable in the significantly greater omission of prepositions by the Turks. Here, SL influence was hypothesised to be indirect, provoking 'avoidance' of preposition use on the part of the Turks.

Processing complexity: ZISA
The exception to the generalisation made above about the lack of detailed examination of the links between linguistic development and determining factors is the developmental sequence of ZISA (see 2.2 above). The following summary of the developmental sequence is taken from an article by Clahsen:

> *Stage 1:* SVO
> None of the German word order rules is applied. The constituents appear in the fixed linear order:
> NP (AUX/MOD) V (NP) (PP)
>
> *Stage 2:* ADV-PREP
> Adverbials (=adverbs and prepositional phrases) are moved into sentence-initial position.
>
> *Stage 3:* PARTICLE
> Nonfinite parts of discontinuous verbal elements are moved into sentence-final position. This rule ... applies to the following structural contexts:
>
> - Separable prefixes
> - Participles in AUX+V structures
> - Infinitives in MOD+V structures
>
> *Stage 4: (Subject-Verb)* INVERSION
> Following preposed complements and in interrogatives the subject appears immediately after the finite verb.
>
> *Stage 5:* ADV-VP
> Adverbials can be placed optionally between the finite verb and the object.
>
> *Stage 6:* V END
> In embedded sentences the finite verb appears in clause-final position. (Clahsen 1984: 224-5)

ZISA's longitudinal study replicates the results of the cross-sectional study, with the following differences of detail: stages 1 and 2 are less clearly separable, as are stages 4 and 5; a topicalisation (object-fronting) rule is observed contemporaneously with stage 3, as is a rule of subject extraposition to final position, which is a precursor of INV (stage 4).

Whereas overall achievement and individual variation within one developmental stage depend on extra-linguistic factors, the developmental sequence itself can be explained by an appeal to the learner's language processing strategies, which operate on syntactic constructions.

ZISA describe learners' production by means of phrase structure rules, which give underlying structures. The closest fit between these and surface orders is [NP [V NP ...] PP], whence the characterisation of the 'canonical' (stage 1) structure as S–V–O–ADV. Constituents then move from this structure, subject to constraints which become less severe the more advanced the learner. Learners initially use a canonical order strategy, which prefers 'direct mappings of underlying structures' (*ibid.*:239); if constituents are moved, preferred orders are those which do not interrupt adjacency of related constituents (such as the verb and the direct object), i.e. an 'initialisation/finalisation strategy'; finally, embedded clauses pose particular processing problems, hence a permutation rule such as V END is acquired late. 'Processing complexity results from reorderings and restructurings of various levels of underlying linguistic units' (*ibid.*:221). These reorderings are not described as transformations because of the categorial nature of both the optional and obligatory transformational rule. Rather, probabilities of movement are calculated, with 'developmental stage' being defined as when a learner uses one of the above rules systematically. The 'systematicity criterion' is defined as use in a minimum of five possible contexts in one data set.

ZISA's approach provides a basis for generalisability, in that processing constraints provide an independent explanation for the development observed, and can be applied (and have been, see Pienemann 1984, Pienemann *et al.* 1988), to other developmental sequences in other languages and learning situations. Moreover, it makes an attempt to describe the structure of the learners' varieties in their own right: the patterns of stages 1 and 2, and those resulting from the object-fronting and subject-extraposition rules are learner-specific constructions.

One may however ask whether all the descriptive apparatus (levels of structuring, TL-functions, 'empty' categories in surface utterances with 'deleted' constituents) provides an accurate description of learners' initial attempts to produce meaningful utterances in a new language. ZISA have no problem with the notion of knowledge of the TL which is available thanks to knowledge of equivalent phenomena in the SL:

> The learner 'knows' of course that there must normally be a verb in each sentence and that it carries morphological information; in his/her L1 this is quite the same...(Meisel *et al.* 1981:115)

The deletion of items as a result of learners' simplification strategies is therefore unproblematic for ZISA, and verb supply would not be an indication of development, as it is really 'there' all the time.

The problem is that processing capacity is in fact required to do a double job. Not only does it constrain the developmental sequence, but it also decides what aspects of a learner's knowledge are immediately transferable, and what aspects have to be re-learned: learners know about subject-verb inversion from their SL, for instance, and yet have to acquire it in TL German. And the result is circular: what is attested early is transferred, what is attested later is re-learned.

The motivation for the movements out of the underlying structure poses a further problem. The early movements are pragmatically motivated. Thus for adverb-fronting, Meisel (1987) entertains the explanation of a 'stage-setting' function for its acquisition, and Clahsen appeals to 'pragmatic production strategies' (1984:241 n.5) as an explanation for the extraposition of the subject. The nature of the motivation changes, however, for PART, INV and V-END. A grammatical analysis of the TL categories and constraints on their positioning has to be supposed for the learner who attains these stages; INV is obeyed because a syntactic rule of German has been learned. Thus, whereas the notion of 'subject' is necessary for the formulation of INV, the early movement rules can be re-formulated pragmatically: 'move the initial referring expression to the end of the utterance if it is old information' would suffice for Clahsen's subject-extraposition rule, for example. The early movements are discourse-contextually governed, the later ones are not.

An examination of *why* one would want to 'move' a constituent thus reveals the same watermark of 'pragmatic to syntactic mode' of organisation as was examined by Dittmar (1984). Here, however, the movements operate on TL-syntactic categories and functions *right from the beginning*. The danger with postulating such initial TL knowledge is that the early data are overinterpreted.

Postulating the TL function of subject right from the beginning, for example, in fact misrepresents the acquisition process. For the grammatically motivated rules such as INV, if the criterion is probabilistic (see above, the systematicity criterion), then it may be questioned whether the learner is operating with the *categorial* functions of subject, verb, object. And it indeed seems to be the case that he is not. HPD (in 2.2 above), Huebner (1983, see below) and Meisel himself (1991, see below) all point to development in the type of referring expression used in pre-verbal position, and to different behaviours of supply and omission depending on sub-categorisation or person. Furthermore, the usual identificational features of 'subject', nominative case and verb-agreement are generally found to be among the last features of the TL to be acquired. It is likely, therefore, that this function is not immediately transferable, but re-learned by precisely those learners who get to the stage where case assignment and verb inflexion are evidenced, not before. This suggestion ties in with the fact that the motivation for ZISA's early movement rules is pragmatic, not syntactic.

Frequency of use has been proposed (for example Meisel 1991) to justify the TL categories from the beginning. Object-fronting occurs not only later, but far less frequently than adverbial-fronting, because it has to be moved out of the syntactic constituent VP, thus interrupting the adjacency of related constituents. The frequency argument depends crucially on the text-type analysed, however. It may well be that object-fronting, or rather the product of object-fronting, is infrequent in conversation (see Huebner, below), but highly frequent in certain types of directions (see the 'stage directions' technique in chapter 6). The choice of text-type as a basis for extrapolation is a non-trivial methodological problem, to which ZISA do not do complete justice.

A major lesson can be drawn from the ZISA study, which is that one cannot ignore the intrinsic motivation for acquisition, that is, not only what constrains it, such as complexity of processing, but also what pushes it. A closer look at the developmental sequence reveals, not a monocausal, but a multicausal explanation. In fact, Clahsen, Meisel and Pienemann (1983), and Meisel (1987) evoke not only syntactic complexity, but also 'pragmatic usefulness' as a possible motivation for development, but without exploring all the implications of this notion. The search for what pushes acquisition entails (i) being more radically sensitive to the originality of learner productions, i.e., not overinterpreting in the direction of TL categories; and (ii) being more attentive to the text type, and the context, for description and for quantification.

Parameter setting

Hilles (1986, 1991) proposes a purely grammatical, i.e., single-cause account of longitudinal development. She studies the longitudinal data of the six Hispanic informants of the Harvard project from the perspective of the so-called 'parameter-setting' theory of language acquisition developed within the framework of Chomsky's 'Universal Grammar' (UG, see Chomsky 1981). For first language acquisition, the theory assumes the child is endowed with a set of general linguistic principles, which must be adjusted to bundles of TL-specific facts; in other words, the 'parameters' must be 'fixed' for the value of the input language. The Morphological Uniformity Principle, the one that Hilles concentrates on, is purported to distinguish languages like Spanish from languages like English in that the former, but not the latter, has a uniform (in this case, a uniformly complex) verbal morphology, with the related grammatical property of allowing the omission of non-lexical subjects. For second language acquisition, the problem investigated is to see whether parameters can be 're-set', for example, in going from a uniform language such as Spanish, to a non-uniform language such as English. Uniformity is 'a property of INFL[exion] (or AGR[eement]), and one of its main effects has to do with the possibility of null-subjects ... null-subjects are allowed in just those languages which are [+uniform]' (1991:311-2).

The evidence Hilles looks for is a correlation between an increase in the use of pronominal subjects and an increase in the use of verbal inflexion in these learners' English production. She calculates the development in supplied pronominal subjects by subtracting from 100 per cent the percentage of 'missing' subjects, those subjects implicit in the production of these learners in contexts where an implicit subject would have been grammatical if their production had been in Spanish, and the percentage of tense and/or agreement markings in contexts which would require them in English. Note that this study adopts the methodological procedures of morpheme order studies (see above, the Harvard study). Even with the detour via the SL, the percentages plotted in Hilles' figures are the correct suppliance of TL items in TL-obligatory contexts.

Hilles' results show that for the youngest learners (Marta, aged four; Cheo, aged five), and for one adolescent (Jorge, aged twelve, the informant of her 1986 study) the two properties indeed correlate, whereas for the three others, they do not. Two informants (Juan, aged ten; Dolores, aged twenty-five) had 90 per cent correct suppliance of both measures at the end of the period of observation, whilst the four others did not. Alberto, therefore, showed no correlation effect, nor did he reach criterion. Hilles' conclusion is that Marta's, Cheo's and Jorge's acquisition is guided by the morphological uniformity principle, hence by UG. This is a strictly monocausal account.

Hilles mentions other components of the acquisition process, namely the TL input, and regulatory mechanisms allowing for its analysis. However, these components are only brought into consideration when the grammatical account fails, allowing her *not* to conclude that the overall unsuccessful learners do *not* have access to UG, as the other components of the acquisition process may have been faulty or unavailable:

> Logically, then, one cannot argue that learners with incomplete acquisition do not have access to UG, but rather that there is no evidence that they do. (1991:307)

Meisel (1991) also examines the question of whether UG plays a role in all types of acquisition, or merely in L1 development, and concludes the latter, that is, he claims that the mechanisms underlying L1 development and ALA are different, and that the onus is on the proponents of UG to provide positive evidence for its role in ALA. What is of relevance for this chapter however is rather his synthesis of results from ZISA's longitudinal study (see Meisel's references), concentrating on surface word order and agreement phenomena (in particular the two phenomena of verbal inflexion and pronominal subjects studied by Hilles). He finds that (in contradistinction to L1 development) the adolescent and adult learners of ZISA's longitudinal study show variable development of subject-verb agreement, ranging from no agreement whatsoever to limited success, and with all learners making numerous mistakes (in relation to the TL norm) over the entire period of observation; the values of use/non-use of subjects in TL-obligatory contexts fluctuate, but independently of the values for subject-verb agreement. In other words, all development is like Juan's, Alberto's and Dolores' of the Harvard study in this respect (with only one learner achieving the correctness of Juan and Dolores). Furthermore, Meisel points out that the calculation of 'correct usage' gives an inaccurate picture of the learner's own system of verbal marking, as in some contexts this marking only coincidentally corresponds to TL marking. This is an inherent flaw in the morpheme order methodology.

Initially, all learners have a marked preference for nominal rather than pronominal subjects, indicating that nominals and pronouns do not have the same status for learners (see above, the criticism of the use of 'sentence subject' by ZISA); during these early stages moreover, subjects do not receive case marking; overall, the 'omission' of subjects is constrained by contextual rather than grammatical factors.

This latter point is inevitable as the identification of null-subject by agreement must be contained in a category which also case-governs the subject position, that is, it must be present in a category which includes tense, the feature which also assigns nominative case, namely INFL; so for identification to be able to take place, finiteness must have been acquired, and it has not been. Hilles addresses this difficulty by hypothesising that learners initially produce ('Chinese-like') topic-comment utterances, and that 'the absence of inflection suggests that they [that is, null-subjects, CP] are being identified through (null) topics' (1991:335).

These are careful, longitudinal studies, from which one may conclude that the LACK of evidence for adult learners' resetting grammatical parameters is impressive. This result is all the more impressive as the methodology used by Hilles encourages a positive result, postulating a binary feature (present/absent) and analysing the data such that for sentence subjects, one value corresponds to the TL, and the other, to the SL, and for verbal inflexion, one value corresponds to 'acquired in the TL', and the other, to 'not acquired in the TL'.

The methodology corresponds to the conception of acquisition where the learner switches from one grammatical setting to another. This conception therefore allows leaps to levels of abstraction for which the data do not seem adequate, where, for example, a null element is postulated by Hilles in order that another postulated null element may be grammatically justified, and it hides, by definition, any systematicity of the learner's own variety which is independent of the settings. Monocausality provokes overinterpretation, and the learner disappears.

Topic prominence to subject prominence
Perhaps, though, Hilles' hypothesis is a notational variant of the following: learners move from an initial topic-prominent (Li and Thompson 1976) organisation of their utterances to a subsequent subject-prominent organisation. Such development has been studied in great detail in Huebner's twelve-month longitudinal study of Ge, a Hmong-speaking immigrant to Hawai'i, from the very beginning

of his acquisition. (Dittmar's 1984, study described above takes a similar 'topic to subject' approach with cross-sectional data from the HPD project). Huebner traces the evolution of three salient aspects of Ge's initial topic-comment sentence organisation: (i) the topic-comment boundary marker *is(a)*, (ii) the determiner *da*, and (iii) the pronominal and implicit means he uses for anaphora.

(i) *is(a)* initially appears before the asserted information (the comment of the utterance), and then its frequency diminishes radically, to re-appear slowly in environments where TL English uses the copula, firstly with equative function, then with attributive function, then with locatives and finally in front of verb + *ing*.

(ii) *da* is an article-like form which is first used to mark specific referents assumed known to the interlocutor, except where this information is redundant, namely, when the referent is in the topic component of the utterance; Ge then radically revises this distribution, 'flooding' all pre-N contexts with *da*, which is then gradually eliminated from all referents except those assumed known to the interlocutor, that is, in TL definite article contexts.

There is a relationship between these two developments (i) and (ii), namely that when article use develops to give independently the information status of NPs, then word order grammaticalises and the TL copula emerges.

(iii) Ge's basic pronoun system at the time of the first recording shows similarities with Klein's and Rieck's 'basic system' described in 2.2 above: Ge has two forms for the first person: *ai, me*, a second person form: *you*, and a third person form: *hii*, this latter covering singular/plural, and masculine/feminine/neuter referents. *ai* is the most frequent morpheme in Ge's first recording. As for anaphora, Huebner calculates the proportion of pronoun use to the total use of pronoun forms and zero in pre-verbal (agent/experiencer) and post-verbal (object) contexts, and finds four unrelated cases of development, depending on the context, and on the person: 'the pattern of use of first and second person pronouns is the reverse of that of the third persons' (1983:176). These differences are explained by an appeal to discourse-processing factors, namely: 'Pronoun anaphora is used in lieu of zero first in those environments in which anaphoric reference is least expected' (*ibid.*).

The development of the expression of anaphora thus follows the other developments studied by Huebner, in that the expression of a function by explicit markers occurs first in contexts where these markers are least redundant. Huebner's conclusion that the *presence* of pronouns is motivated by contextual factors contrasts with Meisel's observation (above) that contextual factors provoke their *deletion*, and reflects these researchers' very different conception of the learner's available knowledge in the early stages of acquisition.

The general explanation for the initial characteristics of Ge's learner variety concerns the communicative requirements of the discourse activity Ge engaged in – conversation, including narratives. However, Huebner does not rule out Ge's SL as a contributing factor, as this is a topic-prominent language. Again, we notice that it is extremely delicate to decide on the weight of SL-influence when the investigation is confined to one SL-TL pair.

Acquisition in (and by) discourse activity

As we said in chapter 1, Hatch and her students (see Hatch 1980 and the references there) were among the first to study how conversations are structured and acquisition proceeds in ALA.

From a longitudinal perspective, Huebner (1983) examined the role of the TL partner's questions on the structure of his informant's answers, 'Sentences in which the presupposed information is most unambiguously distinguishable from the asserted information are responses to information questions' (1983:64). He finds that in the early stages, Ge explicitly repeats the presupposed information, and hypothesises that this is due to the informant's 'need to check on the presupposition, since his listening comprehension is minimal'. The TL-partner's speech also served as a model for Ge's use of the pronouns *it* and *shii*.

The longitudinal study which most systematically examines the role of the discourse activity in the acquisition process is Sato (1990), who studies the weekly conversations she had with two Vietnamese boys (Thanh, aged twelve, and Tai, aged ten) during their first fifteen months in the United States. The linguistic areas she investigates in detail are reference to past time (PTR) and propositional encoding (PE). She terms her approach 'function-to-form', an approach which necessitates a multi-level analysis of both the learner's and the TL-partner's data.

Sato found little development in the linguistic marking of the functions she analyses. For PTR, there was a complete absence of the regular past verbal inflexion, although the learners' use of irregular forms and temporal adverbials increased slightly. In other words, 'very little movement away from contextually embedded PTR was discernible in either learner's data' (76). For PE, there was no discernible development in the proportion of utterances formed of complete propositions, nor in multi-propositional utterances. However, a development was discernible in the expression of these latter, which shifted from juxtaposition of propositions under a single prosodic marker to more explicit marking by conjunctions, and, at the end of the study, a few infinitival constructions. The order of appearance of conjunctions was common to both learners, although speed differed: *and, or, because,* then *when,* then *but.* Thanh alone went on to use *who, if, so, and then.* A 'lexical entry point' to complementation was apparent in the very frequent use of the verbs *think, say,* followed by a proposition. Sato points out that the formal developmental sequence of juxtaposition, co-ordination, subordination does not capture the acquisition process. Complementation (a subordination phenomenon) was more frequent overall than co-ordination, which in turn was more frequent than relativisation (another subordination phenomenon). Referent specification by subordination can be accomplished more efficiently by other means than relativisation in spontaneous discourse, which explains the rarity of spoken language relative clauses generally, and their late acquisition by learners. Thus 'the treatment of subordination as a unitary syntactic phenomenon misses a semantic distinction relevant to the development of complex syntactic structures in ILs.' (114).

Sato examines discourse and SL factors determining the observed lack of grammaticalisation. For both PTR and PE, the role of *discourse activity* was seen as the major determining factor for this lack. Discourse structure makes the morphological marking of PTR redundant; there are only three cases of breakdown due to a lack of such marking, and lack of understanding is regularly repaired by supplying an adverbial rather than a tensed verb, thus 'discourse processes ... may aid in the discovery of lexical but not morphological markers of pastness' (*ibid.*). For PE 'it appears doubtful that conversational interaction is sufficient for learners to develop the full range of morpho-syntactic structures comprising the L2 system', and Sato suggests that written input is necessary to master certain complex cases of subordination. That literacy is a prerequisite for mastery of a language's syntax is a strong claim, as Sato herself writes,but which would have, if it is upheld, far-reaching consequences for the study of untutored ALA. Sato concludes that 'conversational interaction selectively facilitates

IL development, that is, it is variably useful in making L2 coding devices available to learners' (1990:123), the point being that discourse processes make the use of certain markers redundant, therefore low on the scale of communicative urgency for the learner.

In terms of a progression from a pragmatic to a syntactic mode of organisation, Sato is claiming that TL-partner intervention (scaffolding) is *not* a sufficient motor. This is all the more remarkable given that Sato's informants were studied in helpful, friendly, adoptive family circumstances by a co-operative researcher. The typically asymmetrical communication endured by immigrant workers does not include such linguistic 'cocooning' (Long 1983).

So far as discourse processes are concerned, Sato's study is limited to the recognition of those processes favouring redundancy of marking. Although it is not a longitudinal study, von Stutterheim's (1986) is certainly the piece of research which examines discourse processes in most detail; we will however stay with the longitudinal perspective of Meisel (1987), who studied the conversations of José, with summary comparisons with other (less successful) learners of ZISA's longitudinal study. He found that for PTR, learners initially relied on principles of discourse organisation such as order of mention, stage setting and contrast, with explicit time expressions consisting 'exclusively of adverbial expressions at the beginning'. Verbs are initially used in an invariant form, and the acquisition of tense involves many overgeneralisations. The first verbs to receive past tense by José are the auxiliaries, then modals. However, many learners 'never use anything which comes even close to the system of German inflexion'. Meisel points to 'performative complexity' and 'pragmatic usefulness' (see above for the discussion of the motivation for ZISA's developmental sequence) as explanations for the observed development of linguistic means.

2.4   Summary of results

To the extent that the studies summarised above are representative of the available work on spontaneous ALA, either from a longitudinal perspective, or with developmental extrapolations, then their boundaries are quickly drawn. Interest has centred on the morpho-syntax of Dutch, English and German, with some excursions into the analysis of the expressive means of domains such as modality, temporal reference and reference to concrete entities (especially pronominal reference). These boundaries deserve widening.[2]

Two types of study have been undertaken: cross-sectional correlative studies, and longitudinal case studies, with ZISA combining the two approaches. Analytic procedures have ranged from morpheme order counts, to syntactic descriptions of the whole of a variety space (HPD includes native speaker samples) to form-function correspondences. Sato (1990:9-14) discusses the relative merits of form-to-function versus function-to-form analysis, and we turn to a related question in chapter 4. Sato (*op. cit.*) and many others make the point that morpheme order methodology hides the systematicity of the learner variety itself.

Almost all studies concentrate on one type of data: spontaneous conversation, in which narrative sequences are paid special attention by some authors. One exception to this generalisation is Dittmar (1981), whose analysis of an oral translation task brings additional evidence for the lack of morphological marking, and reliance on adverbials and discourse processes in the early varieties of Spanish learners of German. Generally, however, it is difficult to evaluate developmental claims based on one type of discourse activity: it is not to be excluded that those studies which purport to analyse the development of means to express declaratives or interrogatives in the TL *globally* would have had different results to report with different data. Two obvious examples of this danger, given the results of the studies reviewed here, are the frequency of use, and function, firstly of multi-propositional utterances found in narrative, as opposed to argumentative or descriptive activity, and secondly (as we saw in 3.3 above) of utterances with or without extraposed constituents in these different data types. It therefore seems necessary either to restrict one's developmental claims to the discourse type under study, or to compare many discourse types before making global developmental claims.

On the descriptive level, the categories used depend on the supposed closeness of the variety under study to the TL. It is clear, for example, that a study of the acquisition of English which describes the initial stages in terms of (unfilled) INFLEXION (INFL) implicitly assumes a different state of knowledge from one which analyses the

---

[2]Two large projects on spontaneous ALA are actively contributing to the widening of these boundaries, namely *P-Moll*, directed by N. Dittmar in Berlin, (see Dittmar 1991), and the Pavia project *L'acquisizione dell'italiano*, directed by A. Giacalone Ramat (see Bernini and Giacalone 1990). As these projects were started more recently than the ESF project, and as they closely share the overall aims and methodology of the ESF project, we will not discuss them here (other than to state that they are extremely interesting and important studies!).

marking of topic-comment boundaries in the initial stages. Descriptions are correspondingly hard to compare.

One recurring description, which takes various forms in different studies, is of a pragmatic-to-syntactic organisation of learner varieties. The problem with this account is two-fold: a) the features of this development have not yet received sufficient analysis, they take the form of lists of non-interacting features, and b) the explanations of *why* a learner would want to move from a pragmatic to a syntactic mode of expression vary from the strictly grammatical ('movement from a topic-identified to an AGR-identified language', Hilles 1991:335) to the extrinsic (Schumann 1978, and Dittmar 1984 evoke factors such as 'communicative to expressive functions'). We return to this type of description in chapter 4.

It would therefore be desirable in describing development to allow for more systematically comparative statements than have been possible in this summary. The need is for explanatory categories (such as ZISA's processing strategies), and an analytic framework (or frameworks) which can be used cross-linguistically, whilst still remaining faithful to the learner performances that they purport to explain. Some of the analyses we have seen have, through an unwarranted abstraction from the data, run the danger of overinterpreting them. On the other hand, there has been little attempt at systematic cross-linguistic generalisation. Jordens (1988) surveys sufficient studies with sufficient SL-TL pairings to point to cross-linguistic influence. This is otherwise not the case.

However, on a superficial level, and steering clear of underlying assumptions, one may identify some comparable areas of research, producing tendencies which can be expressed most neutrally in terms of the development of the major constituents of the sentence, individually and in interaction with each other.

Development of the noun phrase
For lexical NPs, the initial tendency is the use of a bare noun, contrasting with zero in anaphoric contexts (HPD, ZISA, Sato 1990). These anaphoric contexts are not always as precisely specified as they are in Huebner's study. The marking of quantification precedes the marking of determination generally (HPD, Schumann 1978, Belder *et al.* 1980). The exception is the early use of the determiner *da* by Huebner's informant. For pronouns, forms for 'I' and 'you', plus a strong form for 'I', and an 'all-purpose' third person pronoun are evidenced early (HPD, Huebner 1983). Case assignment is generally a very late devel-

opment. In sum, lexical NPs develop differently from pronouns, and first/second person pronouns develop differently from third person pronouns.

Development of the verb group

The initial tendency is again to use a bare verb. Clahsen (1984) provides for the optional use of auxiliaries and modals from the beginning, but otherwise authors find such use to be a late development, indicating the acquisition of finiteness (analysis of English *do*, or the German or Dutch auxiliary, Lalleman 1983, Jordens 1988). The regular marking of finiteness develops late, if at all (temporal reference is achieved overwhelmingly with adverbs). The finite/non-finite distinction is one of the crucial phenomena determining where the verb is positioned in German and Dutch (see chapter 5.2). Meisel (1991) argues that word order in ALA develops independently of finiteness, in particular with the non-finite verb appearing in verb-second position. Jordens (1988:177) on the other hand, argues that 'INFL has to be reanalysed such that modal and auxiliary verbs can function as instantiations of the finite verb category. The acquisition of the distinction between the finite and the non-finite verb category leads to the positioning of both verbal categories and to underlying ov order'. In the absence of reliable finite/non-finite *oppositions* in the data available, this debate presently seems hard to settle.

For English, the marking of the regular past is completely absent, but irregular past forms are acquired gradually, as is the English progressive. Huebner's original intention was to trace the development of Ge's tense/aspect system, but this aspect of his variety showed too little evidence of development over the year of the study. What development there was converges with the tendencies above. Sato (1990:88) reports similar results from a six-month study of one adult Vietnamese learner by Kessler and Idar (1979), and she sums up this, Huebner's and her own study thus:

> While firm conclusions cannot be drawn on the basis of
> data from only four learners, it can at least be noted that
> inflectional past marking in English is not acquired by
> speakers of Southeast Asian languages for at least a year
> and some months after arrival. (Sato 1990:88)

Word order

Within sentence constituents there is little evidence of idiosyncratic word order (HPD, Jansen *et al.* 1981). Between constituents, learners' early utterances are variously analysed as being ordered SVO (ZISA, HPD also uses 'subject') or topic-comment/theme-rheme (Klein 1981, Huebner 1983, Dittmar 1984). Whichever notation is used, subject-verb agreement is non-existent outside the very last stages of development. For TLs German and Dutch, learners from Romance languages and from Moroccan Arabic tend to place the verb in second or third position early on (HPD, ZISA, Jansen *et al.* 1981), whereas for Turkish learners the early place is utterance-final (Jansen *et al.* 1981). Contextualising (spatio-temporal, modal) adverbials are utterance-initial only at a second stage for ZISA (cross-sectional), whereas their place early on is found to be less constrained in the other studies.

Complete (non-elliptical) utterances are rare in the early stages (HPD), in accordance with the use of zero as an anaphoric device. Which constituents may be left implicit varies from learner (group) to learner (group), and is governed by the discourse context. The verb is absent early on. This is overwhelmingly the case for the copula (HPD), and ZISA characterises the other 'deleted' verbs as 'have, receive, move' (1981:121). Categorical inversion in questions and in German declaratives is a late development (Harvard, ZISA's stage 4). Complex (multi-propositional) utterances are generally rare and show no developmental increase (Sato 1990, ZISA, Jansen *et al.* 1981). ZISA found their use to be subject to inter-personal variation, and therefore not to constitute a developmental stage. On the other hand, HPD observes a global increase in the use of subordination towards, but not attaining, native speaker rates. The earliest attested subordinators are *because/weil*, and *when/wann*.

2.5   Conclusion

So much for the results. Despite the elaboration of possible explanations, the following questions (or variations of a similar question) remain: What pushes acquisition? Why do the developmental tendencies just summarised look like they do? What would motivate development from a pragmatic to a syntactic mode of organisation? Why are processes of syntacticisation found to be variable? Does the variation depend only on the learner's personal orientation? Does it depend on the type of data analysed? Or on the typological proximity of SL and TL? Or on some combination of these? What is the precise relationship between a fossilised variety and the use to which it is put?

Further explanation needs to come from more detailed, examination of the dynamics of *discourse activity*. The idea of many authors that discourse processes selectively push development, postponing the acquisition of communicatively redundant TL-markers, needs to be examined in much greater detail, and involves examining a much greater range of text types than has hitherto been the case. One may predict that certain TL-markers are alternately low or high on the scale of pragmatic usefulness, depending on the type of discourse activity under examination. These markers will moreover be perceived with varying facility, depending on the proximity of the SL and TL. In seeking such explanation, it is essential therefore to adopt a cross-linguistic methodology and to use a variety of data collection techniques.

In summary, constituting an empirical base for analysis, and avoiding the methodological dangers of overinterpretation and unfounded extrapolation pointed out in paragraphs 2.2-4, necessitates a resolutely cross-linguistic design, with sufficient longitudinal case studies, and a battery of data collection techniques, to compare and contrast descriptive statements. We now go on to see how the work discussed here effectively influenced the choice of informants (chapter 3), research areas (chapter 4) and the overall design of the ESF project (chapters 5 and 6).

3 Who are the adult immigrants?

We will mostly be concerned in these volumes with the language acquisition of the following people: Madan, Ravinder, Andrea, Lavinia and Santo are learners of English; Marcello, Angelina, Gina, Tino, Ayshe, Çevdet and Ilhami are learners of German; Mahmut, Ergün, Mohamed and Fatima are learners of Dutch; Zahra, Abdelmalek, Berta, Paula and Alfonso are learners of French, and Nora, Fernando, Leo, Mari and Rauni are learners of Swedish. They are a subset of the informants who were followed longitudinally, having regular encounters with researchers over a period of about thirty months. A short biography and informal sketch of their language development can be found in Appendix B.

As we will explain in chapter 5, the project set out to obtain, and obtained, complete sets of longitudinal data for forty learners, that is, four learners for each combination of source and target language studied. Moreover, the longitudinally studied learners of Dutch, French and Swedish were each paired with a 'control' informant, who was interviewed three times, at the beginning, in the middle and at the end of the period of observation. Appendix B also contains very brief biographical details of the controls and of the longitudinal informants whose names do not occur above.

As a general rule, data from two longitudinal informants per SL/TL pair are analysed in great detail in the various research areas, whose results are therefore based on a total of twenty case studies. Why two informants? Because the empirical outcomes of analysis of couples of informants in different SL/TL pairs, and for different research areas, almost always gave a representative picture of the available data, with specific results having been checked against the data from the less intensely studied informants. We thus obtain, for each linguistic pairing, a class of descriptions which may be assumed to be common to all the learners of that pairing. This is not to say that there are no 'gaps' in the data of individual learners. There are, but they can be filled by comparison with data from other learners. For example, it is often the case that the varieties of slower or less successful learners show clear similarities in their final stages with the pre-final stages of faster, or more successful learners. The slower learners therefore provide more abundant data up to the stages they attained. Applying this 'procedure of mutual compensation' (ESF:Bhardwaj *et al.* 1988:12) completes the picture.

This short chapter will be devoted to a discussion of the original criteria for selecting informants (3.1), followed in 3.2 by a comparison of the 'ideal' informant profile with those of the real informants listed above. This provides a further opportunity for discussion of some of the determining factors mentioned in chapters 1 and 2, in so far as the project was able to investigate them.

3.1　The 'ideal' informant

The informant selection criteria were drawn up primarily to provide safeguards against too much obvious dispersion in the backgrounds and contemporary circumstances of the various informants. To this end, information was culled from previous work involving adult immigrants on the effects of the determining factors described in chapter 1 on the performances of these authors' informants. Age, previous learning experience and potential exposure to the TL were given particular consideration.

The priority which the project set itself (Field Manual:256) was 'to find adult monolinguals with very little TL knowledge and a good prognosis for acquisition.' In relation to the factors hypothesised to determine acquisition (chapter 1.3), the following guidelines for selection were drawn up:

(a) *The cognitive/perceptual disposition of the adult speaker.* Two main factors were taken into account here for the women and men who were selected: age, and previous language experience.

Age has been hypothesised as having a direct or an indirect effect on language acquisition. The 'critical period' for language acquisition (for a comprehensive survey, see Long 1990) is held to have a direct effect. After adolescence, perfect mastery of a new tongue is no longer possible. An alternative point of view is that age is symptomatic of a coalition of other factors (see Schumann's discussion of 'ego permeability' and 'psycho-sociological distance', chapter 2.2) which conspire to hinder acquisition. Under both accounts, the older you are, the less likely your chances of acquisitional success overall (see the results of the *Heidelberger Forschungsprojekt*, chapter 2.2). In the light of such work, the project tried to enroll *young adults* between eighteen and thirty years old for the longitudinal study, that is, adults who were past the 'critical period' but not yet subject to the hardening of habits and hearing which goes with middle-age.

As regards previous language experience, the major factor to control for in a cross-linguistic design was the informants' source language. With very few exceptions, this had not been the case in previous empirical work. This control was to be achieved by pair-wise comparison of the acquisition of one target language by speakers of two different source languages, and also by comparing the acquisition of different TLs by (different) speakers of one SL (for a detailed discussion, see chapter 5). Furthermore, an attempt was made to find informants for whom the new language was indeed a second (rather than a third or fourth) language, and whose metalinguistic awareness had not been developed by schooling (either in the native language or in foreign language tuition). Schooling had been a major determining factor in HPD's analysis, and more recently, Sato (see chapter 2.3) has hypothesised this factor to be essential to the acquisition of certain syntactic phenomena.

(b) *Propensity factors.* It was impracticable to administer standardised questionnaires on the attitudes, motivations and needs of strangers who were in a precarious position in a new country. The only propensity factor taken into account was the researcher's assessment of a potential informant's interest in the project, and motivation to participate regularly over a period of thirty months. The attendant danger is that the most motivated informants select themselves.

(c) *Exposure to the language.* The aim was to study second language acquisition from near the beginning of the process. It was therefore necessary to find informants who had either recently arrived in the target country, or whose stay had not hitherto been propitious to language acquisition but whose circumstances were now changing in that respect. It is very difficult to predict what a newly arrived immigrant's exposure to the language of the majority community will be. An attempt was made to exclude potentially extreme cases of contact or lack of contact, such as immigrants with a TL-speaking partner, those known to be regularly attending language courses, those wives who were neither likely nor encouraged to undertake activities outside the SL-speaking home, and those with children of school age. This last case can provoke considerable variation in exposure to the TL; at one extreme, the TL enters the home via the children, and parents get intensive exposure to it, while at the other extreme, the children shield the parents from contact with the TL, even acting as interpreters if necessary.

These considerations led to the characterisation of the 'ideal informant': she (or he) was to be monolingual with little or no initial knowledge of the TL, with little formal education in the SL and with no TL courses under way. S/he was to be aged between eighteen and thirty, not married to a TL speaker nor with children at school in the target country, whilst entering an environment where day to day contacts with TL speakers were to be expected.

As can be seen, the approach adopted in the project was very firmly that of comparative longitudinal case studies, and the selection criteria were intended to help comparability, where possible. No attempt was made to define representative samples in some statistical sense. Given the tiny number of case studies which have been undertaken in ALA (see chapter 2), statistical measures can perhaps be most usefully employed to evaluate the representativity of results in relation to the available data set. For example, the one major factor which differentiates all the longitudinally studied informants from other adult immigrant learners is the fact that they were studied longitudinally in the project, and this is why the data set contains comparable activities performed by different learners who were recorded three times only, in an attempt to assess, by comparison, what effect the systematic observation of the longitudinal informants had on their language development. This 'control group study' is reported in chapter 8.4.

3.2   Real informants

Ideal informants tend to exist in the heads of researchers. One does not meet them in the street. As can be seen from the characteristics listed later in this section, no informant completely meets the selection criteria. This had been expected, since the situation of potential immigrants from the source countries, interacting with conditions of entry into the target countries made different criteria impossible to meet in different sites, and indeed made it difficult to find informants at all from some of the source languages. Furthermore, different selection criteria may pull in opposite directions. For example, Italian immigration to England and Germany was a well established socio-economic phenomenon, but young Italians are relatively well-educated and have typically received some language tuition. Compromises had to be made. It is this, rather than careless selection from the large number of eager subjects queueing up in front of the project's recruitment offices, which explains the spread of real informants.

The problems to be overcome in longitudinal studies relate to the finding and motivating of individuals within the constraints of a general social context. It is not possible to deal fully with these aspects of the project here, but the following remarks are general enough to be true for the field work in the six sites, whilst doing nowhere near justice to a task which was measured in months, rather than weeks. For more detailed accounts, the reader is referred to Dalmas (ESF:1983), Broeder *et al.* (ESF:forthcoming).

The general social context for immigration at the beginning of the longitudinal study was unfavourable. In France, England, Germany and the Netherlands, various political measures (although prompted in fact by different political motivations) had restricted, and in some cases almost halted, the arrival of workers from outside the EC.[1] Very few new members of some of the most established immigrant communities were to be expected outside family reunions. On the other hand, those immigrants who did obtain permission to join their (immediate) family would have been benefitting from certain measures designed to promote their assimilation into the new country; these measures included language courses. Immigration to Sweden was generally better (or more) organised. There existed an established reception structure for all new immigrants which included language courses. This unfavourable context for immigration provoked unfavourable criticism from certain quarters interested in the immediate applicability of research results. It was claimed that as immigration was not a current problem, the ESF research programme was obsolete before it started. This criticism can be answered by pointing to events of the past decade, both in 'East' and 'West' Europe, which have surely now proved that immigration is a cyclic phenomenon, that there always will be new immigrants, and that it is wise to try to understand the (linguistic and other) problems posed by this phenomenon. It is notoriously difficult to give firm figures for immigration: our informed guess in 1980 was that there were about eleven million migrants living in the industrialised Western European countries; a more recent 'informed guess' (Grillo, 1989:109, the expression is his) is of fifteen million such migrants. The phenomenon did not go away.

Against this temporary background of restricted entry, which had

---

[1]At the time, Greece, Portugal and Spain were not yet members of the EC.

of course repercussions in the attitudes of the immigrant communities, researchers went out into the field in search of individuals. In most cases, it was necessary to become accepted by immigrant networks; approaches through official organisations dealing with immigrants proved to be less fruitful outside Sweden. 'Network' is a term which covers a variety of more or less formal associations which congregate in churches, bars, pubs, schools, refugee centres, and which are characterised by an (implicit or explicit) recognition of who is or is not a member. Some source language researchers were already active in such networks. However, most researchers needed a contact, a 'person of trust' (*Vertrauensperson*) who would vouch for the interest and ethics of the project. Time was needed to get to know such a recognised figure in the network, to explain the aims of the project and to convince him or her to co-operate. During this process, it was possible to obtain a more detailed picture of the match between members of an immigrant community and the characteristics of the 'ideal' informant given above. This person then introduced researchers to potential informants, who in turn had to be convinced of the value and ethics of the project.

Candidates were given a preliminary interview, which allowed researchers to assess their interest, and also their oral and (where relevant) written skills in the TL. These interlocutors were told that the researchers worked at the university, and were interested in achieving a better understanding of how adult immigrants acquire and use the language of the new country, and the problems this can cause them. The immigrants themselves were the experts for such an investigation, and the researchers' work would be to listen to their experiences, although advice and help, where possible, would be forthcoming. Encounters with informants would be recorded in order to keep a faithful record of what was said; no recordings would be made without their prior knowledge, and their anonymity would be guaranteed. Such an introduction meant that to a certain extent, the researcher became a confidant and facilitator. One aspect contributing to the continued motivation of longitudinal informants was that project encounters provided the opportunity to talk, and (with one clear exception, Mohamed) were felt by informants to be enjoyable. Half the teams chose to pay informants a modest sum for attending recording sessions, half chose not to, and such (modest) financial arrangements seemed not to have a decisive effect on an individual's decision to participate or not participate in the project.

It was a major undertaking to set out on a longitudinal study of thirty months, involving members of relatively fragile communities.

It was expected that the dropout rate would be important, and in order to guard against this danger, the net was cast wide at the outset. Twice as many longitudinal and control informants were contacted, and persuaded to start, as were envisaged necessary for the subsequent analyses, that is, over one hundred immigrants in all. Dropouts occurred, but not to the extent anticipated, and this means that complete sets of recordings now exist which have neither been transcribed nor analysed. This 'wasted' work was felt at the time to be a reasonable price to pay to guarantee an adequate basis for analysis, and much of the data are gradually being recycled in the form of practical work for research students.

Conversely, some ten informants who corresponded relatively well to the initial selection criteria, and whose data provided material for pilot analyses during the data collection period did leave the project for various reasons, with the consequence that transcribed, partial data sets from over a year's encounters exist for them. The reasons these learners left the project were of two kinds: firstly, and straightforwardly, a change in their material circumstances (imprisonment in one case) made it materially impossible for co-operation to continue; secondly, and more interestingly, a few learners refused to continue to co-operate in a project investigating how adult immigrants acquire and use a new language. This refusal can be seen as a symptom of a deeper refusal of the new language and culture, which Cammarota (ESF:1986) explains as stemming from the idea that to adopt the new culture is to lose the old. The explanation is reminiscent of Schumann's 'socio-psychological distance' discussed in chapter 2.2. What is different however is that the idea may be provoked by the very *success* of the process of settling into the new country, and hence the sudden refusal of some hitherto successful learners.

This, very briefly, was the context from which emerged the informants whose longitudinal data sets form the basis of the project's analyses. The characteristics set out in Table 3.1 provide some objective information about them at the beginning of data collection. The letters after each name indicate firstly the informant's sex: Male or Female; then his/her source language: Punjabi, Italian, Turkish, Moroccan Arabic, Spanish, Finnish; then the target language: English, German, Dutch, French, Swedish. 'Age' indicates age at the start of data collection. 'Stay' indicates the number of months' residence at the start of data collection. S/M indicates whether single or married to a compatriot, and the following number indicates the number of children attending school. 'SLScl' (source language schooling) and the following number indicate the number of years' schooling in the source country; 'TLScl' and the following number indicates the approximate number of hours' target language schooling (including language courses) the informant could be expected to follow. Finally, there is an indication whether the informant had contact at all with a third language.

Table 3.1 *Informants studied longitudinally in the ESF Project*

	Age (years)	Stay (months)	Fam	SLScl (years)	TLScl (hours)	L3
Madan (M:PE)	25	19	M	6	0	Hindi
Ravinder (M:PE)	21	12	M	7	150	Hindi
Andrea (M:IE)	36	5	M	8	30	?
Lavinia (F:IE)	20	5	M+1	8	600+	?
Santo (M:IE)	25	7	S	8	0	?
Angelina (F:IG)	21	12	M+2	10	0	?
Gina (F:IG)	18	1	S	11	50	?
Marcello (M:IG)	23	9	S	11	0	?
Tino (M:IG)	20	9	S	8	0	?
Ayshe (F:TG)	17	4	S	6	500+	rud. Eng
Çevdet (M:TG)	16	8	S	9	500+	−
Ilhami (M:TG)	17	10	S	8	500+	−
Ergün (M:TD)	18	11	S	5	60+	−
Mahmut (M:TD)	20	9	M	5	0	−
Fatima (F:MD)	25	12	M	2	70	−
Mohamed (M:MD)	19	8	S	6	0	rud. Fr
Abdelmalek (M:MF)	20	13	S	1	15	rud. Sp
Zahra (F:MF)	34	13	M+4	0	30	−
Alfonso (M:SF)	32	10	M+2	6	180+	−
Berta (F:SF)	31	1	M+3	8	180+	−
Paula (F:SF)	32	2	M+2	6	180+	−
Fernando (M:SS)	34	5	M+2	9	400+	rud. Eng
Nora (F:SS)	39	10	M+3	6	600+	−
Leo (M:FS)	18	4	S	11*	400+	Eng
Mari (F:FS)	22	10	M	6	600+	rud. Eng
Rauni (F:FS)	29	7	S	8	300−	rud. Eng

Abbreviations are as follows (from left to right):
M: or F: male or female; Source language code is P (Punjabi), I (Italian), T (Turkish), M (Moroccan), S (Spanish), F (Finnish); Target language code is E (English), G (German), D (Dutch), F (French), S (Swedish); Family status is given by S (Single), M (Married) + number of children; Source language schooling is given in years; Target language schooling is given in estimated hours, with +/− indicating 'probably more/less than'; rud. indicates a rudimentary command of a L3; * Leo received 3yrs' Swedish tuition in Finland.

The overall priorities were to maximise the possibilities for cross-linguistic comparisons, and to minimise the chances of informants abandoning the project. As a basic safeguard, all informants were legally resident in the target country. Comments on the compromises summarised in the above table may be grouped under the headings age, source country schooling and exposure to target language.

Age: The Turkish informants are at the lower end, or below, the desired age range, whereas the Hispanic speakers are all above this range, as are Andrea and Zahra. The overall age range is therefore greater than we would have wished. The contemporary situation in the corresponding target countries was responsible for this state of affairs.

In 1981, the largest immigrant communities in Germany and the Netherlands were Turkish. However, virtually the only potential (and legal) Turkish informants were teenagers being reunited with a parent who had been working for at least three years. They were obliged to attend trade school on arrival, which meant that they were given some language teaching in the Netherlands, and a great deal of language teaching in Germany. But they were available, co-operative, and allowed a comparative study of a similar source population in these two countries, representative of a socially important linguistic community.

In France, the Spanish and Portugese communities were large and well established. But by the time the field work started, it had become extremely difficult to find new (legal) arrivals. A French-Spanish-Swedish configuration was however felt to be linguistically interesting, and significant numbers (for the present purposes) of political refugees from Latin American dictatorships were being accepted in these countries. Many were adults who had already started a family. Many were working class. In Sweden, they received language and practical orientation classes on arrival, just like other immigrants. In France, they received similar classes, unlike other immigrants. Again, the compromise was to opt for available and comparable SL informants in both countries, with the linguistic problems of such informants reflecting in France those of the larger Spanish-speaking community.

Source language characteristics: The source languages of the informants show geographical and sociolinguistic variation, which had to be taken into account. An intractable problem was the absence of new arrivals from Spain, which is itself an area of great linguistic variation of course, hence the choice of Hispanic informants from Latin American countries. Arabic shows great variation. The language acquired in childhood is a local dialect, and these are not necessarily mutually intelligible; so-called 'Standard Arabic' is only taught in schools, and its use is (highly) restricted to formal contexts. The informants contacted all spoke the Moroccan tradition. This desirable homogeneity had the less desirable side effect that the Moroccan learners of Dutch had some rudimentary French.[2] Italian is also a language of considerable internal variation; the majority of the project's informants came from Southern Italy. Finally, the Turkish informants were Turks, rather than Kurds.

Schooling in the source country: Italian and Finnish children benefit from better schooling conditions than children in the other countries. The Italian informants in England and Germany had all completed secondary education up to fifteen years of age (*scuola media*), and this involves foreign language tuition. As far as it was possible to judge informally, the overall effect of this teaching is negligible. When questioned about foreign languages, informants had seemingly forgotten almost all they had learned at the time. This impression is represented in Table 3.1 by a question mark: do they really have any L3 knowledge? It was possible to contact Finnish informants who were relatively poorly educated (for Finns). However, English language teaching starts early in Finland, and the informants had all received three years' tuition. In the case of Rauni and Mari, they had forgotten what they had learned. Leo, however, had only just completed school, and had also received some formal Swedish tuition, which makes him the one problematic informant from this point of view. Finally, Punjabis typically have a rudimentary knowledge of the related language of the Punjab, Hindi, and Madan had received a very small amount of English tuition at school, ten years previously.

Overall, we may consider that informants' active knowledge of a third language is a negligible factor, although there is no way of ascertaining whether contact with another language increased these informants' propensity for language acquisition, or their linguistic awareness.

Exposure to the target language: Informants' exposure to the TL cannot of course be measured directly by their length of stay. As can be expected, those informants in the table who had been resident in the target country for one year or more at the start of data collection were (with the exception of Angelina) from non-EC countries, as newly arrived informants were impossible to find. These informants' command of the TL was judged to be very limited at the outset, with the exception of Madan, who had been working in a factory during the year and a half of his residence, and had adequate speaking and listening skills. No informant was married to a TL speaker.

---

[2] Morocco achieved independence from France in 1957, and the French language tradition is still strong there.

Rauni had a TL partner with whom she subsequently had a child. As far as purely linguistic interaction was concerned, the partner was interested in learning Finnish and spoke a simplified Swedish to her. Mohamed also benefitted from the favourable linguistic environment of living with a TL partner during the course of the study.

As can be seen from the table, the older informants were those with children of school age, and this restriction had to be dropped. It turned out that the restriction was artificial in respect of the young parents in the project, since school provided them with their main source of contact with the TL, in the form of other parents and the relevant authorities.[3] Leisure time contacts with TL speakers was characteristic of the younger informants. For example, some of the young men went out with TL-speaking women for various short periods.

The final aspect of exposure to the TL is TL tuition. Fourteen informants received over one hundred hours of TL tuition. For immigrants to Sweden, this was the norm; it was also the norm for the Turks newly arriving in Germany; for the Latin Americans in France, this was a direct consequence of the choice of type of informant. However, these informants reflected the fact that some effort was being made to help with language problems, and the fact that courses were followed says nothing about their success. Although it proves necessary to evoke TL schooling as a possible determining factor more than had originally been envisaged, the results of this schooling are anything but clear. It seems as if what may be interpreted as a clear influence of language classes is temporary, dying away when classes are no longer being followed, and with the informant continuing contact with the informal, spoken TL variety.

The impact of language classes versus the local vernacular was particularly clear in the case of the young Turkish learners of German. These informants had obligatory schooling at the beginning of data collection, based on a well-known textbook.[4] They had also received informal lessons organised by the social worker, which included lessons dedicated to the contrastive Turkish/German teaching of spa-

---

[3]Lavinia, who had a young child at nursery school in England, put it like this: 'I have a child and I go to the nursery and speak with other people. Not very difficult!'. Selinker (1985:582) judged this restriction to be 'unfortunate if it should cut down their subject pool significantly, as I imagine it would'. He was right. However, it should be pointed out that this particular combination of age and family status correlates with low scores on the lexical richness measures discussed in chapter 8.3.

[4]Demetz/Puente, *Das Deutschbuch. Ein Sprachprogramm für Ausländer*. Niederhausen, 1980. The courses were part of the *Maßnahmen zur beruflichen und sozialen Eingliederung*. ('Measures for vocational and social integration').

tial prepositions and adverbs, including German *in, an, neben, auf, über, unter, vor, hinter, zwischen, oben, unten, rechts, links*. During the first months of data collection, their connected discourse had the stilted character of repetitive use of fixed patterns. Then they left school. As they went out to work later on, they talked progressively less 'correctly', using many of the salient feedback particles like *ne* (roughly 'right?'), vernacular pronunciation like *net* instead of *nicht*, or *gefunne* instead of *gefunden* ('found'), and clusters like *kannsde* (*kannst Du*; 'can you') which when placed in initial position in a statement violate standard word order rules.

These learners were not included in the results of II:I.4 on spatial reference, simply because of the broad repertoire of locative expressions they produced, while the Italian learners of German were making do with a minimum of means. The Turks used *zwischen* ('between') from the outset, whereas the form never appears even with the most advanced Italian learners.

However, what they knew is a repertoire of German forms and their SL 'equivalents', and this knowledge is not always operational. Formal training did not provide these learners with clear and fully-developed conceptions of the functions these forms could serve. Hence, although *über, oben, auf* and *an* ('over/above/on') were taught, the learners had to work out that surfaces constitute a differentiating variable in the German (unlike the Turkish) spatial system. Only then was *auf* used, and it was overgeneralised to apply both to horizontal and to vertically extended surfaces offering support to a theme. This latter constellation is designated in German however by *an*, whose conditions of use in the TL are anything but transparent, and which was not used productively by these learners throughout the data collection period. As we suggested in chapter 1, 'having' a TL word with a meaning attached is not enough, uncovering the appropriate conditions of its use is also an essential part of the acquisition process, and this aspect of exposure was not forthcoming in the classroom setting.

The example of the Turkish learners of German seems then to indicate that teaching can affect the acquisition process in unpredictable ways, but that these effects tend to wear off as soon as everyday discourse activity becomes the main source of exposure to the TL.

3.3   Conclusion

The issues of 3.2 will be taken up again in chapter 8, in an attempt to measure the three types of dispersion discussed there. Overall, the compromises which were necessary did not affect the possibility of making systematic cross-linguistic comparisons, and they resulted in SL groups of very similar characteristics in different target countries.

4 Research areas: some communicative tasks for the learner

4.1 Introduction

We concluded chapter 1 by suggesting that in the quest to identify and explain the horizontal and vertical systematicity of a learner's variety, the analyst encounters aspects of variability which are the reflexion of the learner's current hypotheses about the way the TL functions. Such variability can be attributed, at least in part, to the provisional nature of these hypotheses. The learner's encounters with speakers of the TL will provoke him to take notice of further aspects of the input language which do not fit in with his current hypotheses, or which invalidate one of competing hypotheses.

Adjusting his hypotheses to accommodate the new data ('intake': Corder 1967) will result in a greater or lesser reorganisation of the learner variety. Thus it is the confrontation of hypotheses and input-data which provokes the reorganisation of the learner variety, and this reorganisation becomes visible to the analyst, partly thanks to the learner's variable behaviour in discourse activity. Klein (1986:149) suggests that at a given time, a subset of the learner's hypotheses is 'critical', that is, 'an object of confirmation or disconfirmation'. These are the hypotheses in relation to which the input data are analysed. The input may provide the learner with (perceived) explicit confirmation or disconfirmation for the hypothesis, or with implicit disconfirmation in that no aspect of the input data is (perceived as) relevant for the hypothesis.[1] In any of the cases of strengthening (explicit confirmation), of invalidation (explicit disconfirmation) or of weakening (no relevant evidence), the hypothesis then loses its critical status, and the acquisitional 'spotlight' (Slobin 1979) moves on to other aspects of the input.

What is it that provokes a learner to further analysis of the input?

---

[1]The learner needs no explicitly negative evidence.

What makes a hypothesis 'critical'? We asked these questions in more general terms in chapter 1, and suggested that the general cause is one of communicative need (which includes the learner's desire to remedy communicative failure; to remedy misunderstandings, for example). The discussion of that chapter can be summed up in the following three hypotheses:

(a) acquisition is pushed by the communicative tasks of the discourse activities which the learner takes part in. We suggested that amongst the skills a learner has to master, the capacity to recognise and re-use words denoting various entities, and then to relate them to each other and to their context of use is of primary importance;

(b) the acquisition process will be more or less facilitated by cross-linguistic distance, that is, this factor will selectively determine the speed and success of the process depending on the SL-TL configuration (or, more exactly, on the learner's perception of 'closeness' or 'distance' in respect of some phenomenon);

(c) extra-linguistic individual propensity and environmental factors will have an indirect effect on the process, the effect lending itself less easily to generalisation.

This chapter sets out to make (a) much more precise, thanks to a detailed examination of the communicative tasks selected for investigation. The approach examines, longitudinally, how specific learners set about solving selected tasks in discourse activity. Cross-linguistic generalisations about order of acquisition are then distilled from a systematic comparison of the different SL/TL pairings. For heuristic purposes, we make an initial distinction between understanding and production.

The first problem of the adult beginner is one of *participation and understanding*. Given his cognitive/perceptual disposition[2], how does he go about identifying units of the sound stream and associating them to his present (discourse, situational and background) knowledge? In order to identify such items, he is helped by the non-linguistic clues of the physical context, and also, if he has managed to 'figure out the topic' (Hatch 1980), by his knowledge of how talk about that topic may proceed. These sources of information may

---

[2]The adult learner can draw on 'the mother tongue, plus the entire experience of learning it', as Rutherford (1989:452) puts it.

allow the learner to *infer* relationships between items he recognises in the interlocutor's utterances.

As for the learner's *production*, we may gain some insight into the organisation of the learner variety and into the logic of the acquisition process, by analysing the way he develops linguistic means to perform specific communicative tasks over time. Straightforward as this may sound, there remain the problems of specifying the tasks to be investigated and of identifying the linguistic means used, which in the Field Manual (pp. 18-22) were respectively called *ranking of functions* and *alternatives in expression*. We summarise these problems here.

Ranking of functions. This question concerns how the necessity of expressing relational concepts, such as determination, modality, temporal, spatial, causal and other relations between items, intervenes in the learner's development. There are many such functions, and there is no reason to assume that all of them are equally important for the learner when communicating; the functions he does learn to express will presumably reflect his own communicative needs, and govern the order in which the corresponding linguistic means are developed.

Alternatives in expression. There is no predicting exactly which type of linguistic means will be used to perform a given function. Rather, a language offers a repertoire of different possibilities, which may be used simultaneously or alternatively. Different languages give different priorities to these possibilities, while the functions as such are more or less shared by all languages. Imagine, for example, that a learner of English wishes to express past time reference (PTR). He may achieve this implicitly if such reference can be already inferred from the discourse (as in an answer to a question such as 'What did you do last year?'); or he may himself use a temporal adverbial (deictic, as in 'last year', or calendaric, 'in 1992'); or he may rely on the past tense, in combination with an adverbial or not, these choices depending at least partly on the stage of acquisition.

If the learner by virtue of his first language competence knows how to apply such functions, what he has to learn is how to express them in the language being acquired. The analyst then sets out to identify which of the various possibilities the learner chooses first, and how the balance is shifted from certain elementary devices to more complex ones until he (possibly) disposes of the full repertoire offered by the target language. If the analyst sets out to study the expression of such functions, it follows that the research areas do not, and cannot, correspond to traditional areas of linguistic analysis, such as morphology or lexicon. Rather, the areas must correspond to tasks the learner has to find the means to perform on whatever level of expression. There are recent echoes of this line of reasoning in Sato (1990:14, italics hers) where she states that 'function to form analysis ... automatically commits one to *multi*-level analysis'.

In investigating aspects of the learner's problem of production, we therefore choose recurring tasks that learners have to accomplish in discourse activity, even if expressed idiosyncratically by different lexical-syntactic means. These means vary both as a function of the acquisition stage, and of the different SL/TL pairs, and do not correspond to the traditional linguistic domains of investigation. Rather, they bring together selected questions from each domain which bear interdependently on our general hypotheses about the process of ALA, and about the factors which may explain it, as they have been set out at the beginning of this paragraph. These four broad areas of investigation are described in detail in Volume II; in 4.3 of this chapter, we will offer some preliminary reasons for studying them. But we turn first to the learner's initial problem of analysing TL material.

4.2   Interaction

It was stated in chapter 1.5 that adult immigrants find themselves in the paradoxical situation of having to communicate in the TL in order to learn it, and to learn the TL in order to communicate in it. The process takes place in an indifferent and sometimes hostile environment in which such learners have essentially instrumental goals to achieve. As Grillo puts it:

> In highly industrialised, highly bureaucratised, highly institutionalised societies such as Britain, France or Germany survival is extremely difficult without considerable competence in the dominant language, and many adult migrants lack the wherewithal to obtain that goal.
> (1989:132)

They are disenfranchised from the outset by their lack of the language, and this in turn leads to difficulties in establishing and protecting their rights.

The studies introduced here aim to investigate the ways in which adult learners come to understand TL speakers in encounters which are asymmetrical in that the latter are in command (at least) of the code, and often have the power of decision as to whether resources or facilities are to be accorded. In Erickson's (1976) phrase, such TL speakers are 'gatekeepers'.

How does the learner cope with such encounters? How does he establish himself as an interlocutor? What are the strategies the learner uses in order to achieve understanding?

Feedback mechanisms are a potentially privileged way for the learner to deal with the apparent paradox of learning by communication, in that they give him the wherewithal to participate in dialogue in the TL (to 'keep the partner in the conversation', as Hatch, 1980, put it). Feedback phenomena correspond partially, but not entirely, to the traditional grammatical category of *interjection*. The reason for choosing the term *feedback* is to highlight the systematic organisational role in verbal activity of otherwise unnoticed linguistic items and mechanisms, which are used to enable speaker and hearer mutually to regulate their dialogue. The two main aspects of the feedback process which a learner has to master are *eliciting* feedback, which can be achieved by the use of such little words as *eh?, right?* or by question tags – *isn't it?*, etc. – and *giving* feedback: *mm, yeah,* and other tag phenomena: *yes it is,* etc. The expressive means for feedback include morphemes and words such as the ones mentioned above, but also repetitions and bodily movements, as well as a number of 'secondary mechanisms' such as lengthening, reduplication, and so on (see Allwood 1988).

According to Fechner's law (1860), items that appear either initially or finally in a linguistic string are more easily perceived; these positions could be said to confer salience on the items in question. Since feedback items appear either alone, that is, surrounded by pauses, or in initial position (feedback givers) or in final position (feedback elicitors), and since they are very frequent in spoken interaction, one would expect learners to take them in and re-use them in their own production from very early on. These items are moreover highly multifunctional, allowing the learner to 'fill in' for more explicit expressions which he may not have.

These preliminary considerations and expectations motivate the detailed study of four phenomena (see Volume II:II.2): *the relative weight of feedback mechanisms* in relation to other types of verbal material among both learners and TLSS; the *formal characteristics* and relative complexity over time of the feedback mechanisms used by learners; the *functions of discourse activity* that feedback mechanisms are used to fulfill by learners over time; the *situational determinants* (status of interlocutor, setting, etc.) of the use of feedback mechanisms.

Understanding is largely an invisible process. When two speakers seem to understand each other perfectly, it is difficult for the analyst to get a grip on such smoothness, and to identify all the interacting mechanisms. We therefore also attempt to see whether evidence from non-understanding – its causes, the ways it is indicated and the manner of its resolution – can shed light on the way understanding is achieved. The malfunctioning which non-understanding represents, and the work needed by both partners to repair it, provides a window onto the process of understanding, and may even serve as a 'magnifying glass' (ESF:Trévise 1984) on aspects of the acquisition process.

There is a second reason for studying non-understanding. As we said in chapter 1.3, the learner's 'right to speak' is partially governed by native speakers' reactions in linguistic communication, and the asymmetry of this communication can make it difficult for the speech partners to achieve mutual understanding. Lack of understanding may have a generally positive or negative effect on the learner's motivation to learn, either making him linguistically more aware, or leading him to avoid all but inevitable linguistic contact with TL native speakers, thus provoking fossilisation at an elementary stage.

Early analyses by Allwood and Abelar (ESF:1984) and Trévise (ESF:1984) defined the terminology of 'understanding'. Allwood and Abelar distinguish between understanding, lack of understanding and misunderstanding in the following way: *understanding* 'consists of the processes that connect received information with already stored information and thereby place the incoming information in a meaningful context' (1984:28); *lack of understanding* occurs when a hearer 'cannot connect stored information with incoming information', and the authors distinguish two sub-cases: '(a) relevant information is missing (e.g., one does not know what a Swedish Maypole is since one has never encountered any such thing); (b) a relevant strategy for connecting incoming with stored information is missing (e.g., one knows what a bed is but one has no strategy for connecting the Swedish word *säng* with this information)' (*ibid.*); *misunderstanding* occurs then when a hearer 'actually connects incoming information with stored information but where the resulting meaningful connection must be viewed as inadequate or incorrect' (*ibid.*).

Trévise examines in some detail the discourse consequences of the latter process. She emphasises that misunderstanding is an illusion on the part of both interlocutors that they understand each other. The thread of the dialogue is not broken so long as the other partner's reactions remain ambiguous enough to fit the representation one has built up. A misunderstanding may surface, suddenly, or more gradually as the interpretations of what is said diverge more and more clearly. It may remain unnoticed by the dialogue partners, and remain for ever submerged, or surface afterwards for the analyst. We take as an example of this last possibility a misunderstanding of temporal reference.

Trévise examines the following example of a misunderstanding which went unnoticed by the speech partners, and which serves as a magnifying glass on one aspect of the learner's developing comprehension/production. Gloria (GL) is a Hispanic learner of French who had been resident in France for six months at the time of this exchange with a target language speaker (TLS):

(1) a. TLS: *et vous prenez des cours de français?*
             'and you take French courses?'
     b. GL: *oui *en* la cité université deux *mes* et [se] tout*
             'yes *in* the university village two *months* and
             isa all'
     c. TLS: *c'est toute la journée?*
             'it's all day?'
     d. GL: *oui*
             'yes'

TLS did not know, but the analyst did know, that at the time of the interview, Gloria's two month course was already over. The present time reference of the initial question (a) is signalled merely by the verb ending: the [e] of [proene]. Although Gloria apparently has not understood this, her answer (b) is perceived as appropriate *for the* TLS, in that nothing in this answer situates the event before the utterance time. TLS interprets the time interval as 'for two months', and [se] as *c'est*, apparently. In his next question (c) he therefore naturally continues with present time reference, marked by *c'est*: [se]. This is, Trévise points out, a marker in Gloria's own production at this time which she uses in both present and past time contexts; she therefore naturally interprets TLS' *c'est* as referring to past time, and replies (d) affirmatively to the question.

The verb *prendre* is not part of her (recorded) active vocabulary at this time. Like the other Hispanic learners of French, the first temporal opposition she marks on the lexical verbs she does use is 'past/non-past', and this opposition is carried respectively by the 'base' form of the verb, and by this 'base' form suffixed with [e]. [proene] (*pren + e*) is therefore a good candidate for past time reference in Gloria's developing variety. We see here the closeness fallacy at work from the point of view both of the learner and of the native speaker: [se] in Gloria's utterance is naturally interpreted as 'present' by the TLS, *prenez* in the TLS' utterance is interpretable as 'past' for Gloria. And both have the impression of having understood.[3]

Many individual examples of this type are discussed in published articles (and summarised in ESF:Perdue 1987). The problem is that the type of 'magnifying glass' insight on the relationship between comprehension and production suggested by Trévise's work cannot be undertaken systematically in the frame of a research design where the input is not fully controlled. The data collection window onto the acquisition process is too small, and the vast majority of learners' contacts with the TL environment are beyond the analyst's control. Control can only be indirect, and involves uncovering procedures which are recurrent, and which can contribute to the definition of *types* of encounters which the learner comes to understand more or less well.

At best, 'potentially acquisitional sequences' (Py 1990) can be identified where a misunderstanding surfaces and becomes the object of negotiation. These sequences can only be termed 'potentially' acquisitional; the analyst must attempt to hear them with the ears of the learner whose variety may or may not be at a stage where the metalinguistic information contained in them can be taken in by him. This information may or may not be 'critical', in Klein's sense. Where it is not, one observes what was referred to in chapter 1.5 above as a 'selective deafness' on the part of the learner to pedagogical input.

Input. The 'input' metaphor turned out to be particularly unfortunate in a study of dialogue between people who were working to achieve some level of mutual understanding, as Volume II.II.1 makes very clear. In this context, not only the learner, but also the TLS has to deal with problems of understanding; they are shared and are solved co-operatively, however minimal this co-operation may be. Early analyses in the project centred on TLS' facilitation of understanding for the learner. In particular, Vion and Mittner (ESF:1986) examined their contributions as a resource for the learner by providing words the latter could take up as 'reprises' in his own production (discussed in II:II.1), and Vion (ESF:1986) furthered the notion of interdependency in his examination of the significance of linear versus parallel phases (one-sided versus collaborative sequences) in determining the extent of the learner's comprehension. Voionmaa (ESF:1984) interpreted the one-sided sequences as the learner 'waiting and seeing',

---

[3]Wolfgang Klein points out in personal communication that understanding, itself, is after all an illusion created by language.

and further examined how 'key words' (individual lexical items or unanalysed expressions) for a particular discourse activity come to be identified. These strategies highlight the inferencing work necessary for the beginning learner, who has to work out the relationships between the words themselves, and between the words and the context – between the time of utterance and the event times as in the above example of Gloria's.

The learner then has discourse skills and his knowledge of the world to draw on. However, from a cross-linguistic perspective, it is necessary to keep in mind that these sources of knowledge are at least partly culturally bound, and do not necessarily have a facilitating effect on understanding. Becker and Perdue (ESF:1984), analysing a consultation between a German lawyer and his Turkish client, concluded that the protagonists' differing assumptions about what was at stake, their differing background knowledge, and their diverging goals, created a filter of what the other said which led to persistent and repeated misunderstanding. This type of culturally-based interpretation was therefore hypothesised to be a potential source of understanding difficulty.

This preliminary work resulted in the study on 'Ways of achieving understanding' (see Volume II:II.1), which concentrates on a close, qualitative examination of types of discourse activity which reflect the learners' everyday language use. It examines four main questions on the *causes of non-understanding*, the *strategies used for conveying and managing non-understanding* when it occurs, the factors allowing speech partners to *prevent or repair understanding problems*, and those enabling the *negotiation of meaning*. It also takes a close look at how TLSS speak to immigrant learners. If little is known about the way learners go about solving their analytic task, then very little is known about the way native speakers go about understanding the productions of beginning learners[4] (or misunderstanding them, see example 1). The results of these studies allow an assessment of how a learner uses a TLS as a resource for language acquisition, and also, of the TLS' ways of adapting to the lesser degree of proficiency of the learner. We may say straight away that these results accord more with Meisel (1980, see chapter 2.2) than with Clyne (1984, see chapter 1.3): these learners did not get input consisting of 'foreigner talk'.

The studies of feedback and of ways of achieving understanding relate to the general questions of the project concerning the way in

---

[4]See, however, Roche (1989).

which adults come to acquire a new language while simultaneously having to communicate in that language. The relative novelty of such studies necessitated a heuristic approach, and involved studying aspects of native speaker behaviour which are not well explored. For example, it was necessary at least to attempt to describe the feedback mechanisms of the target and source languages. More generally, we faced the problems of studying psycholinguistic processes in a socially non-facilitative context where problems of mutual interpretation may be exacerbated by the divergent, socially determined expectations of the interlocutors, and can only be resolved through the unequally shared resources of the TL.

4.3   Production

However the learner accomplishes the analytic task sketched in the previous section, he will eventually come up with a certain number of items which are important for his own communication in the TL. These are perhaps the 'key words' (see 4.2) denoting entities relevant for the type of encounter he has with native speakers of the TL. He is then faced with the complex task of arranging these items into comprehensible utterances, and relating these utterances to each other and to the context of speaking, that is, of finding ways to express the 'relational meanings' (Andersen 1984:79) which languages encode. We now examine some aspects of this latter task.

Spatial and temporal reference
The learner's task of *specifying spatial and temporal relations* (spatial and temporal reference, for short) has already been mentioned several times in this volume. The task involves relating a *theme* – an entity or event – to some *relatum*, which is again an entity or event (in particular the speech event itself). Although temporal and spatial reference differ in the degree to which they are obligatory – both with respect to each other and between the various languages under study – any utterance uttered by a speaker necessarily contains at least some aspects of such reference. It is therefore independent of any specific discourse activity, and the acquisition of adequate expressive devices is a central problem for any learner. This immediately justifies the inclusion of spatial and temporal reference as major research topics.
   These areas are particularly interesting from a *cross-linguistic* point

of view. We observe differences in the expression of spatial and temporal reference not only in the choice of particular lexical items but also in the form of quite different preferences which language systems have, and their speakers use. Moreover, such reference systematically exploits the *context dependency* of languages, and in particular the relating of the utterance to the speech act itself. Each instance of language use itself constitutes an event with its own spatial and temporal structure which defines the basic spatial and temporal relatum. We will deal with these two points in turn, before turning to aspects which are more specific to each individual domain.

Cross-linguistic aspects
Except for elliptical sentences, temporal reference is obligatory in all the languages involved, although the grammatical encoding of this reference differs from language to language. For example, the English tense-aspect system is quite different from the French, Spanish or Italian system, or from the German system, which is argued by some researchers to have only tense, not aspect. Tense automatically goes with verb inflexion. As the distinctions encoded in such systems are obligatory, the learner may face one of two problems, either of learning to express a TL distinction which is *not* grammaticalised in his own language, or *not* to express a SL distinction which the TL does not encode. Spatial reference is not grammaticalised in the languages under study. A speaker expresses such reference whenever the need arises to locate some entity, or to describe the movement of some entity from some place to another. In such a frequently occurring situation, the learner then faces the same type of problem as for temporal reference of learning to express or not to express certain distinctions encoded in the system. We give two examples which illustrate the problem of the Turkish learners alluded to at the end of the previous chapter:

a) some spatial configurations may be expressed in a language x, but not in a language y. For example, the general locative suffix -DE of Turkish indicates containment of the theme in the space defined by the relatum, and can be applied to constellations either where the theme is contained within the relatum, or is contiguous to its boundary. The Turkish learner of German then has to work out that the TL has no single equivalent expression, and learn to differentiate between more specific constellations (such as a supporting surface).

b) although an expression of language x may be considered to be the translation equivalent of language y, the conditions of use of each expression differ. One reason for this is that the class of theme and/or relatum to which the relation can apply is more restricted in one language than another. For example, it is possible in both English and German to talk of a photo *on* (*auf*) a table, where the table is conceptualised as a surface whose function is to support the photo. But our Turkish learner of German, having worked out that surfaces constitute a differentiating variable in this language's spatial system, still has to learn that some relations between a theme and a supporting surface cannot be expressed by *auf*. The same conceptualisation of supporting surface is possible in English for expressing the relation between a photo and a wall – *the photo on the wall*, but it is not in German. A vertical surface is not conceptualised as providing support in German, and *an*, rather than *auf*, is required. Such differences in conditions of use between source and target languages may constitute a severe learning problem, as the example of the Turkish learners attests.

Context dependency
We may say that the here-and-now of the speaker/hearer exchange provides a basic relatum (see the *moi-ici-maintenant* of Benveniste 1966, or the *origo* of Bühler 1934. We will adopt the latter term). In this case, linguistic devices (tense, adverbs such as *here/there*, *now/then*) are used as *deictics* which are related to this basic reference point. However, in connected discourse, speakers continually use already established places and times as antecedents for reference in subsequent utterances. This reference-maintaining mechanism (*anaphora*) contributes to bind utterances to other utterances within the discourse, and so contributes to its cohesion. The mechanisms of deixis and anaphora reflect the *indexical* nature of referential devices, that is, the fact that they are anchored in their context of use.

All languages have means to relate what is said to the speech situation and to the discourse context. There is no reason to assume that the way in which this is done is very different from one language to another; these means are however variably complex for a particular referential operation depending on the language one is learning (and its relationship to the language one knows). Studies of child language development show that anaphoric uses of various devices derive from deictic ones, with children using indexical devices at first only as deictics, and very gradually learning to use them also as anaphorics. Thus the ability to use language as its own context is a late development (Hickmann 1991).

In contradistinction to the child learner, the adult has a developed capacity for anchoring his utterances to the speech *origo*, and for using language as its own context. In adult language acquisition, the relationship between the development of deictic and anaphoric means can therefore be examined from a purely linguistic point of view. For deictic reference, what has to be learned are some language specific words and some language specific semantic oppositions (cf. *here-there* in English as opposed to *aqui-alli-allá* in Spanish). At the extreme, the extra-linguistic situation in which an utterance is embedded makes explicit deictic marking redundant. Recall the example of chapter 1:

(2) *aschenbecher + tasche*

We noticed that this utterance is successful in context despite the lack of explicit determination, or temporal marking. Anaphoric reference, on the other hand, is less easy to infer from the external context of speaking. It functions to establish cohesion within discourse, and languages have developed complex systems for marking this function. Therefore, we may assume that it requires more learning than deictic reference, and expect its full use to develop later. If this turns out to be the case, it will be for different reasons from children: for adults, anaphoric use is *linguistically* more complex; for children, anaphoric use is also *cognitively* more complex.

Topological relations
It is possible to express the relationship holding between theme and relatum independently of the origo of the speaker. Relations such as INCLUSION, NEAR, can be expressed by spatial prepositions in all the TLs, and by aspectual distinctions in some of them. A further question is whether explicit expressive means for topological relations are more urgently needed, and receive earlier attention from the learner, than those for deictic ones.

Spatial reference
A major difference between spatial and temporal reference is that spatial relations may hold in three dimensions, whereas temporal relations can hold in only one. The study of spatial reference reflects

this difference. It centres on relations in *perceptual space* in everyday communication (rather than geographical or abstract space, gross though these distinctions are). The speaker may use the vertical, saggital and lateral axes to locate a theme, with the origo as the basic relatum. These *projective relations* correspond to the line from head to toe, the line of vision, and the left to right of the speaker. Such relations may further be extended in order to relate a theme to the interlocutor ('on your right') or to some other entity which has an *intrinsic* orientation ('in front of the T.V.'). The expression of such spatial relations which derive from the deictic origo may constitute an acquisition problem.

Two further aspects of the expression of perceptual space may influence the need for the learner to acquire explicit linguistic means:

(a) The learner may need to describe a particular spatial configuration in a context where his interlocutor may or may not share the same visual field. It is easier for the interlocutor to infer the intended relationship between, say, an ashtray and a bag if they are visible to both speech partners and form part of an instruction, than if they are denoted in a description of an invisible scene. This latter case typically requires more explicit linguistic expression.

(b) The configuration to be described may be static or dynamic. Either configuration needs a degree of explicit linguistic expression consistent with the context and the discourse activity. For example, inferring locomotion or causative motion is possible in instructions if means are available to describe the theme-relatum configuration at goal. These remarks point to the capacity that the learner has for relying on his knowledge of how different *discourse activities* are structured, and to the need for the analyst to contrast contemporary data from different types of discourse activity in studying the acquisition of spatial expressions. The elicitation techniques described in chapter 6 are designed to cover the range of topological and projective concepts typically used when locating an entity in space, or when moving objects from one place to another.

Temporal reference, aspect, Aktionsart
As we have seen, temporal reference involves the locating of events (actions, processes, states, will be termed 'events' for short) in relation to a designated reference time, termed the temporal *relatum*.

The *origo* may be considered to be the basic relatum. The relatum has to be specified in (or inferrable from) the situational or discourse context or the general background knowledge of the speech partners, that is, the time of utterance (deictic reference), a previously situated event (anaphoric reference), or an independently specified time span (a date, or an event whose date and duration is mutually known, such as the French Revolution). Temporal relations may, like spatial relations, be expressed deictically, anaphorically or topologically.

The study of Volume II:I.3 focusses on temporal reference. But it is impossible to ignore the role played by the categories of *aspect* and *Aktionsart* in the expression of temporal relations during the acquisition process, and we make some brief remarks on both.

Aspect refers to the various perspectives the speaker may take with regard to an event, such as viewing it 'perfectively' or 'imperfectively'. The precise aspectual distinctions, and the way they are encoded, vary between the TLs studied in the project. The fact that in some languages aspect is grammaticalised (as with the English 'progressive'), whereas in others, lexical means are used, clearly changes the nature of the acquisition problem.

Aktionsart, or 'manner of action' refers to the quasi-objective time characteristics of an event, which takes as a basis the lexical content of the verb (i.e., 'stative' versus 'non-stative', 'punctual' versus 'non-punctual', etc.). However, the nature of the verb's arguments, and adverbial or particle modification of the verb also play a role (cf. the temporal differences between 'John drank' versus 'John drank up' versus 'John drank tea' versus 'John drank a cup of tea').

These categories interact in the learner's expression of temporal relations. For example, whether an event referred to is interpreted as 'before' or 'simultaneous with' another event often depends on the Aktionsart of both (for example, whether one or both are stative) or on aspect (such as, whether they are marked as completed or not). The inter-relation of these three categories is particularly clear in elementary learner varieties, as systematic morphological marking is typically not used by learners. Thus the different temporal relations which one may infer between the utterances in the following examples:

(3) a *Lie in bed. Phone ring.*
    b *Lie down on bed. Phone ring.*

depend partially on their Aktionsart.

Discourse principles
The fact that the utterances of the above examples are related to each other at all by the reader must mean that he or she has attempted to construct a coherent discourse. In a coherent text, the information to be expressed is distributed over a series of utterances, and the relationship between these utterances depends at least partly on the type of discourse. Interpreting (3)b as a sequence means applying the narrative 'principle of natural order' (PNO: 'order of mention corresponds to order of events, unless marked otherwise') to it. If (3)b were part of the description of a single picture, on the other hand, then an interpretation of simultaneity is possible. We may hypothesise that the adult learner will initially rely on his knowledge of how different types of *discourse activity* are temporally structured, and on his knowledge of the temporal characteristics of events in order to express temporal relations in situation.

These preliminary considerations motivate the studies of 'Reference to space in learner varieties' (Volume II:I.4) and 'The acquisition of temporality' (Volume II:I.3). The research questions of both studies closely reflect the general aims of the project:

- What spatial and temporal relations are expressed in elementary learner varieties and what are the expressive devices used?
- How is this initial interaction of expressive devices re-organised as acquisition proceeds, and what new expressive possibilities are acquired?
- What are the factors which determine the observed process, and how do they interact?

In the light of the above remarks, the factors which are likely to be relevant are the structure of each conceptual domain (for example, deictic versus anaphoric versus topological relations), the structure of different types of discourse activity, and the characteristics of the individual language pairings. This latter point will be taken up in the following chapter.

The learner's problem of arranging words
The problem of synthesis most traditionally researched, although from different theoretical viewpoints, is *the learner's problem of arranging words* into larger units, namely compounds (Volume II:I.2) and utterances (Volume II:I.1). The problem has to do with the 'syntax' of learner varieties – if we take the word 'syntax' in its literal meaning. We will however avoid the term, since it is usually understood in work on ALA in the narrower sense of the formal constraints

on constituent and utterance formation (chapter 2 shows this very clearly).

As in the case of spatial and temporal reference, one source of knowledge that the learner may initially draw on to solve the arrangement problem are the principles governing the way any speaker arranges, or 'linearises' an amount of complex information in temporal order, as they are independent of specific languages and cultures (see Levelt 1982). The original hypothesis (Field Manual:109ff) was indeed that beginners would use such TL-independent principles, and that TL-specific devices would progressively be introduced. In other words, it was hypothesised that learners would first structure their utterances along pragmatic principles, and development would proceed from the 'pragmatic' to the 'syntactic' mode of utterance organisation. This broad hypothesis is affected (at least) by the typological distance between the learner's SL and TL. The interest of the *cross-linguistic* dimension of the study is then to see to what extent common developmental tendencies can be observed over different SL-TL pairs, and to what extent there are clear differences. In this latter case, the typological characteristics of the languages can be predicted to have an effect within major constituents of the utterance (see Jansen and Lalleman, 1980a,b). This prediction is investigated in Volume II:I.2.

Initial analyses highlighted two weaknesses in the original hypotheses:

(a) As we said in chapter 2, the 'pragmatic mode' consists of a list of remarkable features, but at the time, its *functioning* had not received systematic analysis. Contemporary work (Klein 1981, Dittmar 1984, Huebner 1983, and Schumann 1987) had established the prevalence of 'theme-rheme' or 'topic-comment' structure in early learner varieties, and other important features of the pragmatic mode (such as, lack of grammatical morphology), had been attested. But the very notions of 'theme', 'topic', etc., were in need of definition, as Schumann (*op. cit.*) makes clear. Furthermore, there was no principled developmental sequence from the pragmatic to syntactic mode of organisation;

(b) Even if the 'pragmatic mode' and subsequent development could be systematically described, the reasons why this development would take place were not clear. The proposed motivation was, as in Dittmar (1984), the learner's passage from the 'communicative' to the 'expressive and integrative' functions of language, which is itself just as vague as the 'pragmatic to syntactic' development.

In a pilot analysis (ESF:Klein and Perdue 1989), the possible constraints on utterance structure were reviewed, as well as the reasons a learner might adopt them. Informants were virtual beginners: an Italian acquirer of German, an Italian acquirer of English and a Spanish acquirer of French. A semi-guided task was chosen for analysis (the 'Charlie Chaplin retelling' described in detail in chapter 6) which allows some control over the content the informant is attempting to convey. The procedure for analysis was first to establish the linguistic repertoire for each learner, then to characterise the way the learner applies his repertoire to construct utterances to form a coherent text. It was found that no single set of constraints ('pragmatic' versus 'syntactic') was adequate to describe the way these learners structured their utterances in this task. Rather, there was a tight interaction between three sets of constraints, which were termed phrasal constraints, semantic role properties and discourse organisational constraints. These constraints are described in detail in Volume II:I.1.

The varieties of these three learners were remarkably consistent and similar in the way utterances were formed, in that organisational particularities of the SLs and TLs had apparently only a marginal influence on their functioning. The 'basic system' these learners developed is simple in structure, indeed highly restricted in relation to the organisation of the SLs or TLs. It shows a natural equilibrium between the three types of constraint and is apparently easy to acquire.

It was also possible to see the germs of further development. In the functioning of this variety, the three sets of principles coalesced, and learners were very adroit at avoiding contexts where they could clash. But potential contexts could be identified where the constraints might come into competition. For anaphoric reference to people, for example, pronominal reference-maintaining devices need to be developed for contexts where zero anaphor is not sufficiently explicit, and where use of a full NP overspecifies the antecedent.

The existence of such contexts suggest possible lines of explanation for the development observed in some existing studies of second language acquisition, such as the development of verbal morphology, the progressive complexification of lexical NP structure, and the order of acquisition of pronouns (these explanations receive detailed treatment in Volume II:I.1). Indeed, the results of the pilot study for the two latter areas showed that development of NP structure is closely related to its function in introducing and reintroducing referents and maintaining reference, and these functions are in turn so closely linked to the place the NP occupies in the utterance that separate studies on word order and personal reference would have hidden an important interaction in development. Consequently, an adjustment was made to the initially planned research on reference, which comprised three sub-studies on reference to people, space and time (Field Manual:138). The sub-study on reference to people was incorporated into the study of utterance structure.

4.4   Conclusion

In summary, the approach taken in Volume II:I is to see how the learner's repertoire is put to use in discourse activity. The repertoire is studied with respect to the development of lexical and grammatical means for combining words and constituents, and for referring to time and space. These means interact with pragmatic skills providing for the linearisation of information, and for basic spatial and temporal anchoring in the speech situation.

In such areas of investigation, it is possible to see whether the same functions get encoded across learner varieties, to what extent the order (or 'ranking') corresponds from variety to variety and over time, and to what extent the linguistic organisation of the SL or TL affects this ranking. General cross-linguistic developmental sequences would be very good proof of the reality of the notion 'communicative need'. On the other hand, lack of general sequences can be investigated systematically from a contrastive SL/TL point of view. These areas therefore allow us to fully address the general questions the project is concerned with.

Finally we may ask if there is a way of exploring the links between the studies on interaction and language production. We can only point to these links here. The learner's problem in production can be seen to mirror the understanding problem if one imagines the learner interrogating his own procedures for understanding, and expressing himself so that the interlocutor may use the same procedures as he would. For example, the learner can rely on paraphrase and scaffolding from the TLS, on his own knowledge of discourse principles governing the order of utterances in a given type of discourse, on pragmatic constraints such as what information is given at a particular point, as well as on local operating principles such as 'semantically related items are placed together', in order to enhance his understanding of the input. The above principles may function both to facilitate retrieval of pieces of information on the part of the speaker and to facilitate the listener's comprehension. Hence, we may imagine another interpretation of 'comprehensible output' (Swain 1985), as a way that learners have to manage and construct their production from their own comprehension procedures. The learner's output then contains traces of the way he himself comes to understand how to express concepts when communicating in a second language.

5 Research design

As was explained in chapter 1, the project was designed as a cross-linguistic and longitudinal study. It contained three phases: the pilot year (1982), the field work (1983-5) and analysis and report writing (1985-8). The dates are approximate, as there was significant overlap between the phases (in particular, pilot analyses were undertaken right from the project's beginning). Six research teams, based in Aix-en-Provence (French by Moroccan learners), Göteborg (Swedish), Heidelberg (German), London (English), Paris (French by Hispanic learners) and Tilburg (Dutch), participated in the project. The members of these teams are given in Appendix A.

This chapter will concentrate on the cross-linguistic and longitudinal design, and examine problems of sampling and comparability in some detail. We will begin with some short remarks on piloting, which was an important part of the research design.

5.1 Piloting

The project's pilot year allowed the research team leaders to work out and test a complete research procedure, from establishing contacts with immigrant networks, via testing the feasibility and relevance of different data collection techniques with volunteers from these networks, to transcribing and storing the data and starting pilot analyses. The pilot year also served to select and train researchers. A description and assessment of the main data collection techniques used during the field work is given in chapter 6. This work was collected in the form of a Field Manual (ESF:Perdue 1984), whose primary purpose was to provide a framework for the core aspects of the project which would be easily consultable by researchers.

Researchers

The researchers were an integral part of the design. In all teams, there was at least one linguist who was a native speaker of the TL, as well as one for each SL. This allowed the development of each learner to be evaluated from two different points of view. In the same way as cultural background knowledge acts as a filter on interpretation in inter-ethnic communication (see chapter 4.2) so may native language knowledge act as a filter in interpreting a learner variety. In particular, one tends to see the variety as minimally different from one's own. The closeness fallacy had a wide, if diffuse, influence over the analyses of the project right from the preparation of data for analysis. Faced with the same recording, a TL researcher naturally interpreted the learner's production in the direction of the TL, whereas the SL researcher interpreted towards the SL. The simple expedient of having both check the other's transcription led to the clear identification of problems of interpretation which could be given in the form of <comments> in the transcription (see chapter 7). To transcribe is, as is well-known, to interpret.

Much was demanded of the researchers. The SL researcher was usually the guide through immigrant networks, contacting, motivating and accompanying the learner throughout the longitudinal study. The TL researcher organised the data collection encounters. Both were active in transcribing and storing the data, and in the actual analysis. All of these tasks involve specialist skills, and each individual had varying experience with them. This basic fact made the elaboration of a detailed, step-by-step plan of action (that is, a Field Manual) all the more important: it provided a minimal programme to ensure comparability for the core aspects of the project.

Data collection procedures

In a study such as this, comparability is of the essence. On the other hand it is both impossible and undesirable to have a completely regimented procedure applied regardless of differences between informants, their environment and above all their motivation. A compromise had to be reached where a core set of data collection techniques of proven relevance to the research areas were run at the different sites.

A variety of data collection techniques were piloted. Some techniques were 'made optional' (that is, discarded by a majority) because of their lack of suitability for the type of learner studied. In particular, techniques requiring developed metalinguistic and/or metapragmatic capabilities proved difficult to run with such learners. Furthermore, one major lesson was learned, namely, the extreme difficulty involved in getting 'authentic' recordings of the day to day discourse activities of the learners.

The year ended with a training week for all the researchers, based on the shared procedures set out in the Field Manual, as a result of piloting work. It should, however, be clear that field work on such a scale will inevitably pose problems of comparability: the careful reader will notice what these problems were in Volume II, by an examination of the TLs studied in each research area.

Pilot analyses
Pilot analyses continued throughout the writing of the Field Manual and into the data collection phase. As the function of such analyses is to ascertain more exactly what are fruitful lines of research and what are not, it is instructive, with hindsight, to discuss the three research questions which were abandoned after initial analyses. These were all concerned with the relation between intrinsic and extrinsic explanations to ALA, and all encountered the same difficulty: we were over-optimistic about the extent to which it would be possible to follow individual learners' contacts with the TL environment.

The lack of control over the TL environment has already been alluded to several times. For example, it was extremely difficult to foresee the occasions for the 'authentic recordings' mentioned above, that is, recordings involving non-project interlocutors with whom the learners spontaneously had contacts in the TL. The more such contacts are organised (by researchers!) the less 'authentic' they become. On another level, the data collection window on the TL contacts of such informants is bound to be incomplete, and this precluded, as we saw in 4.2, systematically relying on misunderstandings or non-understandings as evidence in describing the acquisition process. Such phenomena are inevitably chance occurrences; they cannot be elicited in the same systematic way as the description of spatial relations, for example.

Thus the first research question to be abandoned was an investigation of 'the effect that understandings and misunderstandings during contacts with TL speakers has on [the learner's] propensity to learn' (Field Manual:68), a sub-area of the chapter called 'Understanding, Misunderstanding and Breakdown'. This question in effect presupposed the analysis of understandings and misunderstandings during asymmetrical encounters, and an evaluation of their cumulative effects on individual development. There was no way of evaluating these effects, as there was insufficient control over a learner's exposure to language. The available data were not equal to the initial aim.

A second area to disappear was a proposed study of the performances of a group of older informants who had been resident in the target countries for five years or more: the 'long residence group' (Field Manual:12). One of the questions to be investigated with this group was whether a change in their external circumstances (family situation, change or loss of job) would have a linguistic effect on what was assumed to be a stabilised variety. This initiative was dropped as the interested research teams completely failed to agree on data collection procedures, a fact which is unsurprising as the difficulty of available techniques in capturing the linguistic environment is compounded by the impossibility of controlling for the relevant parts of life. For the two questions just discussed, participant observation cannot sample validly over time.

Thirdly, a study was planned on the development of the learners' lexicon in relation to various semantic fields, in an attempt to characterise the items important to an individual's own communication. The hypothesis was that communicative needs in various areas of daily life would determine the richness and diversity of a learner's lexicon, and it was decided that the fields of HOME, WORK, and SOCIAL RELATIONS (Field Manual:121) should be studied, with the expectation that home-related vocabulary would remain limited, and that vocabulary related to the other areas would vary significantly according to the personal circumstances of the learner, in particular whether he was in work or not. This question would give an indirect reflection of the links between language and life, if learners' personal circumstances could be carefully documented, and the relevant vocabulary reliably tapped. Techniques which would reliably elicit the active vocabulary of a learner demand a type of metalinguistic skill which these informants do not have, and furthermore, it is not apparent in the face of actually elicited vocabulary which lexical items belong to which field, from the learner's point of view.

Three lessons may be drawn from the previous paragraphs: firstly, that it is wise to conduct pilot analyses; secondly, that it is difficult to go beyond the correlative studies of chapter 2 in assessing the impact of the world on the learner's acquisition; thirdly, it is advisable not to be too enthusiastic when formulating research questions (or rather, be enthusiastic, but do not expect everything to work).

5.2   Cross-linguistic design

In chapter 2 we noticed a recurrent difficulty which previous studies had in identifying with any certainty what features of the learning process are specifically due to SL influence, and features which are shared between many SL/TL pairings, allowing more general statements. As we pointed out in chapters 1 and 2, the main motivation for the project's cross-linguistic design was to allow us to make acquisitional statements over more than one SL/TL pairing with some confidence. It is as follows: The TLs are Dutch, English, French, German and Swedish. For each TL, two SLs were selected. This selection was based on two criteria:

- First, those SLs with the greatest number of speakers (in a given target country) were given priority.
- Second, it was desirable to examine linguistically interesting cases of acquisition; for example, to compare the acquisition of a closely related language – such as, a Spanish speaker learning French – with that of a more distant language – such as, a Spanish speaker learning Swedish.

A compromise between these two criteria led to the combination of target and source languages shown in the following figure:

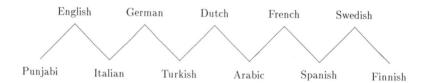

Arabic, Spanish, Turkish and Italian are each represented in two target countries. Punjabi and Finnish are the most important SLs in Great Britain and Sweden, respectively, but they play no significant role elsewhere. Three out of the six SLs are non-Indo-European: Arabic, Turkish and Finnish.

This organisation made it possible to undertake paired comparisons of the learning of one TL (such as German) by speakers of different SLs (here, Italian and Turkish) and the learning of different TLs (such as, German and English) by speakers of one SL (here, Italian), and to achieve overall a systematic comparison of ten linguistically different cases of learning.

Although the above combination was in the circumstances an almost optimal solution, some drawbacks and problems remain which should be mentioned. The linguistic spread of the TLs is narrow. Four of them are Germanic, while French is a Romance language. Although it would have been linguistically more interesting to have a typologically broader range of TLs, these five were nevertheless chosen as they were, and continue to be the most important European languages for foreign workers. In relation to the areas of investigation chosen, moreover, these languages nevertheless pose different acquisition problems, as may be seen immediately.

There are problems of description for all the languages which have to do either with their inherent socio-geographical variability, or the fact that the TL samples relevant to the research areas of chapter 4 are of discourse activity (rather than de-contextualised sentences). We will briefly discuss both problems.

We noted in chapter 3.2 the problems posed by the fact that the SLs are subject to considerable regional variation. The TLs are also subject to variation. Foreign workers in Germany, for example, are usually exposed (in the street) not to standard German but to a local vernacular, which in many cases, if spoken by an uncompromising native speaker, is not completely intelligible to other speakers of German. The variety of Swedish spoken in the Göteborg area has certain word order possibilities and intonational phenomena not found in other dialects of Swedish. The French spoken in the Marseilles and Paris areas show phonological differences. And so on.

The grammatical descriptions which are available for some of these languages concentrate on, and indeed are restricted to, structural properties. They do not deal comprehensively with language in use, that is, with spoken language phenomena such as ellipsis, dislocations, cross-utterance cohesive devices, etc. But it is language in use which supplies the input for the learner.

Hence there were two inevitable consequences for the investigation. Firstly, it was impossible to rely on simple categorisations such as 'speaker of Spanish' when selecting informants. It was necessary to control as much as possible for the native variety, as we have already seen in chapter 3.2. Secondly, it was necessary to collect data about the language which is actually spoken to the informants and in some cases to work out descriptions of relevant features. However, the overriding priority was achieved: having a design where groups of informants coming from relatively homogeneous SL backgrounds could be compared for the acquisition of different languages, and where the acquisition of the same, relatively homogeneous language by learners from different SL backgrounds could be compared.

Such a design remains constant over time. We hypothesised in chapter 1.3 that the learner's SL provides a conceptual and linguistic framework for *initial* analysis of the TL. However, controlling for SL influence cannot come only from comparisons of the SL/TL systems. As the learner progresses his 'psychotypology' (Kellerman 1987) of the TL is recalculated, and different aspects of the SL become relevant in his analysis of the TL. There is a constant interaction between SL-knowledge, TL-input and the changing state of the learner's own variety. In this respect, *a priori* comparisons of SL/TL systems should not be expected fully to predict the path acquisition takes.

We will nevertheless look now at some features of the TLs relevant for the research areas of language production (chapter 4.3), that is, constituent and utterance structure, and reference to space and time, in order to provide some basic information for the reader, and secondly, to point out some potential learning problems.

Utterance structure

In what follows, we concentrate on the order relations between the verb and its arguments in declaratives, as this is most relevant for the study of Volume II:I.1. Despite their close relationship, English, on the one hand, and Dutch and German, on the other, have very different word order constraints, even in simple declaratives. Swedish comes between these two poles, and spoken French utterances are organised differently again.

English has a basic S–V–O word order and its word order, rather than case marking, signals verb-argument relations. Horn (1986) points out that speakers tend to use the subject position for material that is given, familiar, destressed, presupposed, and high on the natural topic-worthiness hierarchy, and that 'left-movement rules' often concern such material.

Dutch and German are said to be 'V2-languages': word order in these languages turns around the distinction between a finite (V_f) and a non-finite (V_i) component of the verb which can, but need not, be fused in one word (V_{if}). In both Dutch and German, V_i often consists of two parts – the 'stem' and a separable particle (PART), such as *herunter, af* in the following examples:

(1) (NP – V_f – NP –   PART + V_i)
    Hans   ist   die Treppe heruntergekommen (G)
    Hans   is   de trap   afgekomen (D)
    'Hans has the stairs down-come'

(2) (NP – V_{if} –   NP –   PART)
     Hans   kommt die Treppe herunter (G)
     Hans   komt   de trap   af (D)
     'Hans comes the stairs down'

The main difference between Dutch and German concerns the position of V_f in subordinate clauses: it immediately precedes V_i in Dutch, whereas it follows V_i in German.

With these few facts in mind, we may state the basic word order rules for these languages as follows:

(I) V_i is clause final.

(II) a. V_f is preceded by exactly one major constituent in declarative main clauses.

      b. In yes/no questions and imperatives, V_f is clause-initial.

      c. In subordinate clauses, V_f immediately precedes V_i in Dutch, and is clause-final in German (overruling I).

(III)   In case of fusion, V_f and PART keep their position; the rest of V_i moves and fuses with V_f to V_{if}.

We will concentrate on simple rather than subordinate clauses. Previous work has shown the latter to be a late and rare development: (IIc) corresponds to the final stage of ZISA's developmental sequence.

Note that the single major constituent, which according to (II)a must precede the finite verb, need not be the subject (hence the 'V2' characterisation). In both languages it can be an object or adverbial, as in the following German example with initial adverbial:

(3) *Morgen gehe ich nach Bonn zurück*
     'Tomorrow go I to Bonn back'

The constraints on what constituents can appear in this initial position are less severe in German than in Dutch, a fact usually attributed to the highly complex case-marking system of German articles and pronouns: semantic role relations between the verb and its arguments are expressed relatively more by case in German, and more by word order in Dutch, therefore. We saw in chapter 2.2 that previous work has established that the German case system presents severe learning problems.

Swedish is typologically between Dutch and English. Although it is verb-second, as is Dutch, all of the verb group (that is, both the finite and infinite part) is found in second position in simple declarative sentences. Subordinate sentences have the same word order as superordinate sentences, with the important exception that sentence adverbs such as the negative *inte*, which follow V_f in superordinates, directly precede it in subordinates.

French has a complex pre-verbal auxiliary-clitic system. The auxiliary combines tense and aspectuals. The clitic pronouns function deictically and anaphorically like the pronouns of the other TLs, but have a third function, central to spoken French, and marginal in the other TLs, which we will call 'pronoun-copy', that is co-referentiality with a full NP (lexical or pronominal) in the same utterance. Pragmatic/discourse phenomena determine the position of the full arguments, while the clitics specify their semantic role relations to the verb. An immediate acquisition problem presented by French is therefore that it has a double system of pronouns: *strong* pronouns which occupy the same positions as lexical NPs, and *preverbal* pronouns cliticised to the verb. In addition, the opaque fused forms of the auxiliary/clitic combinations may be predicted to present analytic problems for the learner.

So for different reasons, French and German show a relative order of arguments and verbs which is freer in than in the other TLs, where 'freer' means more sensitive to discourse constraints such as topicality, givenness, etc. The learning problem that these languages present is morpho-syntactic, with the syntactic and semantic role relations between verb and actants being conveyed less unequivocally by word order.

We have already seen the different problems which the 'alternation' of the lexical verb in Dutch and German present for learners with a Turkish, Moroccan or Romance language background. It should be clear that the acquisition of finiteness in these languages has far greater ramifications for utterance structure than it does in the other TLs, as finiteness governs the position of the lexical part of the verb. Previous research (see chapter 2.4) has left the question moot as to whether word order and finiteness are (Jordens 1988) or are not (Meisel 1991) acquisitionally linked. This question receives further examination in Volume II:I.1.

As far as the internal structure of the actants is concerned, we saw in chapter 2.4 that the determiners of lexical nouns presented various learning problems. A hitherto undiscussed learning problem is posed by the structure of the Swedish NP. It is similar to that of Dutch, but definiteness is marked by a suffix which varies for gender and number: *hus+et* ('the house'); *bil+en* ('the car'); *husna, bilna* ('the houses, cars'). All the TLs have pronouns which are marked for person, number and case. Previous work (see chapter 2.4) uncovered acquisitional differences associated with all three traits: first and third person do not develop in parallel, singular and plural do not develop in parallel, and so on. What was less clear from the results of previous work was the exact relationship between the internal structure of the actants (including zero anaphor), their place in the utterance and the acquisitional stage of the learner. This will be examined in more detail in Volume II:I.1. We may already formulate the same hypothesis (in line with previous results, in fact) as we made in chapter 4.3 for temporal and spatial reference, and for the same reasons: that for adults, deictic use of pronouns will precede anaphoric use.

Temporality
In all of the TLs, the temporal properties of utterances are expressed by (combinations of) discourse organisational principles, the Aktionsart of the verb, by adverbial constituents, periphrastic constructions and by morphology. The latter means are more specific to individual languages.

For *adverbials*, all these languages have adverbials which allow the speaker to specify deictically, anaphorically, or by an independent expression, some particular time span where the utterance is localised – the temporal *relatum* (see chapter 4.3). Previous work summarised in chapter 2 suggests that temporal reference is overwhelmingly marked by adverbials before tense. Von Stutterheim (1986) has shown furthermore that place adverbials may convey a derived temporal specification: 'Turkey' is understood as 'When I was in Turkey', for example. What is less clear from previous work is what type of adverb is used in what context, and whether there is an acquisition order.

Two specific problems which have received virtually no attention are the following:

- There are some frequent and vexing adverbs such as *schon/noch, encore/toujours, still/yet* whose conditions of appropriateness are difficult to specify, as they depend on subtle deictic/anaphoric calculations. These may prove to be a learning problem.
- Still another group are nowhere mentioned in previous work: these are the optional adverbial equivalents of the English 'progressive'. Where English has a grammaticalised aspect marker *be + ing – I am cooking* – French, German and Dutch use semi-grammaticalised adverbs, which are optional, and emphasise the

imperfectivity of the situation which can otherwise be expressed without: Fr. *je suis en train de faire la cuisine* is more explicit than *je fais la cuisine*, for example. The fact that *be + ing* does not present an option poses an immediate problem for learners of English which other learners do not have. Thus we have a TL contrast between optional and obligatory aspect marking, and contrasts of similar nature exist between the SLs. The acquisition of English and German should therefore present different problems for Italian learners, as German has no grammaticalised aspect.

All languages have a verb group comprising auxiliary + main verb, and tense is assigned to the leftmost verbal item, which is therefore finite. Previous research (see chapter 2.4) established that learners tend to use the bare verb first, then combinations of modal + V, auxiliary + V. The cross-linguistic problem here is what counts as an auxiliary, and what the permitted combinations of auxiliary and verb are in the different TLs. In English, the verb optionally combines with modal, perfect, progressive and passive auxiliaries, whereas there is no progressive auxiliary in the other languages, as we have seen. French has aspectual auxiliaries *aller* (=‘be going to’) and *venir de* (=‘have just’), but French modals are full verbs, and French has a grammaticalised future tense.

The tense opposition in the TLs’ cases may be described as ‘present’ versus ‘past’, but the temporal values of this opposition in combination with different auxiliaries – in particular with *have + V_{en}*, and formal equivalents in the other TLs – vary considerably. The present tense in association with the main verb can be used in all cases to refer to specific situations which hold true at the time of speaking (although *be + ing* complicates the picture in English). However, the same is not true of the past: in French, the *passé simple* is no longer used in spoken language, where the *passé composé* is used in aspectual opposition to the *imparfait*. Swedish has a similar opposition to French, whereas the German and Dutch *Perfekt* and *Praeteritum* opposition depends only marginally on aspectual considerations, and mainly on verb and text type.

Over and above the syntactic ramifications of finiteness in Dutch and German which we have examined, the auxiliary + verb complex thus presents different form-function correspondences in all the TLs, which may provoke different learning problems.

Reference to space

Spatial concepts are encoded in the TLs principally by prepositions, adverbs, and static and dynamic verbs. The object of the preposition specifies the *relatum*. Use of adverbs depend on conditions of recoverability of the relatum. Case marking plays a role for German, certain German prepositions alternatively assigning accusative or dative marking to the relatum to indicate a dynamic or a static relation, respectively. For the other TLs, the role of case marking is negligible, and this may prove a problem for learners coming from highly inflected languages such as Finnish and Turkish. Recall that Jansen and Lalleman (1980a,b, see chapter 2.2) observed a tendency of Turkish learners to avoid preposition use in Dutch.

Spatial information is distributed differently over the different categories. In Talmy's (1985) typology of languages, Germanic languages differ from the Romance languages (French, Italian, Spanish) in that they encode a motion event with a manner component in the verb stem. The expression of path/direction of a motion is left to 'satellites', typically prefixes and particles. The Romance languages, on the other hand, typically encode the path/direction in the verb stem, leaving manner to be expressed elsewhere (often in a gerundive complement). Although English is primarily Germanic from this point of view, the Romance influence does become apparent through such highly frequent verbs as *enter, leave, return, descend*. The following examples repeat example (3) and the German variant of (2), and give equivalent French and English utterances for them. They illustrate the different distribution of directional information in the three languages:

(4) *Morgen gehe ich nach Bonn zurück.*
  Demain je retourne à Bonn.
  Tomorrow I'm returning/going back to Bonn.
(5) *Hans kommt die Treppe herunter.*
  Hans descend l'escalier.
  Hans is descending/coming down the stairs.

We saw in chapter 4.3 that deictic adverbs enter into different oppositions in different languages. A further difference in the distribution of deictic information concerns German. A restricted, but central class of verbs in all the TLs conflate deictic anchoring with the motion event within the verb stem: *come/go, aller/venir, kommen/gehen*, etc., but are expressed in German through the use of satellites as well: *hin* (= 'from here to there, away from the speaker');

her (= 'from there to here, toward the speaker', as in example 5), which are further combinable with directional markers in the horizontal: *hinein, herein/hinaus, heraus* (= deictically anchored 'in' and 'out') and the vertical: *hin/herauf* (= 'upward'), *hin/herunter* (= 'downward', as in example 5).

The verb + particle combinations of German and Dutch can therefore distribute spatial information over the utterance, and learners may pick up on one or other of the sources of information. Adverbials and prepositional phrases thus play a different role in the different TLs, and can be expected to present different acquisitional problems.

Further acquisitional problems can arise from the different configurations to which a form does or does not apply. German *auf* 'means' *on*, but is restricted to contexts of vertical support, whereas *on* is not: it is impossible to talk in German of a picture hanging 'auf' a wall, as we saw in chapter 4. This case parallels that of certain auxiliary + verb combinations (such as, *have + V_{en}*), in that a formally similar structure – here, *auf/on* + NP – does not have an identical function in related languages. Recall that we saw in chapter 3.3 that providing 'meaning equivalents' between Turkish and German spatial expressions did not solve the acquisition problem for the Turkish learners. All in all, it appears that the individual TLs pose *a priori* a number of specific acquisition problems in relation to the research areas of chapter 4.3, despite their narrow typological spread.

5.3   Longitudinal design

The motivation for conducting a longitudinal investigation had as its starting point the observations of chapter 1 on the *internal logic* of the acquisition process. The learner variety approach hypothesises that the individual learning process can be construed as a motivated series of transitions from one learner variety to the next, approximating, in principle, more closely to the TL. The logic of an adult's development can therefore be sought in a close examination of the relative success of learner varieties *in use, over time*. In-depth longitudinal studies seeking to identify which communicative factors, in context, motivate linguistic change, and which factors cause the variety to fossilise, were, and remain, thin on the ground, as we saw in chapter 2. Descriptions of adult language development had overwhelmingly been based on extrapolations from the results of cross-sectional studies (studies of different learners at different stages of development), which of course are less time-consuming and easier to carry out.

The advantages and disadvantages of longitudinal case studies are traditionally held to be, respectively, (a) that they better capture the process of acquisition and (b) that their results are not generalisable. We will start with (b), which states that the results of an in-depth case study are in principle valid only for the individual in question, as there is no telling what is truly idiosyncratic from what is generalisable. Cross-sectional studies, on the other hand, give generalisable results because they are designed for and amenable to standard statistical procedures on representative populations.

The problems with cross-sectional studies are that they necessarily analyse the product of acquisition having-taken-place, rather than the acquisition process, and that an *a priori* frame of analysis (typically that of the TL) is applied. This is methodologically unsatisfactory. Firstly, both intra- and intersubject variation tend to be obscured, as we saw in chapter 4 in the discussion of variation potentially due to acquisition. Secondly, idiosyncratic systematicity disappears. A clear example of such a danger would be a morpheme study methodology applied to the analysis of past time reference (PTR) in the production of large groups of beginners, intermediate and advanced students of a language, such as English, that has a past tense. An overall percentage of correct suppliance of the past tense would not identify the following cases (of correct suppliance) which are potentially relevant for the explanation of the acquisition process:

- past tense only occurs on end-state verbs, and expresses an aspectual value;
- only irregular verbs are tensed, regular verbs never are;
- verbs get past tense when the learner is quoting the speech of a native TL-speaker, otherwise not;
- past tense occurs only in hypothetical contexts, and has the value of a mood;
- a learner combines two or more of these possibilities;
- different learners use different (combinations of) possibilities.

This is the point made by Meisel (1991) apropos of subject-verb agreement which we mentioned in chapter 2.3. At the risk of labouring the point, we may say that morpheme studies methodology is at best a blunt tool – but morpheme studies are still actively used (see 2.3 above). Bley-Vroman aptly sums up these problems in what he terms the 'comparative fallacy':

...if a population study uses a single TL scheme for classifying the data of many different learners there is a good possibility that the scheme will not only obscure the structure of the individual interlanguages, but in addition will obscure the structure of each interlanguage in the population in a different way. (1983: 15-16)

For (a), an in-depth study, where the observer tries to place himself 'in the shoes' of the learner, as we said in chapter 1, will in principle better capture the descriptive categories relevant to the horizontal and vertical systematicity of the individual variety (the problem being to evaluate their representativity). It should be pointed out that the identification of the factors determining the acquisition process, and their interaction, depend crucially on the relevance of the categories used to describe the process in the first place. For the first and second aims of the project, a valid and reliable explanation (question I) depends on a valid and reliable description (question II), and vice versa. It is not methodologically sound to describe the productions of a learner with the descriptive framework of what we may term, following Corder (1971), a different dialect: the TL. Such a description necessarily results in a dichotomy of 'error' versus 'non-error', and the learner systematicity is missed. The postulation of 'non-errors' in relation to the TL is the prime case of what was termed in chapter 1, the 'closeness fallacy'.

To overcome the double problem of (a) and (b), we need a methodology where valid results can be generalised, and the obvious way to proceed is to accumulate results from a *number* of *comparable* case studies. This is what the ESF project in fact has done, since the results from each research area are based on approximately twenty case studies. Recall that one of the first questions asked in chapter 1 was whether the very variable outcomes of ALA ('fossilisation') could be put down to varying success along one itinerary, or whether structurally different processes had to be admitted. The way to an answer lies in seeing to what extent individual itineraries are indeed comparable, and the problem becomes that of identifying generalisable stages within an area of cross-linguistic variability. The cross-linguistic design allows the research, in principle, to distil generalised stages (if such stages exist) from pairwise comparisons, provided comparable analyses can be carried out on comparable data.

In the search for comparable data, three minimal assumptions are made: (i) that the learner's activity is fundamentally meaningful; (ii) that meanings can be identified that are shared among learners;

and (iii) that this meaningful activity can be validly sampled. Some of the considerations of how the research design dealt with problems of comparability are set out in the next two paragraphs, which provide an opportunity both for a recapitulation of the approach sketched in chapter 1, and for a discussion of some classic methodological problems. First, we deal with the many sampling problems to be faced, then with our attempts to solve them.

In chapters 1 and 4, we have proposed a view of language acquisition whereby the learner entertains different, possibly conflicting, hypotheses about the TL, and where these hypotheses become critical, leading the learners to adopt or discard them. This process is brought about *in and by* discourse activity: it is the confrontation of hypotheses and input data which provokes the reorganisation of the learner variety, and which may provoke variable behaviour. This view of acquisition immediately poses methodological problems to do with controlling individual variability and sampling the learner's discourse activity. We will discuss the latter first.

Problems of ecological validity
The type of learner we are studying acquires the TL essentially in communication with TL speakers in his everyday environment. Obtaining data representative of this communication is clearly important, and piloting work showed that systematic access to the everyday TL input is well-nigh impossible. What is representative of the everyday input?

Hakuta and Cancino (1977:312) suggest that everyday contacts provoke participation in certain *types* of discourse activity. One can imagine data collection techniques which sample these activity types (participant observation) or which simulate them (role play). However, the problems both of activity selection and recording are severe. The particular difficulty in obtaining 'authentic' recordings which we experienced during the pilot year made us rely more on role-play techniques (of an argumentative or counselling nature), and participant observation was largely confined to everyday trips out and about in town (learner takes researcher on a 'guided tour').

In the resulting recordings, TL-speakers who have nothing to do with the research programme interact with the learners, and this language is available for analysis, both from the point of view of its formal characteristics, and from that of the TL speakers' degree of adaptation to the learner (scaffolding, questions, misunderstandings).

Problems of individual variation
A longitudinal study such as this is faced in a particularly blatant way with the practical problems of analysing recorded spoken language. It is possible in principle that learners' behaviour varies along the 'attention to speech' continuum (Tarone 1984). But as we have already pointed out, this is not the only source of potential variability. Pauses, hesitations, false starts, and self-corrections are not only prevalent in learner speech, but their status is ambiguous. Are they normal speech editing phenomena or are they traces of the learner's activity of system-building?

One way of capturing stylistic variation is to use a combination of data collection techniques for the study of a given phenomenon at a given time. The variability may prove to be systematic. The problem, as we might expect, is when learner behaviour is simply variable in synchrony, either across techniques, or even within one technique. Here, the problem becomes one of ascertaining whether this 'trouble' is indeed due to the learner entertaining conflicting hypotheses about some aspect of the TL, an important decision in the context of acquisition studies.

One may appeal directly to the learner to answer this question. However, there are two major methodological problems with learner intuitions which preclude their being given undue importance in acquisition studies. These are the extreme difficulty of obtaining judgements on (aspects of) the learner variety, rather than guesses about the TL (the learner may also succumb to the closeness fallacy!), and the well-documented discrepancies between spontaneous and judgemental data (see amongst others, Giacobbe and Lucas 1980, Coppetiers 1987). 'Intuitional data' may merely add a further, metalinguistic dimension to possible variability.

Problems of avoidance and ambiguity
Assuming for the moment the problems of variability to be solved, all of a given learner sample is potentially relevant for analysis, but the question then arises whether the sample is sufficient. This classic question with corpus studies may for present purposes be considered from two points of view – quantity (does the sample provide enough relevant data?) and ambiguity (can the data be unequivocally interpreted?).

As far as *quantity* is concerned, 'enough' is when the sample reveals what the learner can and cannot do in relation to a particular linguistic task (here, the research areas of chapter 4). This diagnosis is complicated if, in a situation where the learner is 'not sure', he avoids the task. The data collection techniques of the previous paragraph (role plays and guided tours) were chosen to be representative of everyday contacts; they are not guided systematically, and cannot be expected to give unequivocal evidence both of what the learner can and cannot do.

One way of solving the classic problem of avoidance is to devise quasi-experiments (also known as 'games') where the phenomenon in question has to be dealt with. For example, the 'stage directions' technique was devised in order to make the expression by the learner of a number of spatial configurations inescapable. Another way of controlling for avoidance is self-confrontation, but the technique is very time-consuming and unwieldy when the learner has little idea of what a metalinguistic judgement is. The technique is more useful for *assessing the learner's communicative intentions*: if the analyst is proceeding with a reconstruction of the learner's own construction of meaning, then the learner's communicative intentions need themselves to be assessed, and self-confrontation can be organised to get the learner to comment on recordings of encounters he took part in. Another possible control involves techniques which make available an extra-linguistic 'reality check', as with route directions, stage directions, picture descriptions or film retellings. This is an important reason why some data collection techniques were video-recorded.

As for *ambiguity*, Corder (1973) pointed out the need for 'textual' data to be supplemented with 'intuitional' data in order to circumvent what Bley-Vroman subsequently called the 'ambiguity problem': 'A restricted sample of the learner's production cannot unambiguously determine hypothesis type' (1986:367). Bley-Vroman (*ibid.*:369) sees an answer to his 'ambiguity problem' in the use of '... research methodologies that allow introspection, learner grammaticality judgements, learner explanations, protocol analyses, or other methods that go well beyond corpus collection'. The problem here is that these learner reactions are also finite, and not necessarily less ambiguous than the original data in relation to the functioning of the learner variety, as we suggested above. If learners are testing out competing hypotheses, it is *in principle* unreasonable to ask them to supply an unequivocal answer. So in practice, Bley-Vroman's recommendations do not take us 'beyond' corpus collection, they merely result in a bigger corpus.

Given that the learner's variety is in evolution, the researcher finds her- or himself torn between two contradictory necessities; that of confining the corpus to one moment, and that of keeping the corpus open in order sufficiently to explore the learner's hypotheses. To ignore this contradiction is to equate the horizontal systematicity of the learner's variety with stability, to reason in synchrony, and to cease to do acquisition studies.

The ambiguity problem becomes less acute when the corpus has its place within a longitudinal study where the techniques provide for specific comparisons, and this is where the *data collection cycle cycle* comes in. There was a double motivation for the data collection cycle. Firstly, there was a generally felt need after initial data collection to safeguard comparability in the face of the differing situations in each country, and secondly, we needed to answer as convincingly as possible the challenges of the previous paragraphs. We wanted a tool which would indeed allow longitudinal comparisons of specific activities providing abundant and valid data for each research area.

A *cycle* is a series of *encounters* with longitudinal informants, in which a certain number of *activities* are accomplished in a fixed order. The cycle was scheduled to run for approximately ten months, and was repeated twice. Each longitudinal informant was recorded at four to six week intervals, and therefore did the ordered activities at least three times. Some activities took place more than once per cycle, while others took place more than once within a single encounter. Activity *types* are specified by a single letter code in the data-file naming conventions. Those which were undertaken by all research teams for cross-linguistic analysis will be described in chapter 6.

In principle, the cycle achieves longitudinal and cross-sectional comparability, allowing statements of the type, 'In the first third of the first cycle of data collection, technique x was used with all learners. X was subsequently repeated twice, at nine-month intervals'. In practice, not all learners were absolute beginners at the start, and speed of individual acquisition naturally varied, so the cycles do not in any way correspond to three general levels of 'beginner', 'intermediate', 'advanced'. What the repeated cycle does however allow is to trace the history and geography of a learner's hypotheses in a systematic way, because the communicative tasks can be kept constant over time. Problems of individual variability due to hypothesis testing at a given time should be apparent from an upstream and downstream comparison of comparable attempts. One then begins to observe language change, and to translate at least some aspects of synchronic variability into acquisitional systematicity.

5.4 Conclusion: the research design as multiple controls

The above research design produces generalisations which are distilled from systematic and detailed comparisons: (a) of the performances of one learner in one or more tasks repeated over time, (b) of the longitudinal study resulting from (a), with similar analyses of the same tasks done by other learners sharing SL and TL, and (c) of the resultant description of this linguistic case, with analyses of learners from other language pairings.

Each step of the analysis can be seen as controlling for some aspect of the results. The longitudinal results of each linguistic pairing (b) are controlled from the SL researcher's and the TL researcher's viewpoint. This is not a trivial remark: in one study – temporality – the acquisition of English produced two coherent and independent (but not entirely compatible) chapters from a Punjabi and from a Germanic viewpoint. Obviously, this problem will not arise when only one researcher analyses the data! As we saw, SL/TL influence cannot be detected by simple *a priori* contrastive analysis given the changing nature of the learner's knowledge, which is what motivated the posthoc pairwise comparison of (c). The validity of the data depends on finding techniques which reliably give interpretable data, which motivates the use of data collection techniques that assess the communicative intentions of learners' production by providing 'reality checks', and also the use of the technique of self-confrontation. Finally, the comparison of a learner's performances in relation to an identical technique at different times allows the analysts to check their own synchronic interpretations.

One may finally mention the need to control for the potential effect of observation. Tarone (1979) was among the first to cite the 'observer's paradox' (Labov) in relation to ALA studies. There are two aspects to this problem for present purposes; that of stylistic variation, which we have already discussed, and also the fact that observation itself is an intrusion into the observed. Labovian techniques for overcoming the observer's paradox are well documented (for example, Labov 1972). However, in a longitudinal study such as this, observation is cumulative; it would be strange if regular observation over thirty months did not have some effect on informants' linguistic behaviour, and this consideration prompted the devising of the 'control' study (see chapter 8.4).

In this chapter, we have alluded to several different data collection techniques intended to provide a framework for different aspects of the research design. In the following chapter, we proceed to describe them in detail.

6 Data collection techniques

6.1 Introduction

This chapter describes the data collection techniques used by all the research teams for the three cycles of the longitudinal study. These techniques provided the empirical basis for comparative, cross-linguistic analysis. The data collection took place in a series of regular encounters (every four to six weeks, see chapter 5.3) with learners. These encounters always included *conversation* (coded A) which provided a backbone for the longitudinal study, serving to keep researchers abreast of what was happening in the informant's life. The information required from these conversations meant that researchers asked a lot of questions, at least at the start of each encounter. They came to be referred to by some researchers as 'friendly interrogations'. However these questions also served to establish topics of conversation where the learner was encouraged to give his opinions and experiences. Conversations therefore provided question-answer sequences, argumentative sequences, and above all provided a source of personal narratives. They also functioned to structure the encounter, by allowing the researchers to introduce and explain the other activities to be performed.

Overall, the type of data collected had to be comparable for all the learners over time, and to cover the relevant aspects of the variety established by each learner at various points in development. What was needed was a set of data collection techniques which reflects the learners' everyday language use, whilst providing sufficient and valid data for the individual research areas. There is a tension between these two aims: samples of forms of communication reflecting those in which a learner spontaneously acquires and applies his second language have the disadvantage of providing only chance occurrences of potentially crucial data for a research area, whereas samples from techniques designed specifically to elicit relevant data are less representative of the everyday environment. For most research areas, the procedure was therefore to concentrate on one or two techniques which were predicted to provide abundant and relevant data, and to scan data from other techniques (often conversation) in order to ensure that the main body of data did not show unexpected distortions. Sections 2 and 3 of this chapter describe the main data collection techniques for each research area, and indicate briefly which supplementary techniques were considered.

6.2 Interaction

For the studies of interaction, it had been decided (chapter 5.3) to make a close qualitative examination of types of discourse activity which could be said to reflect the learners' everyday language use, and in particular, cyclic simulations of bureaucratic and other goal-oriented encounters. The studies of interaction ('Ways of achieving understanding', 'Feedback processes', see Volume II, Part II) thus used two main techniques: an extended role play with a project-external professional (coded J), and a 'play scene' with a project researcher (coded C) which was specifically designed to elicit argumentative sequences. These core data were selectively completed by participant (accompanying) observation (coded K) and self-confrontation (coded H).

C, J and K correspond to a type of encounter (or to a simulation of such an encounter) which Erickson (1976) terms 'gatekeeping encounters', where one interlocutor (here, the native speaker) is in a position to grant or withhold goods or services. Thus the linguistic asymmetry between native speaker and learner is compounded by a power asymmetry. We supposed in chapter 4.2 that this type of highly instrumental interaction is the lot of many adult immigrants, and that the native speaker more often than not does not provide the linguistic support which in Long's (1983) terms 'cocoons' the learner. However, it was necessary to examine recordings of native speakers' speech in such encounters in order to test this supposition, which was in fact borne out. For a discussion, see Volume II:II.1.

Role Plays (J)
All the role plays took place in the (audio- or video-) studio with a TL speaker who was not a project worker, and was unknown to the informant. This speaker acted out his or her professional role in a plausible interview with the informant, who was told about the type

of interview to expect. The invited professionals were employers, employment counsellors, opinion pollsters, lawyers, housing officers, social workers, doctors, sales people.

The many different interviews can usefully be divided into two types: interviews where the informant had to apply for goods or services (akin to some of the 'play scenes' described below), and interviews where he was seeking advice. The first type – job interviews, applying for housing accommodation, opening a savings account – had a relatively predictable structure of questions and answers. The second type – counselling, opinion seeking – was more open-ended, and in fact more complex for the learners. In the job centre counselling interviews, for example, the interviewers saw their role in terms not only of assessing the applicants' suitability for a job (that is, questioning about previous experience, qualifications, training, etc.) but also as advisors on the type of training course the learner might realistically apply for. For many learners, this consultation by TL professionals about their own preferences and ambitions came as a surprise.

Play scenes (C)

These short scenes simulate in the video-recording studio an encounter with a TL speaker who has the power to grant or withhold goods or services, and where the informant must argue his case. The source language researcher explained in advance (and in the source language) to the informant what the background to the scene was, and what the desired outcome should be for him. Two examples of the most frequently performed play scenes follow:

The shrunken sweater. This scene takes place in a shop, with a TL researcher role playing a shop assistant. The informant is a customer trying to return a shrunken sweater. He has received the following instructions:

- you recently bought the sweater from the shop;
- you washed it according to instructions and it shrank;
- you want a refund;
- you do not want another sweater;
- you have lost the receipt (easier variant for the informant: here is the receipt to prove your good faith).

The objectives of the informant as customer are thus to convince the shop assistant of his right to complain, and to get his money back. The shop assistant on the other hand attempts:

- to lay the blame for the shrinkage at the customer's door;
- to suggest a straight exchange;
- to give the customer a credit note rather than a refund.

Sending by post. The scene is in a Post Office. A 'counter' has been set up with the appropriate equipment and with the TL researcher behind it. The informant/customer has been told he has a parcel/money order to send back to his home country. Depending on target country conventions, this transaction typically involves making decisions about mode of transfer, insurance, customs' declarations, and may be complicated by a less co-operative clerk in various ways, by announcing, for example, that postal relations have been suspended between the two countries.

Observation (K)
The informant was accompanied into town by the researcher, who covertly recorded certain transactions. In the main, informants were asked to perform small tasks such as making a purchase, visiting the bank, asking for information in travel agencies. On occasion, the informant had a real appointment, and this provided the opportunity for the accompanying researcher to help by intervening if necessary. In the later cycles, those informants who were willing were asked to carry out more complex tasks, such as enquiring how to obtain a mortgage from the Building Society, or obtaining information about buying a house of a particular specification in the town where they lived (ESF:Roberts and Simonot 1987). One Latin American informant, Nora, was recorded being interviewed for a newspaper round.

As can be seen, there is some overlap between the different techniques. They had originally been classified into these three types as a function of the type of TL speaker and the location. In particular, it was hypothesised that informants' familiarity with researchers and their way of speaking (C) would facilitate the task, whereas unfamiliarity with the interlocutor and the setting (K) would make problems of understanding in particular more acute. This hypothesis was partially borne out, but needs to be completed by consideration of two other factors: (a) whether the unknown TL speaker was accustomed to dealing with non-native speakers; (b) whether the interview had what may be termed a 'scenario'.

For (a), the collaborative TL speaker who is accustomed to dealing with non-native speakers (there is of course no necessity for these characteristics to go together) uses various accommodating procedures to favour joint understanding; these are discussed in Volume

II:II.1. Gray (ESF:1986) summarises them as the step by step, overt establishment of shared knowledge. The opposite case is where the TL speaker is used to providing information as a matter of routine in his professional capacity and sees no necessity, or possibly has no time, to depart from the way of speaking that he usually employs with native speakers. It was pointed out by one professional that the content and structure of counselling sessions place such demands on the TL speaker's attention that there is little capacity left for speech adaptation, even in the unlikely event that an awareness of the problem exists. Thus an unknown speaker who is also not collaborative poses a serious understanding problem for the learner.

For (b), during the interviews with a 'scenario' – job interviews, housing applications, etc. – both interlocutors had a goal, and the outcome had to be jointly negotiated. From the learner's point of view, this meant the next move of the interlocutor was often predictable, which in turn lessened problems of understanding. Where the 'scenario' was less clear, or unclear – the 'counselling' interviews described under J above – lack of a predictable development tended to increase understanding problems until an advanced level of proficiency was reached by the learner.

The contrasting combination of 'unclear scenario and unknown interlocutor', versus 'clear scenario and familiar interlocutor' can produce considerable learner variability with a cycle. Kogelheide (ESF:1987), for example, undertakes a detailed comparison of Tino's performance of J and C in cycles 2 and 3. In cycle 2, J was an occupational counselling session with an unknown interviewer, whereas C was his attempt at the 'shrunken sweater' scene described above. Although Tino had made good progress in German at the time, the counselling session is characterised by serious and intractable problems of understanding, whereas the play scene was negotiated with ease. This variability had virtually disappeared in the third cycle. The few instances of non-understanding in J were easily resolved, C again posing no problems of understanding.

This difference between (a) and (b) is indirectly reflected in the measures of chapter 8.1. The negotiated (a) activities demand a constantly high level of feedback activity throughout the three cycles, whereas in (b), the number of utterances containing feedback words, and the overall proportion of feedback words, decrease over time.

The studio techniques proved to be very productive. Both C and J provided long and structured speech, with its own dynamics. The results from K were more variable, depending on the personality and stage of acquisition of the informant, and on the possibility of adequately recording the encounters. Outgoing learners with some confidence in their ability to make themselves understood were happy to engage the TL environment with a hidden microphone, whereas at the other extreme some informants found the experience so painful that it was abandoned for them in cycle 3.

Self-confrontation (H)

Self-confrontation proved to be a difficult technique to use with adult immigrants. This technique involves confronting the learner with an audio- or video-recording of some interaction in which he himself took part (often C or J). This confrontation needs to be carefully prepared, and involves at least a preliminary analysis of the activity in order to select passages relevant for one or more of the research areas. The analysis is done, moreover, under severe time constraints, since it is necessary from the informant's point of view that he have more than a vague recollection of what went on, and from the researcher's point of view that her questions be relevant for the acquisitional stage of the learner. (See the discussion of Bley-Vroman's 'ambiguity problem' in chapter 5.3.)

The procedure we used was to play each pre-selected passage to the learner a first time without interruption. The passage was then played through a second time, with the informant being invited to stop the tape at any point where he wished to comment on something 'of note'. This second run-through served both for the informant to hear the passage again and for the researcher to observe what it was that the learner found noteworthy (see below). The passage was then played through a third time with the researcher asking the specific questions she had prepared. If, however, it was possible to ask any of her prepared questions during the second run-through as a follow-up to the informant's comments, this opportunity was taken, since it was felt to be important that the technique resemble informal conversation to the extent it was possible, rather than a language lesson.

The reason that self-confrontation may lean towards the pedagogical is that it is basically a metalinguistic activity, during which learners are asked to pay attention to stretches of speech as objects to be commented on. This activity therefore potentially raises learners' metalinguistic awareness, and naturally provokes on their part attempts to benefit from its pedagogic potential. As the researchers' aim was to observe rather than to intervene in the acquisition process, the technique was used sparingly.

What the researcher tried to elicit by this technique was three types of information. Firstly, information on the communicative intentions of the learner during the activity under consideration, and also on what the informant thought his interlocutor meant. This information is clearly important for the analyst to be able to construct valid form-function relationships, as we saw in chapter 5.3. Secondly, an attempt was made to capture the informant's attitude to the discourse activity under consideration, and to the TL interlocutor. Such information supplied by two learners during a self-confrontation of K provoked the researchers into abandoning K as a possible technique for them, as we mentioned above. Thirdly, information was sought about what aspects of the TL, or languages in general, are salient ('noteworthy') for an informant: the enunciative properties of an utterance, its appropriateness, its meaning, its form, and so on.

The technique was variably successful. An awareness of, and an ability to comment reliably on, formal aspects of an isolated utterance or vocabulary item is not generally shared among adult immigrants, it seems. The first difficulty is to 'isolate' an utterance or word from the context (simply replaying an isolated utterance is totally unfruitful). The second difficulty is to interest the learner in the precise aspect of the utterance or word that the researcher has carefully prepared (ESF:Vasseur 1990c). Their 'grammatical intuitions' on this level are difficult to capture.

On the other hand, an awareness of how successful a particular activity was from both an interpersonal and instrumental point of view is indeed broadly shared among the informants, and they were able to comment at length on meaning, and the speech partners' intentions. All in all, self-confrontation turned out to be a useful source of supplementary information controlling the studies on interaction, but far less productive as regards the studies on production, to which we now turn.

6.3   Production

Reference to space
For spatial reference, it was necessary to elicit data in a controllable and repeatable way in order to guarantee comparability, to have some control over what the learner intended to express, as well as to ensure that the learners' means of reference with respect to all basic spatial relations were covered (one cannot wait for the chance occurrences

of conversation). These considerations made it necessary to devise specific elicitation tasks. The danger with specific tasks, however, is that learners' performance may not necessarily reflect the whole range of means developed. Therefore, additional evidence has to be sought in a broad range of discourse types.

Correspondingly, two types of data were taken into account:

(1) The core data were provided by two specific, guided tasks, the 'stage directions' task (E) and the 'picture description' (D), which were carried out by all learners. Both tasks were devised to elicit reference to relations in perceptual space.

(2) Complementary data were of two kinds: The teams individually included data from additional guided tasks, such as route directions (L) or film retellings (I). Furthermore, narratives and conversations (A) were scanned with respect to reference to spatial relations. The problem with data from these latter discourse types lies in the fact that it is often difficult to reconstruct the intended meaning on the basis of the context. They could only serve to confirm or discard hypotheses developed on the basis of data from the guided tasks.

Design of the stage directions and picture description tasks

As we saw in 4.3, specifying spatial relations involves relating the place occupied by one object (the theme) to that occupied by another entity, or other entities (the relata). The configurations to be described were selected to cover the basic relations. Here, the frame of analysis of the research area was a necessary prerequisite in the detailed elaboration of the tasks. The following constellations were involved: an entity X is in (or is moved to) a position in/inside an entity Y; near/next to Y; on Y; between two entities; over/under Y; in front of/behind Y; and to the right/left side of Y. In the analysis of the learners' production (Volume II:I.4), the configurations and actions to which they relate and the spatial situations in which they take place are described in detail.

The stage directions task (E)

The stage directions task is a form of role play. The learner is asked to observe a short silent scene performed by one of the researchers (performer). In the scene the performer moves from one place to another while changing the position of various objects. The learner is then required to direct a replay of the scene with a third person who is supposedly not familiar with what has taken place. The learner is thus placed in the role of a stage director, and is instructed to make sure that the actions are imitated as closely as possible.

The presentation of the scene took approximately three minutes, the replay directed by the learner about fifteen minutes. Another researcher was present in the background and could observe whether the learner redirected the scene as required or not. The researcher could intervene directly, if necessary, during or at the end of the replay. The task was video-recorded to provide a reality check in subsequent analysis.

The learners were asked to give the instructions verbally and not to rely on gestures. This requirement could not always be met by the beginners in the first cycle. The extent to which the researcher insisted on verbal directives was left to discretion and depended on the estimation of the learner's actual proficiency, personality and attitude toward the situation. It was generally agreed that the learner should feel self-confident, not frustrated.

The plot of the scene was constructed so that it was easy to follow and to remember the actions involved. It was varied over the three cycles in order to avoid training effects. It also differed in some aspects across the teams (see below). The following variants were common to most teams:

The stolen ashtray. The performer comes into the room carrying two bags. She leaves one bag between two chairs, goes to another chair at a table and sits down, putting the second bag on the floor beside the chair, and taking a newspaper out of it. There is an ashtray on the table. The researcher opens the newspaper and, while reading it, places it vertically on the table so that the ashtray is enclosed and hidden from sight. She then folds the newspaper around the ashtray and returns it to the bag, thus stealing the ashtray. She stands up from the table, picks up the bag at her feet, goes to pick up the other bag, and leaves the room with both.

Missing the train. The performer enters the room carrying a suitcase and a shoulder bag, goes to various places in the room, consults a train timetable which is on a wall and then sits down against the opposite wall and prepares for the night. She takes her coat off and, taking a pyjama top out of the bag, puts it on. She then lies horizontal, using the suitcase as a pillow and the bag as a footrest. Then she wakes up and performs the actions in reverse, taking off the pyjama top, replacing it in the bag and putting on her coat. Finally, she stands up and, picking up her bags, leaves the room.

These scenarios were subject to some variation, due not least to the physical environment for recording (it is easier to set up a railway station in the recording studio than in a researcher's kitchen). The necessity of strict standardisation of collection methods was not that apparent at the beginning of the project. With hindsight, it would have been more desirable to keep the setting, the sequence of actions and the entities serving as theme and relatum identical for all learner groups over time. According to our experience, effects of training are negligible when the sessions are repeated at nine-month intervals, especially as, with increasing knowledge, the learners tackle the task in different ways. What was especially underestimated was the necessity to keep the objects involved constant. For example, the relationship existing between a book 'on' a shelf and an ashtray 'on' a table can be conceptualised by a learner in completely different ways at a certain stage of acquisition. If this cannot be controlled in a systematic way, comparability is restricted. Also, a slight change in the sequence of actions can make the instruction-giver focus on different situational and spatial aspects of the scene. In the data analysis, care is taken to specify in detail under which conditions an utterance was produced, and to what extent comparability can be achieved or not. Overall, the participants in the analysis agreed that the cross-linguistic comparability of the data would have increased if the data collection procedures had been more strictly uniform.

The picture description task (D)
With the picture description, an attempt was made to grasp aspects of the learners' referential procedures which could not become apparent in the stage directions task. The latter task is to a large degree prestructured and the learner has little freedom in choosing the theme and relatum. In the description of the spatial situation in a picture more options are given, and the routines and preferences of learners at a given stage of acquisition are likely to emerge more clearly. What is more, the learner cannot rely on a shared visual context (see chapter 4.3); in none of the variants below was the researcher able to see what was being described. In the task, the learner is asked to describe a picture in as much detail as possible.

The problem consisted of finding an arrangement which made it necessary for the learner to describe the spatial structure of the picture and the positions of entities relative to each other as completely and precisely as possible. In the course of the data collection several possibilities were tried out by the teams:

(a) The learner should describe the scene to someone on the phone such that the addressee could imagine it as well as possible.

(b) The learner was asked to describe the picture to a person who was present but could not see the picture, in such a way that the performer could draw a sketch (this activity is referred to as the 'blind picture reproduction').

(c) The learner was given two pictures from a picture series which shared basically the same scene, but where a number of changes had taken place between the first and second picture. The researcher sat at a distance with a copy of the first picture. The learner was then asked to say exactly in what respect the scene had remained the same and where changes had occurred, such that the addressee could mark these in the copy.

The solutions (b) and (c) were found to work best. They differ with respect to the shared knowledge of the interactants. Arrangement (b) forces the learner to concentrate more on the overall spatial structure of the picture, while the picture comparison (c) demands more detail.

If the picture is well chosen, that is, clearly structured and contains a large number of things to locate, this task is very productive. For example, in the German group, sessions often lasted over an hour and provided up to 250 utterances containing reference to space.

With the picture description, the differing procedures do not affect the validity of the data to the same degree, as the learners were allowed more freedom to structure the task as they wished. Nevertheless, the comparison of the data may have been further facilitated if all teams had chosen the same pictures. The operative modal in the last sentence is 'may', since the strictest procedure cannot guarantee individual interpretation of a picture. One refugee from Chile interpreted a stylised poster of a crowd watching a game of French *boules* as demonstrators throwing missiles at the police.

Despite the problems mentioned, these procedures did specify a common set of spatial configurations the learners were asked to describe, so that a general cross-linguistic comparison was possible. However, with some groups of learners, reference to certain spatial relations is insufficiently represented in the data. In such cases, the description of the development of the learner's system must remain incomplete.

Temporal reference

For this area, it was decided that personal narratives should form the main data base, completed by conversational sequences and film retellings. Narrative is a well-studied discourse type, with a well-studied temporal structure (for a detailed discussion, see Reinhart 1984). The speaker recounts what happened to him, or her, at some moment in the past. Tino's first narrative, for example, is provoked by the explicit question, 'What happened to you last weekend?'. Thus personal narratives favour first person reference, and are anchored in the time before the time of utterance. They consist of a series of singular actions which follow each other according to the 'principle of natural order' (PNO). Unless there is specific marking, the relation between two consecutive utterances denoting actions will be AFTER. The series of utterances related by AFTER comprise the *foreground* of a narrative. Not all utterances in a narrative are in this relationship. The speaker may describe states, make flashbacks, evaluative comments, or use an utterance explicitly to introduce a new time interval. Such *background utterances* need some special marking, however, if their verb denotes an action.

A narrative potentially provides rich evidence of the way learners express temporal relations. There are two major shortcomings, however. Firstly, reference to present and future time will be at best scant, typically confined to quoted speech. For this reason, other passages of conversation were included for analysis, where talk turned to the topics of current interest, or to the learner's future plans. Secondly, the analyst has no control over what the learner maximally wants to express, and to what extent he avoids certain events and relations, if he is not sure how to express them. For this reason, the film retelling described below (and some other available retellings) were also analysed. Here, we may be reasonably sure of what the learner wants to express, and calculate from the film what he does not express. Such retellings are rich in anaphoric and topological temporal relations, but provide scant evidence of deictic reference, as a film is not anchored in the speaker's past. Most learners, like most speakers, readily recount their personal experiences. The conversations were frequently brought round to subjects which provoked narratives. In general, it was unproblematic to get a data base of two per cycle for the informants of the temporality study, the only exception being Moroccan women.[1] On occasion, and in the absence

---

[1] This may be due to cultural reasons. In similar vein, Punjabi informants proved to be very unwilling to refer to future time.

of the TL researcher, the SL researcher was able to get the informant to give a SL version of a previously told narrative, which provides a supplementary aid to analysis.

Utterance structure and compounding
These studies concentrated on one type of data, which represents a reasonable compromise between authenticity, on the one hand, and controllability, on the other: film retelling. The project researchers working in Heidelberg made a *montage* of Charlie Chaplin's *Modern Times*, which lasts about twenty minutes and is divided into two main episodes, described in Appendix C, where some specimen transcriptions are also given. The procedure is simply that a researcher and an informant watch the first episode together, then the researcher leaves the room while the informant watches the second episode. The researcher returns immediately after the end of the film for the informant to tell him/her the second episode. In this way, a common ground was created on which the informant could draw for his retelling.

This retelling (coded I) was found to give rich data for the following reasons:

(a) This is a complex verbal task: the speaker retells part of a relatively complex story, consisting of events whose relationship to each other must be specified (for example, event *a* caused event *b* to happen). Within each event, the speaker has to tell who did what to whom, introducing new characters and maintaining reference to characters who are already on stage. The main characters are male (Charlie) and female (a young girl) and they act and are acted upon. Their stories, which run in parallel during the first half of the film, intertwine during the second half, necessitating a choice on the part of the learner as to which of them is central in which event.

(b) We have partial, although not total, control over what is mutually known to learner and listener at the beginning, and over the retelling of the story by the learner, in that the film is available to compare with his production. This gives us a partial idea of what the learner would maximally want to retell, on the assumption that he wants to get his listener to understand what he has seen.

However, two drawbacks should be mentioned. The first is obvious, the second one less so. The first is that the data are severely limited in a couple of easily identified areas: this is a third person retelling, and unless the learner has recourse to directly quoting the characters' speech, questions and orders are absent, as are first and second person reference, and indeed deictic reference in general. Even a cursory comparison with personal narratives (see ESF:Klein and Perdue 1992, chapter 7) shows differences in the function of pronouns, and of temporal adverbs, past tense marking and their interaction, in what are very similar text types. A further comparison was carried out with the French data by scanning conversation to evaluate the representativity of the phrasal patterns found in the narratives. The evaluative and argumentative nature of much of the conversation clearly differs from narrative style, but it turned out that this difference was quantitative: the same patterns were found, but the ratio was different, with more copula-like and verbless patterns in conversation, directly reflecting the fact that in such sequences the informant tends to answer the researcher's questions.

Secondly, training effects with this technique do need to be taken into account. Despite the time interval of nine months between retellings, if the learner and researcher have already done the activity together, then the learner knows that his listener knows the story, and the motivation mentioned above to retell so that the listener can understand plummets. There were occasions during data collection where such a situation was unavoidable, for example when only one female researcher was available to interview Moroccan women informants, and in those circumstances, the richness of the data suffered. However, the retelling provided a backbone of highly comparable and relevant data, for the present studies, and also for temporality.

6.4   Conclusion

In conclusion, it is useful to summarise the work load of the learners participating in this longitudinal study, which is organised in data collection cycles. Every six weeks or so, they met the project researchers and were questioned on recent events in their lives, and their opinion on various subjects of conversation was sought. In addition to and following this conversation, they were persuaded to take part in a variety of other activities.

For example, on 13 April 1984, two researchers (SLR and TLR) visited Berta in her newly rented flat in the Paris suburbs. First of all, there was a short conversation in Spanish with SLR, from which it emerged that during the past weeks, Berta had finished her job as a replacement cook and had gone on a skiing holiday with her family. The TLR then asked in French about her holiday, and Berta told the story of the skiing accident suffered by her sister-in-law, which resulted in a broken leg. As it was the first visit by TLR to the new flat, Berta showed her round, and recounted all the complications of moving in. Then SLR explained (in Spanish) that she would like Berta to try to play the role of a dissatisfied customer trying to obtain a refund for a shrunken sweater, despite the fact that the receipt had been mislaid (see above, C). Berta and TLR then did the play scene in French. Finally, Berta was asked to describe a poster such that TLR, who was at the table with her back turned, could draw it (blind picture reproduction, see above D). During leave-taking, an arrangement was made to see Berta again at the beginning of June.

The common core of these activities, spread over a nine-month cycle, included role play, guided tour, film retelling, and stage directions, in addition to the play scene and picture description mentioned here. At the end of the nine months, it all happened again. And again.

7 Transcription, storage and retrieval of data

Helmut Feldweg

> *It is planned that transcribed data will be stored on a computer. ... this possibility will not materialise until some time after the data collection period has begun.*
>
> Field Manual:229

This chapter describes a crucial phase in the project. When data transcription started in 1983, the research teams did not even have a personal computer available to them, and transcriptions were handwritten. Ten years later, the fully computerised Second Language Data Bank (SLDB) has about 18,000 pages of transcription available for interested researchers, accompanied by different types of documentation and tools for computer-assisted analysis for such technically diverging platforms as IBM-PCs, Macintoshes, and Unix and VMS mainframes and workstations.

The process of data transcription and storage was contemporaneous with the introduction of personal computers as research tools for the humanities during the 1980s, and with the development of researchers' awareness of the demands of the computer. Mistakes were made, and an exorbitant amount of work was required precisely because computer storage procedures were being worked out at the same time as data were being stored.

The way the project's data are now stored and maintained reflects the process described in this chapter, and determines the ways in which these data can now be exploited by machine.

This chapter summarises the transcription and storage procedures used in the project, with some discussion of their advantages, and of pitfalls to be avoided. It provides a very short account of some of the programmes available for computer-assisted analysis and concludes with some lessons to be drawn retrospectively from the project's experiences.

7.1 Transcription

This section describes how the data were transcribed and why they are transcribed in the way they are, in other words, which methodological and technical presuppositions were made.

The encounters with the informants were recorded with audio or (for activities where analysis of non-verbal interactions were crucial) video equipment in order to preserve the evanescent data. With only minor exceptions, all of these recordings were transcribed, by hand or with a typewriter at the beginning of the project.

During this early phase of the project, the need was for all-purpose, theory-neutral transcriptions, serving as a general basis for different types of more specific analysis in the different research areas of the project. The need for neutral transcriptions was the more compelling because it soon became apparent how valuable it would be to create a permanent data base, available to all interested researchers, including potential users whose research interests could not be foreseen.

Ideally, a transcript should be an authentic representation of all oral, visual, and contextual aspects of the encounter. But as we have already seen for informants, ideals are unattainable. For the amount of data scheduled to be recorded and transcribed by the project, the most economic transcription techniques compatible with interpretability had to be chosen. Estimations of the time required for even a superficial phonemic transcription of the data set collected by the project came to far more than ten (wo)man-years. Hence, the common transcription conventions used were kept relatively simple.

Given the main research topics of the project, the obvious choice was to focus on verbal communication; paralinguistic, non-verbal and actional phenomena were only transcribed when it was felt that this information would be crucial for interpreting the verbal communication. Transcription of the verbal material was based on a compromise between an orthographic and a phonetic transcription reflecting systematic deviations from the standard TL realisation of tokens. How exactly this framework was filled, differed from team to team as the majority of teams engaged in the project had developed differing methods of transcription during the pilot year – or even earlier in Heidelberg. Although no claims were made that the transcribed data could be used for phonetic studies, advocates of a broad phonetic transcription argued that the use of an orthographic transcription forces a lot of decisions which must be made early on in the transcription process, and that this early overinterpretation of the data may lead to problems in its later stages and during analytic work. Advocates of the other side argued that only orthographically oriented transcripts can preserve the most essential information in a clear manner, free from needlessly detailed variability which might overload the user and hinder the analytic process, which would be slowed down by having to re-parse the phonetic representation of the text again and again. In other words, the possible disadvantages of overinterpretation would be offset by ease of use.

Although ideally it would be desirable to have a standardised alphabet for a comparative project such as this, it was felt that the advantages of each team keeping its own alphabet were more important for the following reasons: each alphabet had evolved in order to deal with phonetic phenomena which seem specific to the type of learner variety studied; each team knew its system well, and any time which could be saved in the very time-consuming activity of transcription was precious; all teams involved had familiarised themselves with reading each other's transcriptions; use had been made in establishing each alphabet of characters on the different TL typewriters – ö, ç, å, etc.

Although the alphabet used by each team is still to a certain extent idiosyncratic, the presentation of the text, and the conventions for transcribing non-segmental phenomena, are standardised.

Technical aspects of transcription

Computers offer comfortable ways for editing, correcting and archiving transcriptions, for easy exchange of data between the local teams, and for support in the analysis of the data. When it became possible to buy computers, each team was equipped with a personal computer with two diskette drives. The computers ran the CP/M operating system, which was replaced with some software that emulated MS-DOS when the dominance of the then new IBM-PC became obvious in the market. The text-processing software used was Wordstar.

The format of the transcribed text was to a large extent determined by the capabilities of the contemporary computer hard- and software. Longitudinal data deserves long-term planning of the tools used to store and retrieve it, as the life-span of this type of data easily exceeds several generations of computer hard- and software. In order to keep up with the frequent change of technical specifications in this area, one is either forced to transfer the data from one data format to another, newer, format whenever the technical specifications change, or to use a data format which promises not to be changed too often.

The project decided to follow the second route and started to look for available international standards for text representation. The only standard of this type available at that time was the American Standard Code for Information Interchange (ASCII) – the alphabet most computers use when they talk to each other. Taken seriously, this code allows no other means for text representation than plain text lines consisting of the limited set of characters available in its alphabet. A minimalist system of this kind has a number of disadvantages which are described below. However, its big advantage was, and still is, that use of the data is not restricted to any particular hard- or software, and this is a vital requirement for a long term international project. Moreover, no data transformation has had to be done right up until today, even though the data are no longer being used on the original Victor computers the teams started with, and Wordstar is no longer being used for data treatment.

To use only straight ASCII files puts severe restrictions on any computer transcript, since the alphabet is very limited, containing no more than ninety-six printable mono-spaced characters with no diacritics, and since there are no symbols available which span several lines or characters to mark the scope of supra-segmental material in the transcript.

These restrictions forced a linearity in the data format which did not allow the use of score transcripts (see Ehlich and Rehbein 1976), a system using two-dimensional writing like musical scores to display the flow of time in the transcript in a graphically neat manner. Thus, overlaps and scope had to be marked by various types and combinations of braces in the data. In particular, the symbols < and > were used to establish links between verbal- and non-verbal elements in the transcript, to provide TL translations of SL utterances, etc. Data entry, correction and editing is much easier for such a linear system, since it does not require any spatial alignment across lines as is the case for score transcripts. This gain of entry time, however, is offset by a loss in readability of the transcript (for humans) as it is more difficult to visualise the flow of time and the interactional dynamics. A computer programme was written sometime later which allowed the user to rearrange utterances of different speakers into different columns to get a better representation of the interaction and its dynamics. An example of the output of that programme is given in Appendix C(6).

The limitation of the ASCII to ninety-six characters created even more problems. Having to use a character set based on the English alphabet is a burden for a cross-linguistic study covering eleven different source and target languages – not to mention the need for a phonetic alphabet for transcribing critical items in the learner varieties under investigation.

Common work-arounds that allow customised alphabets such as national variants of ASCII and the so-called 'extended ASCII' were potential viruses in the context of our project. The national variants provide an alphabet for a single language other than English, by substituting some of the less frequent symbols of the standard character set (such as [, |, }, ~) for example German ä, ö, ü, ß, or accents and cedilla in the French variant. This method works wonderfully so long as one can do without the symbols being substituted and one does not have to handle more than one language at the same time. Neither condition was true for the project, simply because it was in the nature of the study that the subjects used more than one language at a given time, thus every available symbol was needed for the wide range of phenomena to be transcribed, each of which had to be marked uniquely. The so-called extended ASCII provides more than twice the amount of printable characters as 'pure' ASCII and covers most of the characters necessary for the alphabets of European languages with Latin script. However, the extension of a standard does not necessarily become a standard by itself, and this is what has happened to extended ASCII. It is supported mainly on IBM-PCs and has never really made its way onto other computers. For this reason, only printable characters from the original ASCII could be used. Any character not contained in that set had to be represented by a combination of existing characters and by defining one of the characters as an escape character, which has no other function than to serve as a marker for sequences of characters, that is, to define characters that are not available in ASCII. For instance, common Swedish characters such as å and ö are represented as \aa and \"o, so that a word like *utegångsförbud* appears as uteg\aangsf\"orbud in the text. To spare the reader's eyes, we will not follow this convention in the examples given in the remainder of this chapter or in Appendix C.

Layout of transcriptions

This section describes the layout of the transcription, how the data were arranged within the given technical environment and what efforts were made to prevent the above restrictions from masking the content of the file.

All data files have a well-defined document structure. Data and meta-data are strictly distinguished. In this context, *data* is considered to be the transcript in the narrower sense, that is, the verbal and non-verbal actions that took place during the encounter; *meta-data* is any information about the transcript, such as place and date, overall setting, participants. A sample page of a transcript file for each language studied is given in Appendix C.

Transcript files start with a file header giving basic information of the episode described in the file. The transcription follows the header and is terminated by a one line trailer indicating the end of the transcription and the end of the file; this is needed to guarantee that no material has been lost at the end of the file.

The transcript of the activity distinguishes three major types of information: (i) speakers' utterances, (ii) comments on and interpretations of speakers' utterances (these are the types of information linked by < >), and (iii) lines serving as speakers' turn markers. Separate lines are used for each information type. The first character of each line defines its information type. Lines containing speakers' utterances have a lower case letter in the first column, which is a one-letter abbreviation of the speaker's name. Comments and interpretation have a hyphen in the first column, lines with technical and situational information are marked by a plus sign, and turn markers are indicated by a sharp sign in that position. The following text of the transcript may be broken into lines at any word boundary. Continuation lines are not specifically marked: they use the same markers in column one as their predecessors, so a continuation line by speaker a would be marked a. All these identifiers in the first position of the lines are followed by a blank space in the second position.

This information serves as a frame for the words uttered by the speakers. As noted above, the transcription method used varies from almost standard orthographic (TL Dutch) to almost phonetic transcription (TL German). (See Appendix C for illustration.) Over and above the words, prosodic and metalinguistic phenomena are added together with some linguistic analysis of the words transcribed. The complete transcription conventions are listed in Feldweg (ESF:1991: 22ff.). The examples given in Appendix C are annotated, giving the most important transcription conventions.

7.2   Organisation of the data bank

The data were recorded, transcribed, double checked, and anonymised by the six research teams, and were finally centralised in the Second Language Data Bank (SLDB) housed at the Max-Planck-Institut für Psycholinguistik. The centralisation process covered transformation of local varieties in the data format to the proposed standard, whenever this was possible, without losing information present in the local variety. The SLDB is the central archive for the data collected during the course of the ESF project. It ensures long-term storage, makes the data available for interested researchers, and provides documentation and computer programmes for data analysis. It also provides an organisational framework for collaborative research on adult language acquisition and use.

The *data* in the archive are organised into a large number of plain, semi-structured text files. The basic organisational entity is the *episode*, a part of an encounter devoted to one of the pre-defined data collection activities described in chapter 6. Navigation in the huge amount of data files is facilitated by an elaborate file-naming system yielding ready access to the basic *meta-data* of the episode transcribed in the file. The file name gives information about the subject's group – whether the informant belongs to the longitudinal, control, native speaker, or other group –, source and target language, subject, data collection cycle, encounter, activity type, sequence of activities in the encounter, the language spoken during the activity and the file type. Each of these items is encoded with one letter – except for the two-letter abbreviations used for subjects' pseudonyms. This makes a total of eleven characters, which is the most that can be used on computer systems with limitations in the length for file names. Though a file name like lsfbe24a.ltr might seem cryptic at first, it can easily be decoded with some basic knowledge of the project's design (see chapter 5): subject from Longitudinal group, source language is Spanish, target language French, the informant's name is BErta, the session took place in the 2nd data collection cycle and it was the 4th encounter in that cycle, the activity transcribed is a free conversation (activity code A), it is the 1st conversation in the encounter, carried out in the Target language and the file contains a Raw transcript. All the information encoded in the name of a file is also contained in the file itself and is as such redundant. However, keeping the most essential meta-data of a transcript in the name of the file is a mechanism yielding ready access to this information without the need to look at the contents of the file itself, which is a much more time-consuming process. This is especially relevant for many computer programmes, as files can easily be selected – or excluded – from analysis by specification of the file name or parts of it. In fact, these file-naming conventions fulfill some of the functions of database management systems.

Inspection of the format of the transcripts explained above show that specific data types (such as header information, annotations and transcribed utterances) in the transcript can easily be selected by the type of the first letter of each line in the transcript. In this position, capital letters originate from keywords yielding header information, and lower case letters stand for speakers' lines, so that specific information types from within the file can be selected by the specification of the first character of a line.

Raw transcript files containing the transcribed episodes are the primary file type in the data bank. Information about the overall structure of every encounter, covering the sequence of activities, setting, general observations and commentaries, is given in a separate protocol file having the extension PRT. This file had a specific function during the actual project; it was created immediately after an encounter took place in order to organise data for subsequent transcription and analysis, and to note other relevant aspects of the interaction (Field Manual: 245). Socio-biographical information for each informant, including developments during the observation period, is available in files with the extension BIO. They provide a structured list of relevant biographical information based on a guided conversation held with the informant at the very beginning of the data collection cycles. This information was updated regularly during the conversation which usually started the subsequent encounters between researcher and learner. These files provide the raw material for the mini-biographies of each learner given in Appendix B.

Technically, all data files are stored as plain text files containing only lines made up of printable ASCII characters. Control information such as record structure, record delimiters and end-of-file markers are not specifically defined in the Databank, as this information is system-dependent and can easily be adjusted during data transfer across different computer systems.

7.3   Programmes for computer-assisted analysis

At the time the data were entered into the computer only a few computer programmes for computer-assisted analysis of transcribed data were available. These programmes, such as the Oxford Concordance Programme or William Tuthill's Humanities Concordance and Text Analysis Package, were bound to mainframe installations and as such could not be used by the project with its distributed design, working with personal computers at different sites. As a consequence several computer programmes were written by members of the project, although programme development was not one of the objectives of the ESF project. These programmes and prototypes of programmes facilitated data (re-)formatting, data reduction, creation of concordances and type/token frequency tables. Most were different types of search programmes, which allowed the user to scan the data sets for occurrences of specific patterns in the data. Within the project, most of these programmes were used to demonstrate what the computer could do with the data, rather than being used as an actual tool for data analysis. Extensive coding and preparation of the data would have been necessary for most of the software to work properly. Under these circumstances it was not always obvious that the use of a computer was saving any time. For the project itself, the main use of the computer was as a typing, archiving, and data exchange tool – with the exception of some computational analysis for quantitative lexical studies described in the following chapter. Researchers working on post-project research with the SLDB, or indeed with other data, benefit from the work invested, whilst the researchers of the project benefitted by acquiring know-how about computer-assisted analysis of transcribed data.

   With the exception of the reformatting programme (see Appendix C for an example), all programmes developed during the project were replaced by standard software offering the same functionality when it became available. The use of standard software freed the project from software development and maintenance tasks, and, more importantly, it allowed the researchers to get acquainted with software that has also proved to be useful for project-external data.

   The major tasks are now performed by a set of such programmes which have been culled from various public sources and ported to different operating systems. All of the programmes described are available within the SLDB for the operating systems DOS, UNIX, VMS, and Macintosh-OS. These programmes perform the lowest and most useful levels of computer analysis, the humdrum tasks of searching through a text for a specific word or pattern, determinations of word frequencies, and creation of concordances.

What will be attempted in the following paragraphs is a summary of the experiences we have had with computer-assisted analysis of the transcript data in the SLDB. The topics discussed are text searching, the creation of frequency tables and concordances, and some basic problems of analysing transcript data. Without going into too much detail about the programmes, we will show how to solve at least some of these problems with standard programmes available in the SLDB.

Searching
Searching through a text for a pattern, word, character combination, number, etc., is a basic function offered by a large number of available computer programmes. However, only a few of these programmes offer the right combination of features necessary to cope with natural language data, and even fewer are able to combine these features with those necessary to cope with the semi-structured text files of the SLDB. Three basic bits of information are necessary for a search programme: (i) where the programme should search; (ii) what it should be searching for; and (iii) how the results should be presented. A search programme operating in the context of the SLDB must have features allowing it to provide these three types of information, and in particular, the ability to use wildcards in file names, a syntax to specify complex search patterns, and a way to display the results of the searches together with some amount of context.

Wildcards allow the researcher to specify a group of file names without having to name each of the files in that group explicitly. A user of the databank frequently does not know precisely which files exist for a type she wants to examine. Even if she knows, she certainly would not be willing to list all the names of the fifty-four data files available containing free conversations of Spanish learners of Swedish from the longitudinal group. With wildcards (or 'jokers') available, it is sufficient to provide only the information necessary to define that group and to have some programme unfold this pattern into the available items.

Search patterns need to be defined precisely in order to get only relevant instances as a result. Finding the precise pattern is frequently a non-trivial task. For instance, if one is aiming to get all occurrences of the preposition *in* in a text, it is not sufficient just to search for the character combination **in**, since this pattern would also match undesired instances such as *interest, binding* or *Chaplin*. To solve this problem, modern word-processing software usually allows the user to specify whether complete words should be matched during find operations, that is, it has some definition of *word*. For the purposes of the SLDB, a programme must allow the user to define much more complex search patterns. The user must be able to define what constitutes a word, and it must be possible for her to search for prefixes, infixes or suffixes only – and all this in combination with other constituents.

Finally, the user needs control over both the format and amount of the results of a search job. Different types of output must be provided, such as a global binary indication as to whether there was any match or not, the number of matches found, or display of every line containing a match – with or without some lines of context before and after the line containing the match, with or without line numbers.

One of the best known programmes meeting most of these criteria comes as a complete family named GREP (Global Regular Expression Print). The basic GREP programme allows fast searches for patterns of limited complexity, EGREP (Extended GREP) allows the researcher to use more complex patterns at the cost of processing speed, and FGREP (Fixed GREP) allows a search for a set of different strings at one time. One offspring of this family of programmes is named GNU-GREP (GNU is a project developing public domain software, see Stallman 1985), a free programme offering the functionality of GREP and EGREP with some extensions that are particularly helpful for natural language processing. The most significant additions are the possibility of displaying the results with some context, and simple means to restrict the search pattern to match full words only.

As an illustration, let us assume that a user of the SLDB wants to search for utterances of Zahra, a Moroccan learner of French, containing the conjunction *mais*. Given the elementary syntax:

    grep *pattern file-specifier*

for calling the GREP programme, it might seem reasonable to suppose that the command:

    grep mais lafza*.*tr

yields the desired output, that is, the researcher calls up the search programme GREP on the string *mais* in any (* = wildcard) raw data where Zahra is communicating in the TL. But in fact the results contain a great deal of information which is not relevant for the given question, as we see from the first lines generated by the command:

```
lafza11a.1tr:c  oui + ?  mais oU ?
lafza11a.1tr:c  maison ?  + dites moi comment c est
lafza11a.1tr:c  avez les clefs ?  + ?  est ce que vous avez les clefs
de la maison ?
lafza11a.1tr:c  ?  non ?  + mais alors euh si vous travaillez tous les
matins
lafza11a.1tr:c  vous faites 1 aprés midi ?  + ?  vous restez à la
maison ?
lafza11a.1tr:c  et du sel + mais c est pas du pain + alors pour
faire du pain
lafza11a.1tr:c  assiette + voilà + mais c est pas du pain
lafza11a.1tr:-  < dit en LS qu'elle a compris les propos de c mais
qu'elle ne sait
lafza11a.1tr:c  oui mais ?  comment je fais pour faire du pain ?
lafza11a.1tr:h  elle a parfaitement compris mais elle sait pas
comment le dire
lafza11d.1tr:c  oui + oui + mais alors euh vous / ?  vous pouvez me
dire euh
lafza11d.1tr:-  < dit en LS que la dame s'épile les sourcils mais
qu'elle ne
lafza11d.1tr:z  la maison
lafza11d.1tr:c  ?  oU elle est à la maison ?  + ?  elle est oU ? + ?
est ce qu elle
lafza11d.1tr:-  <=m= mais sous la table je n'ai pas su le dire >
lafza11d.1tr:c  oui mais ?  quelle piéce ?
lafza12a.1tr:z  euh non + mais mercredi \
```

Obviously, the transcriptions contain the native interlocutors' (c, h) contributions, and transcriber's comments (< ... >). What is needed is some device that allows us to restrict the searches to informants' lines only. GREP uses a syntax known as *regular expression* for specifying search patterns that allows us to restrict the searches to lines starting with the letter z, the one-letter abbreviation used for the informant Zahra. This syntax assigns special meaning to certain symbols, a *circumflex* (^) represents the beginning of a line, a full stop (.) is a 'joker' for any single character, and an asterisk (*) permits the preceding symbol to occur any number of times to match the pattern. The command to use then is:

```
grep '^z .*mais' lafza*.*tr
```

that is: use grep to search for any lines starting with a lower case z followed by a blank space followed by any numbers of any character followed by the character sequence `mais` in all files matching the given file specification. This yields the following output:

```
lafza11d.1tr:z  la maison
lafza12a.1tr:z  euh non + mais mercredi \
lafza13a.1tr:z  <# destE #> à la maison
lafza13c.1tr:z  mais <# ZE kuprc #> [ ( x ) ] et <# parle #>
lafza13c.1tr:z  euh l atelier <# kup #> pas + et à la maison <#
kup #> moi
lafza13c.1tr:z  maison oui
lafza13c.1tr:z   <# i travaj #> à la maison
```

This output contains only utterances of Zahra, but it also includes instances of *maison*: we are now faced with the problem of word-oriented searches and need to restrict searches to instances where the character sequence `mais` constitutes a word. A simple answer would be to enclose the character sequence with spaces as in:

```
grep '^z .* mais ' lafza*.*tr
```

but this solution has a double disadvantage: (i) it excludes instances of *mais* at the edge of a line, since there are no spaces used in that position; (ii) it also excludes tokens with suprasegmental markings such as `:mais`. Regular expressions offer the concept of character sets to deal with cases of this kind, the search pattern is not restricted to a simple sequence of characters, it is also possible to specify lists of characters to occur in one position so that we can formulate that the character sequence *mais* must be preceded by either a space or a colon. Such character classes are specified within brackets as in the following example:

```
grep 'z .*[ :]mais[ $]' lafza*.*tr
```

which reduces the output to the following more appropriate set:

```
lafza12a.1tr:z  euh non + mais mercredi \
lafza17a.1tr:z  euh non mais maintenant et <# sE #> <# sE #> /
le le patron <# sE #>
lafza18k.1tr:z  ja:mais / + euh ja:mais <# part #>
lafza21a.1tr:z  [ mais euh ] aujourd hui
lafza23r.1tr:z  ja:mais euh ja:mais <# travajE #> <# a #> moi /
avec la patronne
lafza24a.1tr:z  <# se #> pareil :mais <# se #> / <# se #>
pareil <# se #> pas
lafza24a.1tr:z  <# se #> pas comme le cocotte + cocotte vite +
mais <# se #> bon
lafza24a.1tr:z   mais <# se #> :pas < ga > <# se #> bon
```

```
lafza24a.1tr:z  :mais euh le poisson aussi
lafza24r.1tr:z  la maison à moi + mais la patronne <# kalE #> <#
tErESerSe #>
lafza24r.1tr:z  ah oui + mais <# travaj #> bien <# e sury #>
<# eparl #> e
```

Note that the search pattern used still generates matches for instances other than the word *mais*. As the pattern allowed a colon to be on the left edge of a word to cover the use of this symbol as a marker for lengthening of the word (as in :mais), it retrieved cases where a colon is used within a word to mark lengthening of a single syllable (as in ja:mais). It is possible to construct a pattern handling the use of the colon in the data correctly (i.e.: 'z .* :*mais[$]'), and even more complex search patterns can be specified but we will not go into further technical details here.

The two most notable technical limitations of the GREP family of programmes are that they cannot combine patterns with logical operators, and that the scope of a search pattern is always limited to one line only. It is indeed possible to construct patterns of the type *x* FOLLOWED BY *y*, but not possible to specify a logical AND relationship between pattern *x* and *y* where the order of the elements is irrelevant. Logical OR conditions are only realised at a one-character level in the form of character classes. However, the effects of logical operators can be achieved by other means. FGREP allows one to specify multiple search patterns which are internally linked together by a logical OR condition, and AND combinations may be realised by running sequences of the same programme where the output of a preceding run is used as the input for a subsequent run.

The importance of such technical limitations diminishes in many concrete situations where the programmes are used to pre-select the data for further human analysis since additional false matches can be tolerated during these steps of data analysis. It is, after all, the analyst that does the analysis.

The one serious limitation in the context of the SLDB is the fact that search patterns are compared with only one line at a time. This means that it is not possible to search for any pattern spanning lines. This limitation is overcome by another programme available in the SLDB: SFIND can search for patterns within 'sentences', that is, user-defined units which may span lines (see Tuthill 1981).

Finding what to search for: making frequency tables

Search programmes help only when one knows what to search for. Having a list of the lexical forms used in a corpus is a useful tool when working with unfamiliar data. It is even more useful when working with transcribed data, since it is not always obvious which tokens are used in the data for a given type since, as we saw, the data reflect learner-specific use, and so are often not transcribed in standard orthography. Such inventories of lexical forms can easily be generated by programmes known as frequency table generators. These programmes read a set of specified data files and build up a list of all word forms contained in these files and also provide a frequency for each form. When reading is finished, all words are listed, together with the frequency. This list of words and frequencies is usually given in alphabetical order of the word forms, but ordering by descending frequency is also possible. Additional programmes facilitate lists in alphabetical order by reverse spelling of the word forms, that is, the words are ordered according to their endings, so that *Saba* and *Jazz* make up good candidates for the first and last entries in such a list of words. All words with the same ending (such as *-ing*) are therefore grouped together. As a statistical extra, frequency table generators also compute the total number of words and the number of different words.

Given that a word form is the elementary unit for a frequency table generator, the definition of a word form becomes the crucial part of the programme. Programmes of this kind avoid the hazards of a more linguistically oriented definition by defining a written word by its edges. As a text is nothing but a sequence of characters, a word gets defined by whatever is enclosed by characters that have previously been defined as non-word constituent characters. This set of characters is sometimes also referred to by the term *punctuation set*. We have seen that the GREP-programme requires the user to define the delimiters to the left and right of a word as a part of the search pattern. Most computer programmes generating frequency tables use a pre-defined set of word delimiters such as any blank space and the symbols , . ; : ? ! " ( ) [ ] { }. This default value can be overwritten by the researcher by specifying a *punctuation file*, a text file with just one line containing any symbols which should be used as delimiters instead of the pre-defined set. This method allows the user to keep the set stored for later use. Moreover, different sets can be stored in different files having different file names for different analyses: users might want to consider liaison markers – such as ^

in the SLDB – as word constituent characters for one type of analysis and as a word-delimiting character (by adding it to the punctuation file) for another task. A drawback of this technique is that there are no means to make a distinction between the left and right edges of a word.

Within the ESF project, work has been done with a frequency table generator named FREQ, which is part of a set of computer programmes facilitating computational analysis of text files developed by William Tuthill's HUM-package (see Tuthill 1981). The complete HUM-package of programmes is available in the SLDB.

In the following, we will trace down some realisations of Zahra for the French conjunction *parce que*. A command like:

```
freq lafza*.*tr
```

generates a very long list, from which we will show only a few lines around the word *parce* and the end of the list giving basic statistical information for the whole list:

```
  ...
  3  parant
  2  parc
656  parce
  1  parceque
  1  parcouru
 10  pardon
  1  pare
224  pareil
  2  pareille
  2  pareilles
  4  pareils
 34  parents
  ...
-----------------------------
390773 Total number of words
12081  Different words used
```

In practice, data need to be prepared before being fed into the FREQ programme. The data shown come from all the text in the input files, and not just the utterances of Zahra. Unlike the GREP programmes, the FREQ programme cannot restrict its analysis to specific parts of the file(s) it is reading. But it is easy to combine the data selection features of a search programme with the qualities of FREQ by first using GREP to select the utterances of Zahra only and then having

FREQ use the output of GREP as its input. This can be done by the command sequence:

```
grep '^z ' lsfza*.*tr | freq
```

producing a much shorter list from which we show the relevant passage:

```
     ...
  77  par
   1  para
   4  paradis
   4  parapluie
   1  parawdis
   3  parawpluie
 247  parce
   1  parceque
   1  pare
  68  pareil
   3  pareils
   2  parents
   7  paris
   1  parisiens
   2  parki
  84  parl
 191  parle
   1  parlent
   1  parsku
   2  parsque
  14  part
   1  partaz
   9  parte
     ...
------------------------------
145112 Total number of words
  4656 Different words used
```

The list shows at least four forms (`parce`, `parceque`, `parsku`, and `parsque`) which are good candidates for different realisations of *parce que*. These forms can then be used to build up patterns for search programmes to verify their use and to allow quantitative analysis in context.

The procedure described is a standard procedure for computer-assisted analysis of transcript data. Search programmes are used to narrow the input for a frequency table generator, the output of which is than analysed for subsequent search-runs. This kind of modularity is in fact one of the most convincing characteristics of the software category presented here. Rather than implementing each and every feature into one programme, the system offers a set of small programmes, each of them performing a specialised task.[1] The real power of the system is best exploited by the combination of several individual programmes.

Other Programmes

The SLDB offers more than just the programmes described above. We have already mentioned SFIND, a programme allowing a search for patterns spanning one line. Other programmes like KWAL (KeyWord And Line) and KWIC (KeyWord In Context) produce types of concordances which consist of a blend of the lists generated by search programmes and frequency table generators, where one line with three fields is printed for every word in the data. The first field contains the word itself, the second field gives information on where the word was found (page and/or line-numbers), and the remaining field is used to display the word with some context. The main difference between KWAL and KWIC is the way in which they format the third field. While KWAL displays the lines in the same format as they were found in the input data, KWIC centres the keyword and displays the same amount of context to the left and right of the keyword. As an illustration, we give some selected lines of output generated by KWAL and KWIC for words starting with `pars`:

KWAL:

```
    pars            | 12063    c et si tu vas en vaWcances / + ?  est ce
    que tu pars en vacances
    pars            | 12078    c ?  tu pars au maroc en juillet ?
    parsque         | 16756    z <> parsque euh <# uenc e pase #> + et
    ma fille <# a #> huit ans
    parsque         | 16957    z euh + parsque + et le centre <# i di
    kla #> / + et
    pars            | 33744    c quand tu pars pas toi
    pars            | 49731    c là y a plein de choses ++ ?  qu est ce
    que c
    est ga / ga enfin pars
    parsku          | 54897    z parce que moi moi quand <# raSete #>
    les :  choses <# parsku #>
    pars            | 67521    c \ moi je pars
    pars            | 78094    c hm hm + ?  tu / tu pars au maroc là ou
```

---

[1] After all, the system is processing language!

```
      + cet été ?
KWIC:
    pars              |172,108|     / + ? est ce que tu |pars en
    vacances/c cet iété
    pars              |172,123|     - <=m= oui >/#/c ? tu |pars eu maroc
    en juillet
    parsque           |238,118| x ) ]/#/u allez y/#/z <> |parsque euh
    <# uenc e pase
    parsque           |238,319| u aéré aussi ?/#/z euh + |parsque + et le
    centre <#
    pars              |702,405|  "partir" >/#/c quand tu |pars pas
    toi/#/k <* *>
    pars              |1070,19|  que c est ga / ga enfin |pars/c  oU tu
    veux/-< présentation
    parsku            |1154,156| raSete #> les :choses <# |parsku #>/z
    <# kuprc #>
    pars              |1348,62|  #> + euh c \ moi je |pars/-
    <= tu , partir >
    pars              |1460,37|  >/#/c hm hm + ? tu / tu |pars au maroc
    là ou + cet
```

Limitations

These examples not only show what can be done with elementary programmes of the type of GREP, FREQ, KWAL, and KWIC, they also demonstrate the common drawbacks of all-purpose programmes of this kind. These programmes are designed to deal with any kind of text data files, no knowledge of the layout of transcripts has been coded into these programmes and hence the programmes cannot take advantage of the structured format of the transcript files in the SLDB. As we have shown, a user not only has to tell the programme that she wants to search in informants' lines only, she also needs to tell the programme how to identify an informant's line, a task it could easily do if only it knew about the structure of the transcript. The same holds for the intricate method of defining word boundaries: although it is desirable to gain control over what defines a word, it seems wasteful to have to define these boundaries anew for every search.

These difficulties can be avoided by use of customised software. But the development of such software not only costs a lot of time and money, it also requires a precise definition of the functions to be performed by such a programme, which in turn presupposes an exact knowledge of the detailed layout of the computer-assisted analysis to be done in the course of a project before any data transcription and programme development can start. Advance definition of the exact tasks to be performed in a large-scale project with numerous research areas is an ambitious project by itself, all the more ambitious if exploitation of the data by project-external users is envisaged. Such a study could not have been part of the ESF-project. However, work has since been done in this area by other projects and some of these projects have clearly benefitted from the pioneering experiences of the ESF-project. They have also gained from improved hard- and software technology. As a result we have seen the advent of first applications which overcome some of the major technical restrictions alluded to in this chapter.

One of these restrictions is the data format. The transcription conventions used throughout the project were a compromise between the goals of readability of the transcript, ease of data entry, and ease of computational analysis, which were of course subjectively evaluated in the light of each team's previous fieldwork experience. Accordingly, these conventions did not fully satisfy anybody. A clear conflict exists between the readability of a transcript for humans and its potential for computational analysis. Computer programmes do not understand the contents of the transcript and they still have problems perceiving two-dimensional patterns. For computational analysis, markers and labels must be provided for information which is retrieved by humans through their understanding of the contents of the transcript, or by its spatial layout. It is exactly this additional information which disturbs the reading process of humans.

Computer-based transcription systems have been developed which go for readability, others are oriented towards the ease of computational analysis, and only very few tread the stony path to provide both. We see a solution in meeting the computer halfway, letting the machine do what it is best at, that is, using the computer's strength in computation of linear data to produce non-linear data which are more accessible to human beings. In such a system, data are stored with all the tags necessary for the computer, but this format is then used only for an internal representation of the data. What the researcher sees and reads is a nicely formatted transcript, tabulated on the basis of the data entry format, which has become the internal format. This also allows the researcher to select only the information which is needed for a given research purpose. Information that is not relevant for a given type of study will be hidden, but become instantaneously available upon request. This idea of allowing different users different views over the same data becomes even more important when data are shared. Shared data get richer over time as different research projects add coding to the data which corresponds to their particular research interests. This coding may be completely irrelevant for other purposes. Without re-formatting programmes allowing the reader to scan particular aspects of the data, the words actually uttered by the informant get hidden in a huge amount of secondary coding.

Such an approach is in the spirit of a joint enterprise of The Association for Computers and the Humanities (ACH), The Association for Computational Linguistics (ACL), and The Association for Literary and Linguistic Computing (ALLC). This *Inititiative for Text Encoding Guidelines and a Common Interchange Format for Literary and Linguistic Data (TEI)* is in the process of setting up standards for the encoding of not only written, but also spoken text (Sperberg-McQueen and Burnard 1990). The mark-up language developed by the TEI is considered to be an internal format, and the various types of computer programmes for text exploration and text formatting only operate on the internal format.

The transcript conventions used by the Child Language Data Exchange System (MacWhinney 1991) is a good example of such a growing system of shared data. Originally focussing on the actual utterances of the informants, more and more symbols and tiers were added to reflect the growing range of research interests working with the data, and to allow easy computational analysis. At some point the data were so deeply buried in their codes that it was considered to be necessary to introduce yet another coding line which had no other purpose than to display the data without any coding to allow fluent reading! These problems are being solved now within CHILDES by a growing number of programmes that allow the data to be reformatted in different ways.

Score transcripts have long been used by another transcription system known as *Halbinterpretative Arbeitstranskripte* (HIAT), (Ehlich and Rehbein 1976). Although HIAT was not originally designed as a computer-based transcription system, two computer programmes have become available that support data entry and analysis of HIAT score transcripts on personal computers (Ehlich *et al.* 1991; Grießhaber 1991). Compared to the CHILDES system, HIAT focusses on neat formatting of the data and has less options for computer-aided analysis, although all basic functions such as search functions, frequency tables and concordances are implemented.

Both systems, CHILDES and HIAT, have learned from the experiences with computer-assisted analysis of transcript data during the past decade. They are not only easier to use, they also offer more extensive tools for data analysis. This is achieved by having some knowledge of the transcripts' format built into the programmes: the programmes 'know' where utterances start and end, what constitutes a word etc., and how to differentiate between the raw transcript and additional coding. The cost for this comfort is that the data must conform with the rules of the transcript system used. The transcription conventions used by the ESF-project are not compatible with these systems since the data were transcribed and stored at a time where CHILDES was not yet established and HIAT was not yet applicable for computer-based transcriptions. Pilot work has shown that a conversion of the ESF-data into one of these, in order to take advantage of the functions these systems offer is not easy for three reasons: (i) the original transcript conventions were only approximate in many areas, and formats for data entries blossomed. For example, the user encounters dates in an amazing number of different formats: 22-01-85, 25.8.83, 21 01 83, 1 Feb 1982, etc; (ii) the variations in the original transcription conventions across the teams add to the plurality of formats; (iii) the transcripts still contain a certain number of mistakes, and some of them, like missing parentheses, cause computer programmes to abort. Normalisation of these phenomena is not just a matter of time, in many cases decisions can only be taken by people who are very familiar with the data collected, and these people have now gone their different ways.

7.4 Conclusion

The computer is a valuable tool for analysis. The quotation with which this chapter begins describes a situation which was common a decade ago, but which is unlikely to be experienced by any future, large-scale project interested in analysing transcribed, spoken-language data. Given the experiences of this (and other) projects, the computer-related problems which have been described in this chapter can be foreseen and avoided, provided the place of the computer in the research design is defined at the outset.

Three points can be made in conclusion:

(1) We have been discussing computer-*assisted* analysis. The computer does not *do* the analyses. Given the value of the computer, a potential danger should be pointed out of overcompensating and setting up research procedures merely because certain programmes for data analysis exist. Obviously, the research questions come first.

(2) The transcription conventions of the beginning of the project were developed for the specifics of local learner varieties, but they also reflect clear, if diverging, research interests of the different research teams. It is certainly desirable to strive for theory-neutral transcriptions, but such transcriptions are a mirage, and it is vital to take the necessary steps to preserve the recordings on which the transcriptions are based (while continuing to preserve informants' anonymity).

(3) The mistakes made with data storage were mainly due to an initial lack of awareness of the importance of (often low-level) standardisation procedures. Over the years, the organisation of the database gained most where the contributing teams agreed on standards. The importance of standardisation for large-scale, long-term projects should not be underestimated.[2] Where standards do not exist, it is important to try to define them, in co-operation, before the empirical work begins. It was, after all, the agreements in this area which allowed the project to move from handwritten transcriptions to the SLDB – the largest and richest, ready-to-use, computer-based collection of spoken adult language acquisition data available.

---

[2] See also Wells (1985) on this question.

8   Measuring language acquisition

In this chapter, we return to a methodological problem first raised in chapter 5.3. In quantifying learners' performances, we incur the danger of hiding the systematicity of individual learner varieties at any given point in the acquisition process. On the other hand, it seems desirable to many researchers of ALA to have some general measures of proficiency available in order to compare learners between themselves, and learners with native speakers. Moreover, any attempt to gauge the effect that socio-biographical factors may have on the speed and success of the acquisition process requires some measure or another of learner proficiency.

The measures presented in this chapter provide a quantitative assessment of learner proficiency which runs parallel to the qualitative analyses of learner varieties in evolution presented in Volume II. They take the *word* as a basic measurement unit. The first questions to be asked are purely quantitative: Does the length of learners' utterances reflect their proficiency? Is there a connection between proficiency and text length? Is it possible to measure the richness of learners' vocabulary over time? These questions lead on to a consideration of the frequency and distribution of specific classes of words in the learners' repertoire. It was found that measures of words functioning as feedback, and articles, conjunctions and verbs are sensitive to learners' development.

The authors of the contributions to this chapter continually question whether the proposed measures do provide a valid and reliable picture of learners' proficiency, and in doing so, bring to light some methodological pitfalls of often-used measures such as the mean length of utterances (MLU) or the type/token ratio. They also demonstrate the need for comparison with other populations for specific purposes, in order to see, for example, whether the frequency and distribution of a class of words is specific to the type of learner under study, or not. Comparisons are made with native speakers (8.1), and with learners who had not been subjected to the constant observation of a thirty-month longitudinal study (8.4: the 'control study'). For the latter study, it was found that effort-related or motivational measures were sensitive to differences in the observation situation, but that observation had no substantial effect on the structure and success of the acquisition process itself. These assessments of learner-specific performances are not intended to be, and should not be interpreted as, measures of how 'far away' from some TL norm the learners are.

Finally, an attempt is made to assess whether variation in the informant selection criteria of chapter 3 which could not fully be controlled for – age, source country schooling, exposure to the target language – is linked to the learners' scores on the two most robust measures of vocabulary richness. It was found that there was a significant effect for the two first variables. However, there was no effect that could be traced to the amount of TL courses the learners had been exposed to. These results are discussed in 8.3.

8.1 Type and quantity of feedback use as a measure of language proficiency

Jens Allwood

MLU as a measure of language proficiency
A rough solution to the problem of assessing developing proficiency is to consider the development of the so-called mean length of utterance (MLU) for a certain learner, cycle by cycle. This measure, although it has many problems (see below) has often been used to give a very rough idea both of differences in proficiency and of the extent to which acquisition is taking place. In this chapter, an utterance is defined as a stretch of uninterrupted speech produced by one speaker bounded by silence or by contributions from other speakers.

The performances of twenty learners, whose names are given below, are examined in this study. The activities studied are conversations (A), role plays (J) and play scenes (C), which are described in chapter 6. Further discussion of the internal dynamics of these activities can be found in Volume II:II.2. These performances are compared with those of a small group of native speakers (the 'controls') in identical activities. This group is composed of two working-class native speakers of English (Martin and Sheila), and of Swedish (Adam and Eva). In addition, Mari and Nora performed these activities in their native language as well as in Swedish.

In Table 8.1 we reproduce the results concerning mean length of utterances for learners grouped according to pairs of source and target languages. The table contains the means for the individuals, as calculated over two activity occurrences in cycle 1 and cycle 3, and the differences between the means in cycle 3 and cycle 1 in order to give an idea of the change that has taken place between the two first and two last recordings.[1] The table reports on individual learners rather than on SL-TL aggregations since there are too few individuals and too many potential differences between them really to justify anything but a report on the individual level. Table 8.1 shows that there is indeed considerable individual variation both between learners of a given target language and between learners sharing a source language. Compare Berta and Alfonso who are both Latin American Spanish-speaking learners of French, or Lavinia and Andrea who are both Italian-speaking learners of English. It is not unlikely that these differences reflect a difference in target language proficiency at the

---

[1]See chapter 5.3 for the data-collection cycle.

beginning of the period of observation and that there are different rates of acquisition for different learners. The differences between the learners with regard to the MLU for cycle 1 results in the following ordering, which we provisionally take to be a first, rough indicator of differences in proficiency in cycle 1: Ravinder (2.0), Çevdet (2.4), Ergün (2.9), Fatima (3), Madan (3.2), Leo (3.3), Fernando (3.5), Mari (3.7), Berta (3.7), Zahra (3.7), Mahmut (3.8), Ilhami (3.8), Andrea (3.9), Marcello (4), Tino (4.3), Mohamed (4.4), Abdelmalek (4.4), Lavinia (4.9), Nora (7), Alfonso (15). A general point to notice is that all the learners except one – Mohamed – show an increase in MLU between cycles 1 and 3.

Table 8.1 *Development of* MLU; *cyclic mean per activity occurrence (Learners grouped by source and target languages; twenty learners)*

			C1	C3	C1-C3
Sw	Fi	Mari	3.7	6.6	2.9
		Leo	3.3	5.1	1.8
	Sp	Nora	7.0	9.2	2.2
		Fernando	3.5	5.8	2.3
Fr	Sp	Berta	3.7	17.2	13.5
		Alfonso	15.0	17.5	2.5
	Ar	Zahra	3.7	5.5	1.8
		Abdelmalek	4.4	7.9	2.5
Du	Ar	Fatima	3.0	3.4	0.4
		Mohamed	4.4	3.5	−0.9
	Tu	Ergün	2.9	3.7	0.8
		Mahmut	3.8	4.8	1.0
Ge	Tu	Çevdet	2.4	6.2	3.8
		Ilhami	3.8	5.9	2.1
	It	Marcello	4.0	4.3	0.3
		Tino	4.3	7.2	2.9
Eng	It	Lavinia	4.9	9.0	4.1
		Andrea	3.9	5.0	1.1
	Pu	Ravinder	2.0	4.0	2.0
		Madan	3.2	3.7	0.5
Total mean:			4.3	6.8	2.5

In sum the data, both on an individual level and on a more aggregated level show an increase in MLU which is compatible with a gradual increase in individual linguistic proficiency. Comparing the learners with the controls we find that the overall MLU for the controls is 10.7

as compared with a total overall MLU of 5.5 for the learners. This indicates that MLU is a measure which is sensitive to whether one is learning a language or not and therefore perhaps can be used as an indicator of differences in language acquisition.

As we have already said, all learners except Mohamed show a higher MLU in the third cycle than in the first, which is surprising since Mohamed has been characterised as a fast learner of Dutch. If we accept this assessment of Mohamed as correct, it is not obvious how one should reconcile it with his MLU decrease in the third cycle. One possibility is that MLU does not reflect linguistic proficiency. Another possibility is that MLU only indirectly reflects linguistic proficiency and that we should try to locate other factors that might also be reflected by MLU. In Mohamed's case, we know that he was the one learner whose motivation fell away sharply during the third cycle, and he was minimally co-operative during project activities. The low MLU may reflect this fact. To the extent that MLU reflects general proficiency, we see that it does so only given an assumption of a constant level of co-operation between researchers and informants.

Some of the expectable differences in MLU scores can perhaps be elucidated by reference to differences between source and target languages. In particular, lexical similarity (and to some extent grammatical similarity) between source and target languages is likely to facilitate fluency in the learners' TL communication and, thus, probably also MLU. For example, Punjabi and English are somewhat less closely related than Swedish and Spanish, and are considerably less closely related than Spanish and French. This might, *ceteris paribus*, mean that it is easier for Spanish speakers to learn French and Swedish than it is for Punjabi speakers to learn English. This might further mean that one should expect Punjabi learners of English to have lower MLUs than Spanish learners of Swedish, who in turn should have lower MLUs than Spanish learners of French. Table 8.1 supports these expectations.[2]

However, the relation between utterance length and complex syntactic-semantic cohesion is not one-one. So even though some types of syntactic-semantic cohesion require long utterances, there are also short utterances with great complexity with regard to syntactic-semantic cohesion and long utterances with little complexity with regard to such cohesion. The relation between MLU and proficiency is therefore an approximation and should wherever possible be sup-

---

[2]It should be said that Alfonso was an exceptionally talkative and sociable person, who already had a fairly rich repertoire at the first recordings analysed here.

plemented by other measures. We turn now to one such measure; feedback use.

Feedback as a supplementary measure of language proficiency
One of the areas under investigation in our study is feedback. Feedback can briefly be characterised as specialised linguistic mechanisms (for our present needs, *words*) which enable speech partners to give and elicit information on the basic dialogic requirements of contact, perception, understanding and attitudes. The phenomenon ('narrow feedback') is briefly described in chapter 4.2, and discussed in detail in Volume II:II.2. This area not only has interest, in its own right, as an aspect of linguistic communication but it can perhaps also provide data that can be used as a measure of linguistic proficiency to supplement MLU. The reason for this is that the relative share of narrow feedback in a given learner's output, in general, seems to decrease as the learner increases his linguistic proficiency. Possible explanations for this decrease are that:

(i)   narrow feedback is among the first linguistic means available to a learner;
(ii) narrow feedback can be used to substitute for or to accomplish other linguistic functions; and
(iii) as the learner acquires other linguistic means he will use these to accomplish what he earlier accomplished by feedback.

The two main measures we have used to get an idea of the relative share of narrow feedback expressions in the learners' linguistic output are FBU (relative share of feedback-containing utterances in relation to total number of utterances in an activity occurrence) and FBW (relative share of feedback words in relation to total number of words in an activity occurrence). Using these two measures, Table 8.2 gives us an idea of the relative percentage amount of feedback expressions for the different learners. The table contains the cyclic means for the individuals, and the per cent unit difference between the means in cycle 3 and cycle 1. As in Table 8.1, what Table 8.2 presents could be viewed as a number of case studies in tabular form.

Table 8.2 *FBU and FBW, mean relative shares per learner and cycle (twenty learners)*

			FBU			FBW		
			C1	C3	C1-3	C1	C3	C1-3
Sw	Fi	Mari	74	56	−18	23	12	−11
		Leo	81	79	− 2	42	26	−16
	Sp	Nora	74	63	−11	21	5	− 6
		Fernando	65	59	− 6	29	15	−14
Fr	Sp	Berta	69	57	−12	31	6	−25
		Alfonso	63	56	− 7	11	7	− 4
	Ar	Zahra	79	63	−16	33	15	−18
		Abdelmalek	69	53	−16	34	17	−17
Du	Ar	Fatima	67	55	−12	27	20	− 7
		Mohamed	63	73	10	19	28	9
	Tu	Ergün	54	66	12	23	27	4
		Mahmut	69	80	11	27	27	0
Ge	Tu	Çevdet	64	53	−11	35	11	−24
		Ilhami	58	51	− 7	25	11	−14
	It	Marcello	57	55	− 5	26	17	− 9
		Tino	51	53	2	22	11	−11
Eng	It	Lavinia	80	72	− 8	27	17	−10
		Andrea	51	74	23	27	24	− 3
	Pu	Ravinder	61	84	23	40	37	− 3
		Madan	76	75	− 1	43	42	− 1
Total mean pr cycle			66	64	−2	28	21	− 7
Total mean controls			62			16		

The table shows that there is a small overall FBU decrease and a somewhat greater FBW decrease. The trend is clearer for FBW than for FBU. This judgement is motivated not just by the numerical difference, visible in the table, but also by a consideration of the base for the calculation of the relative shares of FBU (9,772 utterances) and FBW (49,474 words). Although both measures rest on secure grounds, we see that the absolute numbers required for a decrease in the relative share of FBW (as measured in percentages) are much greater than those required for a decrease in the relative share of FBU.

A comparison with the total means of the controls (native speakers' data) for FBU and FBW supports the analysis we have made of the trends for learners concerning FBU and FBW. The controls have both a lower mean FBU score and a lower mean FBW score than the majority of the learners exhibit, even in cycle 3. This means that high initial and successively decreasing scores of FBU and FBW can perhaps be taken as something which is indicative of acquisition. We will return to why this might be so below.

Let us now look a little more carefully at the FBU and FBW scores. We observe that six learners (Mohamed, Ergün, Mahmut, Tino, Andrea and Ravinder) increase their FBU from cycle 1 to cycle 3, while only 2 learners (Mohamed and Ergün) increase their FBW rate. Mohamed's lack of co-operation in cycle 3 is manifested here by his use of minimal feedback.

Table 8.2 does not allow for any statistically sound inferences to be drawn. It can, however, be used to look for trends which can then lend support to certain hypotheses. The data can also be used to check for compatibility with and to gain initial support for hypotheses which can be proposed on partly independent grounds.

The following are possible hypotheses which can be seen as an attempt to specify the three explanations put forth initially in this section:

(i)   FB words often have simple phonological structure. They can therefore be learned early and used fairly easily.

(ii) There is a constant need and use of feedback in most types of spoken interaction. FB words are therefore usually available in the spoken input which the learners are exposed to and they have a high need to make use of this input.

(iii) Initially, basic feedback functions and basic linguistic feedback mechanisms can be used to substitute for other more specific linguistic functions.

(iv) Initially, feedback functions are also used by the learner as a means for language acquisition.

(v)   The reasons given in (iii) and (iv) but not in (i) and (ii) can be expected to diminish in importance as the learners proficiency increases.

The data in Table 8.2 seems compatible with these assumptions. The total FBU rate remains fairly constant with a slight decrease. Both learners and controls have a high FBU rate, with an average difference of only 4 per cent.

This result can be taken as weak support for the hypothesis that there is a constant and fairly high need of feedback for everyone and that this need is slightly higher for language learners. However, the fact that there is a fairly high degree of variability between learners with regard to FBU (for example, six learners increase their rate from cycle 1 to cycle 3) seems to indicate that FBU is sensitive to factors other than proficiency. Such factors could, for example, include motivation and the kind of activity in which the learner is engaged.

The relationship between FBU, FBW, MLU and proficiency
Turning to the FBW rate, we should first note that there is a conceptual relationship between FBU and FBW. The FBU rate is the relative share of utterances containing feedback words and the FBW rate is the relative vocabulary share of the FB words. Thus, the two measures have a common base in the FB words, which in the FBW measure are used directly in relation to the total vocabulary of a learner in a specific activity occurrence, and in the FBU measure are lumped together relative to the utterance containing them, and then compared with the total number of utterances of the learner in a certain activity occurrence. There must, therefore, on analytical grounds, be a relationship between the two measures.

In spite of this relationship, the two measures also show some differences which are interesting to note. The FBW rate shows a more consistent decrease than the FBU rate (only two learners show an increase). This could be interpreted in the following way: whereas the FBU rate reflects a fairly constant need for feedback which can be affected by such things as motivation and type of activity, the FBW rate, although also sensitive to the same factors, shows a more direct relation to language acquisition. This interpretation is supported both by the fact that the difference between controls and learners is slightly larger for FBW than for FBU and by the relatively uniform decrease in FBW for the majority of the learners.

The reason that FBW should show a closer connection to language acquisition than FBU is that the former, according to our hypothesis, should initially be usable both as an instrument for language acquisition and to substitute for linguistic functions other than feedback. As acquisition proceeds the learner will acquire more specific linguistic means for these functions. Since the need for feedback is fairly constant the changes should affect FBW (the relative share of FB words of the total vocabulary) more directly than FBU (the relative share of feedback-containing utterances). The FBU rate can remain high and permit many functions, other than the basic feedback functions, to be performed sequentially or simultaneously with feedback, while this can not be the case for the FBW rate, which will immediately be affected by the addition of other functions when they are lexically encoded.

There is a negative correlation between MLU and FBW (Pearson's product moment: $-.67$), that is, when MLU is high, FBW tends to be low. The longer utterances a learner has, the smaller the share of FB words in his vocabulary (although it is always possible to give FB by repeating the interlocutor's words; see below). As one learns to produce longer utterances, one also learns to make greater use of non-feedback vocabulary. In this connection, it is interesting to note that the only learners who have a higher MLU score in cycle 3 than the controls, that is, the Spanish-French learners, are also the learners who have the lowest FBW rate. The connection between high MLU, low FBW, and proficiency receives further support from a comparison of learners and controls with regard to the correlation MLU-FBW. The controls exhibit an even stronger negative correlation than the learners (Pearson's product moment: $-.76$ versus $-.67$).

Another clear way of demonstrating the fact that feedback seems to have a special function in language acquisition is to compare linguistic data for one and the same learner, in one and the same activity in SL and TL. The data exhibited in Table 8.3 come from the only two informants for whom we have control data of this type available.

Table 8.3 *Comparison of* MLU, FBU *and* FBW *in SL and TL (Mari and Nora)*

	SL			TL		
	MLU	%FBU	%FBW	MLU	%FBU	%FBW
Mari	13.7	56.0	7.5	5.1	63.9	20.2
Nora	18.6	54.7	5.9	8.6	71.2	18.4

The status of MLU as a measure of proficiency is corroborated. For both learners there is a mean difference of almost ten words per utterance between speaking their first language and speaking the target language. The same differences are present if we observe the share of feedback-containing utterances and feedback words. We see that the share increases dramatically, especially in relation to feedback words when learners are using the target language. There is also an increase, although a smaller one, in the amount of feedback-containing utterances in the TL data.

Further refinements

Over and above the use of FBW (and to some extent FBU) as an indicator of linguistic proficiency, two other aspects of feedback also show a correlation to changes occurring in language acquisition, namely, the functions of feedback words and repetitions as feedback.

Let us therefore take a look at how the two main FB functions – giving and elicitation – are distributed with regard to utterance status and utterance position. The data base for the learners is 7153 tokens used with FB function. The developmental patterns in relation to the crossing of the two dimensions is shown in Table 8.4. *Initial, medial, final* are utterance positions, while *single* indicates that an utterance has no other function than feedback. The functions are: (i) pure feedback giving (FBG), (ii) pure feedback elicitation (FBE) and (iii) utterances which have both a feedback giving and a feedback eliciting function (FBG/FBE).

Table 8.4 *Development of FBG, FBE and FBG/FBE in relation to utterance status and utterance position (percentage of FB units, twenty learners)*

	Pure FBG			Pure FBE			FBG/FBE		
	C1	C3	C1-3	C1	C3	C1-3	C1	C3	C1-3
Single	59.5	51.1	−8.4	0.8	0.8		9.0	3.1	−5.9
Initial	23.4	32.6	9.2	0.1	0.3	0.2	0.9	5	−0.4
Medial	0.8	1.7	0.9	0.1	0.6	0.5		0.1	0.1
Final	1.3	1.7	0.4	0.4	2.9	2.5	0.1	0.2	0.1
% Total FB units	83.0	87.4	2.4	3.6	6.7	3.1	11.4	5.9	−5.5

The decrease of the relative shares of singles – utterances consisting only of FB material – is clearly indicated. We see that it concerns singles as pure FBG and singles used in a vague way (FBG/FBE). The singles that are used for pure elicitation, on the other hand, retain a small but constant share. There is a small increase in all utterance positions, above all in initial position, of pure FBG. There is a concurrent but much smaller increase in all positions, especially final, or pure FBE and, finally there is a decrease among singles and in initial position of FBG/FBE.

The data supports the following generalisations about language acquisition and feedback: (i) that there will be a gradual functional differentiation of giving and eliciting; (ii) that both of these functions will be manifested with increasing complexity in relation to other linguistic material (that is, occur embedded in utterances rather than as single-word utterances); (iii) that 'pure FBG' will tend to be manifested either in single utterance or in initial utterance position, where the initial utterance position will gradually take over some of the 'pure giving' function from the singles; (iv) that 'pure FBE' will tend to be manifested in single utterances or in final utterance position and (v) that the vague category, FBG/FBE, will be manifested primarily as singles and that it will show a decrease from cycle 1 to cycle

3 connected with the learners' increasing differentiation of feedback functions. These generalisations will be further discussed in Volume II:II.2.

Besides the utterance status of feedback, repetition as feedback could provide another refinement in attempting to measure language acquisition through feedback. Repetition, as a means for feedback giving and elicitation, is important for second language learners. We find repetitions of many different linguistic structures and they can have several functions (see ESF:Allwood and Ahlsén 1986; ESF:Vion and Mittner 1986). Repetition is a simple means of feedback giving for the learner who does not have many other means of expression. In this function, it is used by learners early in their acquisition. By adding a questioning intonation to the repetition, the learner also has a way of eliciting, for example, showing non-understanding or asking for clarification. All of these functions of repetition are probably acceptable in most languages, but they will be more or less common. Some learners start out with more attempts to use repetition than other learners, perhaps through source language influence. In a similar way, some learners will find more support for their use of repetition in the target language than others. The use of repetition in the different languages also has to be put in relation to the availability of other types of feedback in both source and target languages, as well as to factors like learner characteristics and activity type.

The use of repetition as feedback was studied in two ways. The total amount and share of repetition among the feedback units for the twenty learners in the three cycles was calculated and used as a basis for a general overview. Let us first have a look at the number and the relative share of repetitions in the feedback of the learners and the controls (see Table 8.5).

Table 8.5 shows a clear decrease in the number of repetitions used for feedback from cycle 1 to cycle 3 for fourteen of the twenty learners and for seventeen for the twenty learners if reformulations are left out and pure repetitions alone or in combination with simple feedback is included (the second of the two C1-C3 columns in Table 8.5). This tendency is clear enough for it to be safe to assume that second language learners use repetition as an especially prominent type of feedback in early stages. This is also supported by the low shares of repetition for the controls.

Table 8.5 *Repetition – percentages in relation to total number of feedback units. Total number of FB units for each individual is given in brackets.*

			C1	C2	C3	C1-C3 (incl. re-formulations)	C1-C3 (Pure repetitions excl. reformu-lations)
Sw	Fi	Mari	12(77)	5(94)	18(155)	6	−6
		Leo	10(170)	5(130)	6(176)	−4	−4
	Sp	Nora	6(65)	4(145)	5 (83)	−1	−4
		Fernando	7(71)	4(97)	12(200)	5	7
Fr	Sp	Berta	16(86)	14(65)	17 (51)	1	−5
		Alfonso	36(55)	17(82)	14 (56)	−22	−36
	Ar	Zahra	16(195)	13(261)	10(220)	−6	−3
		Abdelmalek	63(139)	28(109)	11 (67)	−42	−46
Du	Ar	Fatima	58(195)	5(239)	5(282)		−1
		Mohamed	10(246)	4(299)	6(155)	−4	−2
	Tu	Ergün	13(161)	17(151)	15(193)	2	2
		Mahmut	30(252)	14(322)	13(296)	−17	15
Ge	Tu	Çevdet	50(46)	17(58)	6 (78)	−44	−37
		Ilhami	20(41)	2(47)	6 (64)	−14	−14
	It	Marcello	69(49)	13(84)	6 (83)	−63	−49
		Tino	50(67)	28(67)	11(112)	−39	−27
Eng	It	Lavinia	69(26)	14(14)	2 (41)	−67	−32
		Andrea	43(21)	10(59)	10 (79)	−33	−6
	Pu	Ravinder	3(69)	6(89)	5 (40)	2	3
		Madan	33(86)	4(70)	14(123)	−19	−5
Mean relative share			31	11	10		

TL Controls: SL Controls:
Swedish Adam   7(81)   Spanish Nora   7(91)
       Eva   12(60)   Finnish Mari   16(61)
English Martin   9(34)
       Sheila   0(34)

Conclusions: Supplementing MLU with feedback derived measures
MLU gives a fairly indirect measure of linguistic proficiency. It therefore needs to be supplemented by other measures. In this section, we have suggested that some such measures could be derived from the study of interactional linguistic (narrow) feedback. The reason for this is that various aspects of feedback show a great sensitivity to the needs of naturalistic adult language acquisition. We have found the following correlations between feedback phenomena and language acquisition.

1. The relative share of feedback as measured through FBU and FBW regularly decreases as a learner gets more proficient.
2. The relative share of singles, that is, utterances consisting only of feedback, and repetition used for feedback purposes decreases as the learner gets more proficient.

This means that an increase in MLU which is combined with a decrease in FBU and FBW, a decrease in feedback singles and the use of repetition for feedback or a subset of these, is a more reliable measure of language acquisition and increase in linguistic proficiency than MLU alone.

However, in order to be really useful, what is said above should also be made sensitive to differences in activity demands. Activity must, therefore, be kept constant in using any of the measures under consideration as indicators of linguistic proficiency. The problem of activity variation will be examined in detail in Volume II:II.2.

Thanks are due to two members of the Swedish team, Elisabeth Ahlsén and Joakim Nivre, for reading and commenting on this section.

8.2 Richness and variety in the developing lexicon

Peter Broeder, Guus Extra and Roeland van Hout

Introduction
In this section quantitative data on the learner's lexicon will be discussed. Three arguments can be put forward in favour of a macro-oriented approach to the lexicon. A macro-level study will give us: (i) a (descriptive) macro-picture of the learner's lexicon; (ii) the opportunity to test the overall effect of some aspects of the project's research design; (iii) a point of comparison for the qualitative studies of Volume II.

After the description of the lemmatised data base, the analysis starts with some evaluative comments on a number of global lexical measures. The results of several measures were unsatisfactory, especially the best known of these measures, the type/token ratio. Two measures (Guiraud's index and theoretical vocabulary) proved to be more satisfactory indexes of lexical richness. Their outcomes were used to trace the effects of cycle (time) and activity type.

All word forms were assigned a grammatical word class category. Some analytic results based on word class distinctions are to be found in the section following the global measures. Finally, the lemmatised data base is used to trace morphological development by weighing the number of lemmas against the number of word types.

Data base
The quantitative analyses are based on the complete lemmatisation of six language activities (three cycles × two activities) for twenty learners (the same learners as in 8.1, minus Ilhami, plus Ayshe). The two activities are conversation (A) and film retelling (I). In the resulting lemmatised data base, every word form in the transcripts of the language activities was assigned a specification of place of occurrence, word class category, lemma and, if necessary, a hypothesised learner meaning. The total data base contains 109,920 word forms.

The lemmatised data base consists of a set of records. A record has a fixed number of fields (seven). The data on a record always belong to one and the same language activity. The identification of informant and activity is encoded in field 1. The remaining six fields contain the linguistic information and the frequency of occurrence of the word form encoded in the record. The fields distinguished are:

field 1	pos. 1-12	record identification
field 2	pos. 13-30	word form
field 3	pos. 31-35	obligatory word class code
field 4	pos. 36-40	optional word class code
field 5	pos. 41-57	hypothesised learner meaning
field 6	pos. 58-76	lemma
field 7	pos. 77-80	frequency

Field 3 includes a language code which indicates whether the word form in question belongs to the target lexicon or is to be assigned to another language.

It is important to note that the lemmatisation has been conducted per informant per activity. Given two activity types (film retelling and free conversation) and three cycles, six lemmatised activities are available for each learner. The language activity will be the central unit of analysis. A lemma is defined as the combination of the entry in the lemma field (6), the language code and the first grammatical word class code (3). Any mismatch between these elements implies that the records in question contain different lemmas. For instance, 'work' coded as '01' (noun) is not the same lemma as 'work' coded '02' (verb). As a consequence, one lemma may enclose different word forms. Because of the different levels of transcription used by the research teams, the lemma was chosen as the basic lexical unit in our cross-linguistic comparisons.

The procedure for the lexical analysis in the present study was spelled out in internal project papers (detailed information is given in ESF:Broeder *et al.* 1988). Decisions have to be made about which word forms should be left out from the data base. In this study, false starts have been excluded from the data base, whereas repetitions (see 8.1) and non-target words within target language utterances have been included. On the text level, non-TL utterances, based on intersentential code-switching, have been excluded. In segmenting and coding the data problematic items occur of course, and considerable familiarity with the data is needed to solve them.

A first problem concerns the description of learner data. Even though the basic unit of coding for this study – the word – is as theoretically neutral as possible, it is not always straightforward to identify words, nor to assign them a category. In coding, one has to steer a course between the Scylla of the closeness fallacy and the Charybdis of superficial overinterpretation of the data. For this reason, the additional field 5 'Hypothesised learner meaning' was introduced into the coding scheme, as it allows the coder to indicate (without extensive, time-consuming analysis) that a word appears to be used by the learner in a non-TL way.

A good example is the Dutch verb *betalen*. In the film retelling task in the second cycle, Mahmut uses *betalen* (to pay) which is, according to standard conventions, a Dutch verb. However, Mahmut uses this word together with the verb *geven* (to give) in this retelling. The same verb occurs in the retelling in the third cycle, but now in combination with the standard Dutch noun *geld* (money), as is illustrated by the following examples

Cycle 2: *jij betalen geven*
       'you pay give'
Cycle 3: *jij geld geven*
       'you money give'

In cycle 3, the word *betalen* has disappeared in favour of the noun *geld* and it seems reasonable to interpret the word *betalen* in the film retelling in the second cycle as a noun. (This and other examples of Mahmut's are discussed in detail in ESF:Coenen and van Hout 1987.)

A further problem is that it is necessary to decide which word forms are taken into account in further analyses. In Table 8.6 the word forms are classified in three categories.

Table 8.6 *The number of tokens of the lemmatised data base*

| | intended language | | other language | total |
	clear cases	unclear cases		
L2 longitudinal group	104751	245	4924	109920

The unclear cases were left out from the analyses as well as the 'other language' data. The Spanish learners of French are mainly responsible for the frequency of tokens found in this category. The number of word forms used in the lexical analyses is 104,751.

It turned out that team-related differences for the longitudinal informants are rather sharp with respect to the numbers of tokens for free conversation. The number of tokens varies between 52 and 3652 in this activity, a gap which makes comparisons between the informants far from easy. The film retellings appear to be more comparable, although their size still varies between 144 and 2004. Table 8.7 is provided to give the reader a general picture for the film retelling, since this activity also represents the 'core' data base for thirteen of the learners of Volume II, chapters 1 and 2.

Table 8.7 *Number of tokens and number of lemmas in film retelling*

informant	data collection cycle 1		data collection cycle 2		data collection cycle 3	
	tokens(N)	lemmas (V)	tokens(N)	lemmas (V)	tokens(N)	lemmas (V)
Madan	1523	199	953	182	1249	209
Ravinder	144	58	579	146	600	159
Lavinia	662	139	530	137	324	98
Andrea	548	123	521	158	677	180
Marcello	802	297	649	242	1030	345
Tino	219	121	626	229	982	337
Ayshe	1312	367	2004	517	1660	493
Çevdet	393	163	934	288	1494	407
Ergün	963	139	1235	189	1065	182
Mahmut	891	155	753	148	937	163
Fatima	369	96	642	134	341	97
Mohamed	745	136	904	160	843	174
Abdelmalek	429	99	772	160	717	158
Zahra	398	92	468	98	288	82
Alfonso	856	142	652	126	638	149
Berta	221	54	417	93	937	170
Fernando	541	131	552	118	690	155
Nora	310	86	1094	184	904	189
Leo	187	83	545	143	702	174
Mari	640	153	983	193	1638	243

Global measures of lexical richness

The lexical richness of a text is usually defined as the number of types (V), given a number of tokens (N). The number of tokens constitutes the text length. Lexical richness (or vocabulary richness) has been investigated especially in lexicometric and stylostatistic research. As Arnaud (1984) states, the results in these areas can provide useful guidelines, in spite of the fact that the texts examined in these studies bear little resemblance to the speech produced by language learners. Nevertheless, in studying the developing lexicon of language learners two questions deserve some special attention.

The first question concerns the reliability problem. What kind of measures assess the lexical richness in a speech sample in a stable and unbiased way? A problem inherent to texts produced by language learners is the length of the text. Given a specific task, for instance a film retelling, a beginner will use a small set of short utterances, only a few function words and a restricted set of content words to get his message across. The amount of words produced will grow as the learner becomes more proficient, which implies that the text length itself reflects, to a certain degree, the language proficiency and the richness of the vocabulary of the language learner. On the other hand, it is precisely the difference in text length which causes enormous problems when comparing the lexical richness of fully proficient speakers. The increase in number of types is normally not proportional to the increase in number of tokens, but the precise relation is far from clear and many measures meant to correct for text length turn out to be unsatisfactory (Menard 1983).

The second question concerns the validity problem. Is it possible to generalise the findings from a specific speech sample? To what extent is one allowed to draw conclusions about the size and variety of the learners' lexicon on the basis of performance in a specific activity? This problem has at least two facets, both related to sampling. On the part of the learner, the point is how he selects words from his lexical stock. A real beginner may proceed by trial and error, while a more advanced learner may carefully pick out the words he needs. Moreover, the mark of a good speaker is that he selects words from his word stock in an optimal way in relation to the communicative situation, rather than produce as many different words as possible. The second facet can be seen as being of a statistical nature. In a running text, there is a dependency between successive occurrences of words. Such dependency produces redundancy in the sample. It is remarkable that this facet has received hardly any attention in lexicometrics and stylostatistics.

These questions cannot be solved in this study, of course. They are discussed here to make the reader aware of the many complicating factors hidden in the measurement of lexical richness.

In the lexicometric and stylostatistical literature, a variety of measures has been proposed for spelling out the lexical characteristics of a text. In our study, a set of lexical measures has been selected, mainly based on Menard (1983). The set of eleven measures applied to our lemmatised data base is given in Table 8.8.

The measures 2–7 in Table 8.8 are all in some way related to the number of types in a text. The lexical measures 8–10 belong to another family of measures, which are all directed towards the variation in the word frequency distribution (more information on the variation indices can be found in Herdan 1966). The variable X is the token frequency of a lemma. $\bar{X}$ is the *mean* token frequency of the lemmas, which is $\sum X/V = N/V$. The mean frequency is simply the inverse of the type/token ratio. Finally, the theoretical vocabulary measure belongs to the first group of measures.

Table 8.8   *The lexical measures applied*

1. *number of tokens*: the total number of words in a speech sample	N
2. *number of types*: the total number of different words (= lemmas) in a speech sample	V
3. *number of hapaxes*: the total number of lemmas occurring only once in a speech sample	V_1
4. *type/token ratio* (TTR)	V/N
5. *index of Guiraud* (indice de richesse)	$V/\sqrt{N}$
6. *index of Herdan* (logTTR)	$\log V / \log N$
7. *index of Uber*	$(\log N)^2/(\log N - \log V)$
8. *variance in the frequency of the types*	$\sum(X - \bar{X})^2/(V-1)$
9. *coefficient of variation*	$\sqrt{\text{variance}}/\bar{X}$
10. *coefficient of variation of the mean*	coeff.of var./$\sqrt{N}$
11. *theoretical vocabulary*	V'

This last measure is relatively unfamiliar, and additional information is probably needed (an extensive description can be found in Menard 1983:107–117). Suppose that we have a text with 1000 tokens. Suppose that we also want to reduce the text length to 500 words. How many different words will survive this process of reduction? The number of word types with a frequency of occurrence of 1 is symbolised by V_1; the number of word types with a frequency of 2 by V_2, etc. So, the number of word types with a frequency of n is symbolised by V_n. If the text length is reduced by half, the probability that a particular token is found in the reduced text is $p = 500/1000 = .5$; the probability that it does not re-occur is $q = 500/1000 = .5$. The binominal distribution makes it possible to calculate the probability that a certain lemma (or type) will not reoccur in the reduced text. This probability is dependent on the frequency of occurrence of the lemma in the original text. On the basis of probability calculations, the expected number of lemmas or the theoretical vocabulary can be calculated for the reduced text. The advantage of this lexical measure is that all texts investigated can be reduced to the same text length, giving us a measure independent of text length. The disadvantage is that the size of reduction is determined by the shorter texts, if texts are compared.

The most famous measure of lexical richness or diversity by far is the type/token ratio. Surveying the literature on child language, Richards (1987) concludes that type/token ratios have been extensively used but that this measure has frequently failed to discrimi nate between children at widely different stages of language development. As an alternative measure he mentions Carroll's (1964) diversity measure $(V/\sqrt{2N})$. This measure is in fact equal to Guiraud's index $(V/\sqrt{N})$; the use of the multiplication factor 2 makes no sense. Given the results in acquisitional studies, the general conclusion is that the results of global lexical measures of lexical richness and diversity should be handled with great care.

Guiraud and theoretical vocabulary
In selecting the best measure of lexical richness, there is a real danger of circular argumentation. Because of the absence of clear and directly comparable findings in other studies, one is inclined to rely on the attractiveness and interpretability of the outcomes of the measures applied. Nevertheless, it is obvious that a valid and reliable measure should signal progress in vocabulary in our data: at least some of the informants should show progress over the thirty months during which they were observed.

The most promising results in our data are found for theoretical vocabulary and Guiraud's index. Independent evidence exists in favour of the validity of both measures. Vermeer (1986) found that of the several lexical measures he applied, Guiraud's index produced the highest correlations with a vocabulary test and with other language proficiency tests. Meara (1983) compared the quality and properties of a range of lexical measures. He did not analyse texts of language learners, but his positive judgement on theoretical vocabulary as a measure for lexical richness is not without value for us.

An obvious disadvantage of the theoretical vocabulary measure relates to the reduction of the text length. Because of this step of reduction the smallest texts determine the size of the reduction required. The smallest text in film retelling contains 144 tokens, but in free conversation, four texts have a number of tokens of even below 100. The more the text size is reduced, the more the variation in the data is reduced and the more the reliability of the measurement will decrease (see Arnaud 1984). A base of 100 word tokens is chosen and the option for this lower limit has the consequence that for four texts in free conversation no theoretical vocabulary can be calculated.

An analysis of variance has been carried out to trace the effects of cycle, activity type and the interaction between those two factors on the vocabulary measures. The outcomes for number of tokens, number of lemmas, theoretical vocabulary (100 word tokens) and Guiraud's index are presented in Table 8.9. The analysis of variance

Table 8.9 *Analysis of variance of four lexical measures*

	mean square	error	F	df	p
tokens					
activity	1493431.40	1168520.90	1.28	1,19	.272
cycle	586624.67	119443.68	4.98	2,38	.013
cycle∗activity	84294.61	61494.08	1.37	2,38	.266
lemmas					
activity	7007.41	20103.18	1.28	1,19	.562
cycle	33152.16	3104.18	10.68	2,38	.000
cycle∗activity	4092.51	1578.75	2.38	2,38	.088
theor.voc.$_{100}$					
activity	718.37	9.97	72.03	1,15	.000
cycle	82.77	12.41	6.66	2,30	.004
cycle∗activity	14.13	9.01	1.57	2,30	.225
Guiraud					
activity	5.60	1.89	2.96	1,19	.101
cycle	6.48	.63	10.22	2,38	.000
cycle∗activity	.61	.31	1.96	2,38	.155

of the theoretical vocabulary relates to sixteen out of the twenty longitudinal informants. Madan, Ravinder, Marcello and Zahra had to be excluded, because their free conversation was too short.

Both the number of tokens and the number of lemmas show a cycle effect, and this effect holds in general for both film retelling and free conversation. The probability value of the interaction effect of the lemma analysis is less than .10, which could be interpreted as an indication of a difference in growth of number of lemmas between film retelling and free conversation. The theoretical vocabulary shows a very large effect for activity type and cycle. The activity effect in the Guiraud analysis is absent, but the cycle effect looks stronger.

An adequate interpretation of the outcomes of the analysis of variance of theoretical vocabulary and Guiraud's index requires the inspection of the individual results as well as the global results. In Table 8.10 the individual outcomes for the theoretical vocabulary measure can be found. Table 8.11 contains the outcomes with respect to Guiraud's index. The mean scores split up for activity type and cycle are plotted in Figures 1 and 2 respectively. The exact mean values for both measures can be found in Table 8.12; the mean values of the type/token ratio are given too.

The differences in outcomes between theoretical vocabulary and Guiraud's index seem largely reducible to the effect of text length

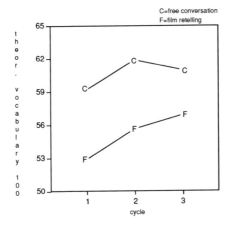

Figure 1. *Mean theoretical vocabulary of 100 tokens according to cycle and type of activity (n=16; those cases which have a missing value are left out)*

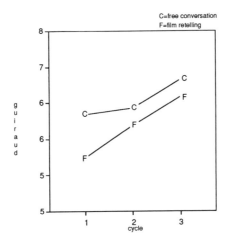

Figure 2. *Mean index of Guiraud according to cycle and type of activity*

Table 8.10 *Theoretical vocabulary for 100 words ('—' means that a value cannot be calculated because of too small a number of tokens)*

informant	film retelling			free conversation		
	cycle 1	cycle 2	cycle 3	cycle 1	cycle 2	cycle 3
Madan	59.512	57.035	58.484	59.136	—	57.340
Ravinder	46.592	55.732	59.337	—	53.158	60.084
Lavinia	53.080	56.442	52.631	52.201	59.951	56.260
Andrea	49.488	60.267	59.524	56.439	58.304	61.496
Marcello	69.514	66.266	68.818	67.270	—	63.393
Tino	68.364	68.301	70.732	71.213	74.751	72.898
Ayshe	63.772	67.530	67.625	60.666	74.318	72.050
Cevdet	63.731	62.874	64.204	70.535	75.509	68.957
Ergün	45.653	52.773	53.016	56.000	62.154	60.598
Mahmut	51.256	53.169	53.613	57.197	59.767	63.049
Fatima	48.830	49.305	48.265	54.260	53.053	60.371
Mohamed	50.040	48.434	52.959	51.636	58.377	60.047
Abdelmalek	47.367	57.129	53.804	61.518	59.594	53.305
Zahra	48.584	49.375	46.688	43.419	—	55.712
Alfonso	49.816	52.887	54.969	60.600	59.647	56.634
Berta	38.170	47.878	53.987	48.859	58.015	55.681
Fernando	51.977	45.229	54.615	62.102	59.554	59.396
Nora	52.499	54.215	55.969	60.208	54.626	54.001
Leo	55.964	54.991	56.836	61.285	61.123	54.566
Mari	57.268	58.801	59.040	62.422	61.239	65.466

which is still perceptible in the Guiraud scores. Because increase in text length is partly inherent to progress in acquisition, this outcome is not by definition objectionable. Regarding the differences in the results of the analysis of variance, it should be taken into account that four informants were not incorporated in the analysis of variance of the theoretical vocabulary. The resulting picture may therefore look better. It is hard to decide which of the two measures should be preferred. The best solution seems to be to take both into consideration in studying the developmental pattern of the lexicon. A reassuring factor is that the correlation between both measures is high. It is .89 in film retelling and .87 in free conversation.

As can be seen in Table 8.12, the type/token ratio delivers counterintuitive results. The ratio decreases in time, a result also found by Broeder and Voionmaa (ESF:1986) in the analysis of data on the learners of Swedish. The type/token ratio is already a questionable measure for texts produced by fully proficient speakers, but certainly in language acquisition research this measure has to be rejected as a

Table 8.11 *Index of Guiraud* $(V/\sqrt{N})$

informant	film retelling			free conversation		
	cycle 1	cycle 2	cycle 3	cycle 1	cycle 2	cycle 3
Madan	5.099	5.896	5.914	6.108	5.8	6.029
Ravinder	4.833	6.068	6.491	4.160	5.525	7.090
Lavinia	5.402	5.951	5.444	5.364	6.420	7.098
Andrea	5.254	6.922	6.918	6.473	6.288	7.074
Marcello	10.487	9.499	10.750	8.253	5.889	7.392
Tino	8.176	9.153	10.754	9.863	10.380	12.264
Ayshe	10.132	11.549	12.100	7.386	10.418	12.364
Cevdet	8.222	9.424	10.530	8.125	9.092	8.032
Ergün	4.479	5.378	5.577	6.854	6.507	6.307
Mahmut	5.193	5.393	5.325	6.106	6.642	7.040
Fatima	4.998	5.289	5.253	5.778	6.187	6.352
Mohamed	4.983	5.322	5.993	6.014	6.260	7.044
Abdelmalek	4.780	5.759	5.901	6.820	6.413	5.880
Zahra	4.612	4.530	4.832	4.463	4.313	5.872
Alfonso	4.853	4.935	5.899	6.702	6.572	5.916
Berta	3.632	4.554	5.554	5.715	6.455	6.152
Fernando	5.632	5.022	5.901	7.612	6.378	6.660
Nora	4.884	5.563	6.286	6.389	6.082	5.981
Leo	6.070	6.125	6.567	6.714	6.527	6.522
Mari	6.048	6.156	6.004	7.228	6.678	6.817

proficiency measure.

The occurrence of a general cycle effect for Guiraud and theoretical vocabulary is self-evident and as a general effect needs no further explanation. Further interpretation would be interesting on the level of differences between individual informants. We will return to these differences (see 8.3).

The type of activity turns out to be an influential factor too, especially regarding theoretical vocabulary. This effect is explainable,

Table 8.12 *Mean scores according to cycle and type of activity of theoretical vocabulary, Guiraud and type/token ratio*

measure	film retelling			free conversation		
	cycle 1	cycle 2	cycle 3	cycle 1	cycle 2	cycle 3
theor.voc.$_{100}$	52.95	55.64	56.94	59.20	61.87	60.92
Guiraud	5.89	6.42	6.90	6.61	6.71	7.19
type/token ratio	.27	.24	.24	.32	.35	.28

so it seems, by the type of pooled data: all the informants retold the same film stimulus, whereas the pooled conversations took place on a large variety of topics, between different people, at different places and times. Consequently, the probability of variation in content words will increase and this effect seems observable particularly in the theoretical vocabulary measure.

Word class categories

The literature provides ample evidence of the fundamental role of word class distinctions in speech production and language competence. Studies on the (mental) lexicon demonstrate that in addition to semantic features, grammatical word class features are part of the major organisational categories that determine the selection and retrieval of word forms (Hatch 1983:63). In speech error data, repairs and corrections operate more often within than between word classes (Garret 1982; Maratsos 1982:255; Hatch 1983:63).

Only very global word class distinctions are usually applied in language acquisition research. A distinction is often made between content words (nouns, verbs, adjectives) and function words (including articles, pronouns, prepositions, conjunctions, quantifiers), or open and closed word classes respectively. Many studies on first language acquisition show that words belonging to closed word classes emerge later than words from open word classes (see, Carey 1982:380). A more specific distinction is the difference between nouns and verbs. Verbs are acquired more slowly than nouns. Gentner (1982) argued that as the referents of nouns are commonly concrete objects, they are more easily accessible in a cognitive perceptual sense than the referential value of verbs and other relational categories. Bloom (1981) claimed a strong dependency between the acquisition of verbs and grammatical development.

Dietrich (ESF:1989b) investigated the difference between learners' use of nouns and verbs in German data gathered in this project. He concluded that verbal elements emerge in later phases of acquisition than nouns, but he also raised another explanatory factor in adult second language acquisition. Adults will have the cognitive maturity to understand relational concepts. Nouns would be learnt first for a pragmatic reason. In general, the most crucial information to give explicitly in communicating a message are entities, represented by nouns, and not the relations between them, represented by verbal elements, as it is generally easier to infer the latter.

One may use the lemmatised database to explore whether the specific word classes distinguished show a developmental pattern. Given the global growth rate in lexical richness over time, the quantitative developments in particular word class categories may be related to the two most successful global indices of lexical richness, theoretical vocabulary and Guiraud's index. This relation was investigated by computing correlations between these two measures and the proportion of both the number of lemmas and the number of tokens within the various word class categories. The proportion (or relative share) of a word class was calculated by dividing the number of tokens or lemmas within that word class by the total number of tokens or lemmas of all the word classes together. The correlations between theoretical vocabulary and Guiraud's index and the proportions of the word classes are given in Table 8.13 (number of tokens) and Table 8.14 (number of types). The correlations were calculated over both activities in all three cycles and over all informants ($n=120$).

Table 8.13 *Correlations between relative share of word classes for number of tokens and lexical richness (theoretical vocabulary and Guiraud)*

number of tokens	film retelling		free conversation	
word classes	theor.voc.	Guiraud	theor.voc.	Guiraud
nouns	−.13	−.21	−.21	−.22
verbs	.36*	.29	.43**	.42**
adjectives	−.09	−.15	−.13	−.16
articles	.46**	.48**	−.02	.05
pronouns	.22	.16	.11	−.15
prepositions	−.05	−.08	−.10	−.05
conjunctions	.29	.29	.12	.14
quantifiers	−.05	−.18	.05	−.04
adverbs	−.36*	−.26	−.09	−.34*
interjections	−.36*	−.27	−.28	−.13

Most correlations in Table 8.13 and Table 8.14 are not particularly high. This may have been partly brought about by the method of calculation. The relative share is related to the total set of tokens or lemmas, which means that the relative share is sensitive both to internal developments in the word class involved and to (external) contributions from other word classes. Despite this suppressor effect, some word classes have a significant correlation, in particular verbs, and also nouns and articles. The most consistent effect is found for the verbs. A relative increase in verb lemmas and in the number of verb tokens is correlated to an increase in lexical richness. This result supports the idea that verbs have a crucial role in the overall devel-

Table 8.14 *Correlations between relative share of word classes for number of types and lexical richness (theoretical vocabulary and Guiraud)*

number of lemmas word classes	film retelling		free conversation	
	theor.voc.	Guiraud	theor.voc.	Guiraud
nouns	−.34*	−.36*	−.44**	−.28
verbs	.55**	.68**	.55**	.60**
adjectives	.01	−.08	−.30	−.19
articles	.41**	.51**	.22	.03
pronouns	−.17	−.12	−.01	−.28
prepositions	.03	−.02	−.03	−.08
conjunctions	.18	.17	.19	.12
quantifiers	−.28	−.37*	−.18	−.12
adverbs	−.21	−.20	.15	−.13
interjections	−.23	−.27	−.08	−.12

opment of the lexicon, also in the case of spontaneous acquisition by adults. Furthermore, it is noteworthy that the relative size or share of some word classes is inversely related to the measured richness of vocabulary (the correlation is negative). This is particularly true for nouns.

A more global distinction between word classes can be made on the basis of the sign of the correlation coefficients. Positively correlated are verbs, articles and conjunctions. With respect to the number of tokens, the pronouns belong to this group as well. Prepositions have a correlation of about zero. A negative tendency is evidenced for nouns, adjectives, adverbs, quantifiers and interjections. The position of the quantifiers is not surprising, since this word class contains numerals for a large part. The differences between the word classes are not very sharp, but the following tendency toward a bipartition seems to emerge:

> + verbs, articles, conjunctions
> − nouns, interjections, (adverbs, quantifiers, adjectives)

This bipartion reflects the urgency of the tasks which we hypothesised (in chapters 1 and 4) the learners to be faced with over time. Their priority is to acquire words denoting relevant entities (and attributes of these entities) in their environment, and this corresponds especially to the initial, preponderant share of nouns. Then comes the need to express relational concepts explicitly, which can be seen in the increasing vocabulary share of articles, conjunctions, and especially verbs.

However, the direct calculation of the noun/verb ratio in these data showed no clear developmental pattern. The number of verbs used by our informants is relatively high compared to findings in child language acquisition, which may be attributed to the fact that not all the learners were beginners. Above a certain level of proportion of verbs, the verb/noun ratio seems to become an unreliable index. Whereas Dietrich (ESF:1989b) did observe some increase for three learners of German, it is not implausible that the verb/noun ratio is an effective measure only at the very early stages of spontaneous ALA.

Notice, finally, that the above bipartion contrasts with Gentner's (1982: 302) distinction between 'the category of nouns and the composite predicate category composed of verbs, prepositions, adjectives and adverbs': children learn nominals before predicates because of the perceptual accessibility of the former. Here, adjectives and adverbs cluster more with nouns, and prepositions show no clear tendency. As Dietrich (*op. cit.*:19) points out, 'adults are no longer struggling with perceptual bits of relations and processes', and 'adults have established verbal concepts' – the explanation for initial adult development closely depends on communicative urgency. An increase in the proportion of verbs corresponds to a development in the *structuring* of learners' utterances, as we shall see in Volume II:I.1.

Lemma variation and morphology

In the lemmatised database a lemma may contain different word forms. Before analysing the relation between the number of word forms and the number of lemmas, it has to be clear how the variation within the lemma should be defined. The lemma is defined by the entry in the word lemma field and the first obligatory word class code, that is field 6 and part of field 3 in the lemmatised database respectively (see above). Next, the variation within a lemma can be defined as the number of different forms occurring in the word form field (field 2). This definition implies that all types of variation are taken into account. Identical word forms are taken together, even if some additional notes are put in the field of the hypothesised learner meaning (field 5) or if the word forms have a different second obligatory word class code (part of field 3). Because different records in the lemmatised data base may be merged by this definition, a new term should be introduced to indicate this level between the standardised lemma and the raw word forms: the word type. A word type is a set of identical word forms within a lemma. The lemma variation is then the number of different word types belonging to that lemma.

The variation in the occurring word forms belonging to the same lemma may be caused by quite diverging factors. First of all, the word forms may reflect morphological variation, such as singular versus plural forms or present versus past tense. Since the database derives from language learners, variation in word types may also be caused by mispronunciations, by a deviant word form for a specific lemma meaning, and by faulty affixation. If the transcripts contain phonetic details (for example, the German transcripts), even purely phonetic variation can be the source of word form variation within the lemma. Because of this rich mixture of possible sources of variation, it seems reasonable to hypothesise that the number of different word forms has a fairly opaque relation to the number of different word lemmas. That is precisely the reason why in this study the lemma was chosen as the basic element for studying the developing lexicon. A procedure of standardisation by means of lemmatisation offered a firmer base for cross-linguistic comparisons, especially given the fact that the local project teams allowed for different levels of phonetic detail in their transcripts.

Nevertheless, an interesting hypothesis would be that random variation on the phonetic and phonological level at the first stages of second language acquisition is gradually replaced by variation produced by the acquisition of proper morphological rules. The lemmatised data base makes it possible to carry out the rough test of this hypothesis despite the different degrees of phonetic detail in the transcripts. If phonetic/phonological variation is the main source of differentiation between types and lemmas, this source of variation will be operative independent of the word class category of the lemma involved. If morphology develops, it is to be expected that the morphological rules will become operative in specific word classes. In the target languages involved the class of verbs is the word class category par excellence in which the morphological component can show development. All the TLs show tense, participle and infinitive forms, and to a certain extent, number. If the indifferent phonetic/phonological variation is gradually replaced by morphological variation, this should be observable in the differentiation scores of the verb types and the verb lemmas.

Differentiation scores (number of types divided by the number of lemmas) were calculated for (a) the whole set of word classes, (b) the word class of verbs, and (c) the remaining word classes after having removed the verbs. The correlations between these three differentiation scores can be calculated, as well as their correlations with the two measures of lexical richness (theoretical vocabulary and Guiraud's index). It was expected that the verb differentiation score would have a higher correlation with the measures of lexical richness, indicating that progress in lexical richness is accompanied by progress in morphology. The correlations found for film retelling and free conversation are presented in Table 8.15 and Table 8.16 respectively.

Table 8.15 *Correlations between measures for type-lemma differentiation and lexical measures for the film retelling data*

	diff.$_{total}$	diff.$_{verb}$	diff.$_{rest}$	theor.voc.	Guiraud
diff.$_{total}$	—	.90	.91	−.39	−.53
diff.$_{verb}$	—	—	.64	−.48	−.61
diff.$_{rest}$	—	—	—	−.26	−.38
theor.voc.	—	—	—	—	.89
Guiraud	—	—	—	—	—

Table 8.16 *Correlations between measures for type-lemma differentiation and lexical measures for the free conversation data*

	diff.$_{total}$	diff.$_{verb}$	diff.$_{rest}$	theor.voc.	Guiraud
diff.$_{total}$	—	.88	.94	−.32	−.41
diff.$_{verb}$	—	—	.70	−.36	−.45
diff.$_{rest}$	—	—	—	−.29	−.36
theor.voc.	—	—	—	—	.87
Guiraud	—	—	—	—	—

The highest correlations in Tables 8.15 and 8.16 for the differentiation scores are found for the word class of verbs. This first and rather global test does not contradict the hypothesis. The correlations of the verb differentiation scores with the lexical richness measures are higher than those of the differentiation scores of the remaining lemmas, despite the fact that this category still contains word class categories which are marked by morphological variation (such as nouns). Further research is required, to test the hypothesis whether random variation is gradually replaced by a variation produced by morphological rules, given the different transcription conventions. These figures do, though, give more evidence that the verb takes a crucial position in lexical development.

Conclusions and perspectives

In this section, various analyses based on the lemmatised data were presented and discussed. These quantitative analyses gave a macro-picture of the developing lexicon on three main aspects of the lexical data: (1) the global lexical richness, (2) the distribution of word class categories, (3) the differentiation of the number of different word forms in relation to the number of lemmas. Two main variables in the design of the project (cycle, activity type) proved to be influential factors regarding specific aspects of lexical development.

Global lexical richness was investigated by applying a wide range of lexical measures. Primary concepts in the analysis were the number of lemmas and the number of tokens used by a language learner in a specific language activity. Two measures proved to be fairly satisfactory, viz. Guiraud's index and theoretical vocabulary. It was impossible to decide which of the two measures should be preferred. Guiraud's index seems more sensitive to the length of a text (the number of tokens). One may have the impression that such an effect is pernicious, because it is precisely the text length factor which should be neutralised by measures of lexical richness. However, the increase of the number of words used in a specific language activity by a language learner is partly inherent to progress in language acquisition, as we shall see again in the control group study (8.4). Both measures were therefore used in the analysis of lexical richness.

It was possible to test the effects of two main factors in the research design (cycle and activity type) by the two more successful measures. The effects observed for these two measures, as well as the effects observed for the number of lemmas and the number of tokens, can be summarised as follows:

	cycle	activity
number of tokens (N)	+	–
number of lemmas (V)	+	–
theoretical vocabulary	+	+
index of Guiraud	+	–

A '+' means that a significant effect was found. In case of a cycle effect, '+' means that an increase was found between the first and third cycle. A '–' means that no effect was found. A clear cycle effect was observed for the group of learners as a whole, which indicates that a general increase in vocabulary richness was found. Activity type turned out to be a statistically significant factor regarding theoretical vocabulary. On average free conversations gave higher scores on lexical richness than film retelling for reasons discussed under *theoretical vocabulary* above.

On the basis of the grammatical word class categories assigned to the word forms in the lemmatised data base, the distribution of word classes were investigated. The class of verbs seems to play a crucial role in lexical development. First of all, the relative share of this word class showed the highest correlations with the two measures used for lexical richness. These correlations were positive, meaning that an increase in lexical richness was accompanied by an increase both in the relative number of verb tokens and verb lemmas. It highlights the special role of the verb in the developing lexicon. Secondly, the verb lemmas showed an almost significant effect for cycle, despite the fact that in general the effect of activity type overshadowed the cycle effect in the analyses of the distribution of the word class categories. Thirdly, progress in lexical richness was correlated with progress in the differentiation scores (= the number of types divided by the number of lemmas) found for verbs. This differentiation is conspicuous given the fact that no change in the differentiation score was found for all word classes together.

8.3   The influence of socio-biographical factors

Roeland van Hout and Sven Strömqvist

In this section we will discuss the usefulness of socio-biographical information for explaining the variation in lexical richness and rate of lexical development between the learners.

Studies of individual differences in language learning or acquisition often focus on psychological variables such as aptitude, motivation, attitude, personality, intelligence, cognitive style and affect (see, for example, Skehan 1989). Systematic socio-biographical information available for the learners of the present study includes more sociologically oriented variables, such as age, sex, education, and family status – the 'bias' factors of HPD's study (see chapter 2.2). The socio-biographical notes kept for each informant also include information on types and amount of contact with target language speakers, and occasionally information about attitudes and emotional states. This latter type of information, however, is less systematic.

Among the many factors which can be hypothesised to influence the structure of language acquisition, some were systematically varied and some were ideally to be kept constant in the design of the project. The systematically varied factors were source and target languages. Factors to be held constant included education (preferably very low), family status (preferably no children attending school), length of stay in the target country before entering the project (preferably very short, say, less than half a year), and participation in training courses in the target language (preferably none). In the actual implementation of the project, however, we saw in chapter 3 that it was impossible to hold many of the latter type of factors constant. There is variation between the informants. Thus, the age of the learners studied ranges from sixteen to thirty-nine; their length of stay in the target country before entering the project ranges from one to nineteen months; their education in their source countries varies from nought to eleven years; their participation in training courses in the target language ranges from 0 to more than 600 hours, some of them are married to compatriots whereas others are single, some have had contact with a third language, etc. (see Table 3.1 for more information).

Given that the informants do vary with respect to these characteristics, it becomes possible to explore these characteristics as hypothetical explanatory factors underlying differences in the success observed among the informants. We want to stress, however, that this exploration should be undertaken with great caution.

First, assume that we want to use socio-biographical information for explaining differences between two individual learners. We would then be able to use this information with a greater degree of confidence if the other factors influencing the performance of the two learners were controlled for. This means that the two learners compared should share the same source-target language characteristics. Similarly, differences in socio-biographical characteristics between learners may be attributed greater reliability as an explanatory factor if the data from the learners are collected by the same research team – on the reasonable assumption that project activities, on a detailed level, have been carried out with greater consistency within teams than across teams.

Now, if we find statistically significant correlations between the socio-biographical characteristics of the learners and their language proficiency measures to hold across target languages, source languages *and* research teams, then these findings should be taken seriously in view of the many factors which influence the measure of language proficiency. Or, put somewhat differently, if we find certain correlations to hold across all learners despite the many factors not controlled for, then these correlations represent strong findings.

In the remaining parts of this section, we shall first illustrate the use of socio-biographical data for shedding light on differences between learners who share the same source-target language constellation (and who, by implication, also experienced project activities implemented by the same research team). We shall then proceed to explore correlations between socio-biographical data and lexical proficiency measures which prove to be valid across all learners.

Pair-wise comparisons

With respect to the measures of lexical richness of the previous section, we observe a difference in progress between the two Italian learners of English, Andrea and Lavinia. Lavinia made faster progress than Andrea. The socio-biographical notes kept for these two learners provide a candidate explanation for this difference. Andrea appears to have had very few contacts with target language speakers, whereas Lavinia did have contact with target language speakers.

A difference in lexical development is also observed between the two Turkish learners of Dutch; Ergün and Mahmut. Ergün makes faster progress than Mahmut, although his level of lexical richness in the first cycle is lower than that of Mahmut. The socio-biographical records state that Ergün, in contradistinction to Mahmut, had frequent contacts with native speakers of the target language.

Similarly, the two Moroccan learners of French, Zahra and Abdelmalek, show a difference in lexical development which is matched by a difference in degree of contact with native target language speakers. Abdelmalek showed a clear increase in lexical richness, whereas Zahra did not. Abdelmalek, a bachelor, had many opportunities to use and practice French both at his work place and during his leisure time. Zahra, in contrast, had far fewer opportunities. Her primary reason for coming to France was to join her husband, who had already been working there for some time.

A comparison of the lexical development in the two Latin-American learners of Swedish shows that Fernando is a slow learner throughout the period of observation, whereas Nora, after an initial period of very slow learning, has a rapid increase in lexical richness. Fernando's socio-biographical record states that he had no Swedish friends and that he had a strong wish to return to Argentina. Nora, on the other hand, was initially married to a compatriot, whom she later divorced. As a consequence of her divorce she had more contact with the Swedish speaking society than previously. This period in Nora's life coincides with the period of rapid increase in her lexical richness scores.

Judging from these four examples of pair-wise comparisons, intensity of contact between learner and target language speakers seems to be a potential factor for explaining differences in acquisition success. This finding is in accordance with, for example, the conclusions of HPD (see chapter 2.2).

General patterns

A statistical analysis based on the socio-biographical information available from the project yields a number of systematic correlational patterns. In Table 8.17 the socio-biographical variables used in the analysis are defined. The correlations between these variables and our two main measures of richness of vocabulary, that is, theoretical vocabulary and index of Guiraud (see Tables 8.10-11), are then presented in Tables 8.18 and 8.19. Tables 8.18 and 8.19 show that there are systematic correlations between our measures of lexical richness on the one hand and the variables *Age, Married, Children* and *School* (source country) on the other. The correlations are consistent. They hold across the two main measures (Theoretical Vocabulary and Guiraud) and they hold across the three cycles. With the exception of

School they also hold across the two activity types (film retelling and free conversation). The fact that *School* correlates with film retelling across all cycles, but not with free conversation, is interesting. The pre-set instruction task of film retelling is a communicative task which has a greater similarity to traditional classroom interaction than free conversation has.

Table 8.17 *Definition of the variables used in the analysis*

Variable	Definition
Sex:	(1) male
	(2) female
Age:	Years, varying between 16 and 39 years
Married:	(1) single
	(2) married
Children:	(1) has no children
	(2) has children
School:	Years of education in source country,
	varying between 0 and 11 years
Literate:	(1) illiterate
	(2) literate
Courses:	Target language courses in the target country
	(1) none
	(2) between 15 and 200 hours
	(3) more than 200 hours
Stay1:	Number of months between arrival in the target country
	and the first project session; varying between 1 and 19 months
Stay2:	Number of months between arrival in the target country
	and the first project session used for analysis in the present
	study; varying between 7 and 27 months
L3:	Knowledge of a third language
	(1) no knowledge
	(2) rudimentary knowledge
	(3) (moderate) proficiency
Distance:	Typological difference between source and target language
	(1) Indo-European, very close: Spanish-French
	(2) Indo-European, more distant: Italian-English,
	Italian-German, Spanish-Swedish
	(3) Indo-European, remote: English-Punjabi
	(4) different language families: German-Turkish,
	Dutch-Turkish, Arabic-Dutch,
	Arabic-French, Finnish-Swedish

The variables *Age, Married* and *Children* all show negative correlations with the lexical measures. We know from chapter 3.2 that

Table 8.18   *Correlations between socio-biographical variables and vocabulary richness (1)*

THEORETICAL VOCABULARY				* = significant at the .05 level, one-tailed		
	Film retelling			Free conversation		
	Cycle 1	Cycle 2	Cycle 3	Cycle 1	Cycle 2	Cycle 3
Sex	−.17	−.13	−.28	−.47*	−.13	−.08
Age	−.43*	−.45*	−.33	−.35	−.57*	−.45*
Married	−.47*	−.49*	−.49*	−.47*	−.64*	−.39*
Children	−.38*	−.50*	−.43*	−.42*	−.29	−.50*
School	.44*	.40*	.63*	.49*	.33	.25
Literate	.29	.26	.51*	.36	.27	.31
Courses	.07	.01	−.01	.14	.18	.02
Stay1	.09	.05	−.11	.08	−.17	−.15
Stay2	.31	.07	.07	.27	.19	.19
L3	.22	.23	.14	.09	.02	.05
Distance	.07	.02	−.18	−.06	.17	.18
	N=20	N=20	N=20	N=19	N=17	N=20

these three variables are inter-related. The older the learner, the greater the chance that (s)he is married and the greater the chance that (s)he has children. We will therefore tentatively conceive of these three variables as aspects of a more complex variable which we might call *Age and family status*. The variable *School*, in contrast, shows a positive correlation with the lexical measures. In effect, two main generalisations can be made on the basis of the results from our correlation analysis:

(a) if the learner is older, married to a compatriot and has children, (s)he is less likely to receive high scores on the lexical richness measures than if (s)he is younger, single and has no children;
(b) the more education a learner has received before starting to learn a second language, the more likely (s)he is to receive high scores on the lexical richness measures.

Variables tested for which do not show significant correlations with the lexical measures are *Sex, Literate, Courses, Stay* (Stay1 and Stay2), *L3* and *Distance*. The fact that *Distance* does not show a systematic correlation with the lexical measures should not come as a surprise, given that typological distance is calculated on the basis

Table 8.19 *Correlations between socio-biographical variables and vocabulary richness (2)*

GUIRAUD	* = significant at the .05 level, one-tailed N =20					
	Film retelling			Free conversation		
	Cycle 1	Cycle 2	Cycle 3	Cycle 1	Cycle 2	Cycle 3
Sex	−.09	−.08	−.14	−.32	−.03	.02
Age	−.44*	−.47*	−.39*	−.33*	−.49*	−.42*
Married	−.57*	−.59*	−.62*	−.58*	−.53*	−.47*
Children	−.38*	−.47*	−.38*	−.29	−.29	−.33
School	.45*	.42*	.47*	.41*	.29	.26
Literate	.25	.28	.31	.30	.30	.27
Course	.12	.13	.07	.05	.24	.05
Stay1	−.17	−.17	−.20	−.15	−.37	−.28
Stay2	.23	.17	.14	.11	.02	.05
L3	.24	.22	.13	.20	.15	.21
Distance	.07	.09	−.02	−.12	.05	.04

of properties of grammar and not lexicon. Also, from cross-linguistic research, we know that the presence of similarities in vocabulary between two languages does not imply similarities in general typological traits between the two languages. Rather, lexical similarities tend to imply socio-cultural contact between the linguistic communities in question.

The L3 knowledge of our learners was assessed to be negligible in all cases but one, and the lack of a significant correlation here certainly does not contradict this assessment. The lack of correlation of the *Stay* measures can be partly attributed to variation in intensity of contact (see above), which is concealed by such a measure.

The most striking result is surely the lack of correlation between our lexical richness measures and *Courses*. It is unlikely, from what we know, that the courses taken by learners in any of the target countries concentrated on grammar, or pronunciation, to the detriment of vocabulary. We cannot, of course, exclude the possibility that courses do influence aspects of TL proficiency except vocabulary. What seems however more plausible is that in competition with the cumulative effect of everyday exposure to spontaneous use of the TL, the effect of such courses is negligible. This result tends to confirm the subjective assessment of language tuition given in chapter 3.2. This is not at all to treat TL tuition as *quantité négligeable*, but rather to underline the power of the spontaneous acquisition process for learners such as those studied here.

An ordered picture

In order to produce a more individualised picture of the impact of socio-biographical characteristics on lexical richness, we will now proceed to order the learners according to the variables which we found to be systematically correlated with our lexical measures. This ordering makes it possible to explore how the individual learners conform to the expectations on lexical richness generated on the basis of their respective scores on the four variables *Age, Married, Children* and *School*. To this end, we redefine the variables *Age* and *School* in such a way that they take two and three values respectively.

Specifically, we expect low values to facilitate lexical acquisition and the achievement of high scores on the lexical richness measures. Similarly, we expect high values to make the achievement of high lexical scores more difficult. The redefined variables used to obtain the ordered picture are presented in Table 8.20 and the resultant order is presented in Table 8.21. Table 8.21 also shows the mean value of Guiraud for each of the learners. The mean value is calculated on the basis of the Guiraud scores for all six activities.

Table **8.20** *Redefined socio-biographical variables*

Variable	Definition
$A = Age$	(1) 25 years or younger
	(2) 26 years or older
$M = Married$	(1) single
	(2) married
$C = Children$	(1) no children
	(2) children
$S = School$	(1) 7 or more years of education
	(2) between 3 and 6 years of education
	(3) 2 years of education or less

Table 8.21 shows that, by and large, the expectations are borne out. The correlational pattern between socio-biographical characteristics and lexical scores can be most clearly seen at the extremes, that is, the lowest and the highest values. Thus, those learners who belong to the youngest age group, who are unmarried, have no children and who have the most amount of years of (secondary school) education are also the learners who score the highest on the lexical measure.

Table 8.21 *An ordered picture*

A^3	M	C	S	Informant	Mean value Guiraud[4]
1	1	1	1	Çevdet	8.90
				Leo	6.42
				Marcello	8.71
				Tino	10.10
1	1	1	2	Ayshe	10.66
				Mohamed	5.94
				Ergün	5.85
1	1	1	3	Abdelmalek	5.93
1	2	1	2	Mahmut	5.95
				Madan	5.70
				Mari	6.94
1	2	2	1	Lavinia	5.95
1	2	2	1	Ravinder	5.69
2	2	1	1	Andrea	6.49
2	2	1	3	Fatima	5.64
2	2	2	1	Berta	5.34
				Fernando	6.20
2	2	2	2	Alberto	5.80
				Nora	5.86
2	2	2	3	Zahra	4.77

In contrast, those learners who belong to the oldest age group, who are married, have children and who have the least amount of years of education are also the learners who score the lowest on the lexical measure.

Conclusions
In conclusion, we found clear correlational patterns between the socio-biographical characteristics of the adult second language learners and their scores on the lexical richness measures. The statistical testing of the correlational patterns proved *Age and family status* on the one hand and Education (*School*) on the other to be significant factors influencing lexical richness. The impact of these factors on lexical richness was also illustrated by the result obtained from ordering the learners according to their relevant socio-biographical characteristics. By and large, this order matched the way the learners would be ordered according to their lexical richness scores.

---

[3] A = Age; M = Married; C = Children; S = School
[4] The mean value is calculated on the basis of the Guiraud scores for all six activities.

The correlational patterns were found to remain constant over time (across the three cycles), thus allowing the use of the mean value of Guiraud in Table 8.21. The absence of developmental dynamics in our data may have to do with the fact that the adult learners had already been living in the target country for several months (on average nine months) at the time they entered the project. And at the time of their first project activity analysed in the present study, the learners had been living in the target country for an even longer period of time (on average seventeen months). This, perhaps, also contributes to an explanation for the lack of significant correlations with the two *Stay* measures. And overall differences in developmental rate between the learners may well have levelled out by the time the learners contributed their first data-point to the present study.

8.4 The control group study

Jane Edwards and Willem Levelt[5]

Introduction
We noted in the Field Manual (p. 32) the inescapable fact that participation in the ESF project would provide the longitudinal informants with additional target language experience of a somewhat different type and a somewhat greater amount than that they would have obtained in everyday contact alone. They were involved in a continuing relationship with target language speakers, and knew they were important participants in a large research project. Such factors could be expected to increase their motivation to learn the target language. Furthermore, they received practice in the target language, in the form of performing the task activities in the presence of target language speakers during each of the encounters, circumstances which might have enhanced their awareness of their linguistic productions and particular difficulties than would otherwise have been the case.

It was necessary for this reason to assess whether the 'Longitudinals' differed from individuals who had minimal (or no) contact with the project, in terms of the speed and nature of target language acquisition. In addition to providing an indication of how project results could be generalised to individuals not exposed to such experiences, the present investigation may also shed light on the permeability of particular aspects of the acquisition process to environmental influences, or relevant aspects of the input.

For this purpose, comparable data were also gathered from a second group of individuals who were socio-biographically matched to the Longitudinal informants, but who were observed only three times during the entire project. This second group of individuals, who were called the 'initial learner group' in the Field Manual, provided a control with respect to the amount of intensive contact with ESF project researchers and data gathering tasks. The present chapter reports the results of comparisons made across two different activities, and over time, to assess the strength of effects of contact experience.

Two classes of variables were used: (a) linguistic and (b) non-linguistic, or motivational. The linguistic variables used here include the following:

---

[5]This section is a version of the control group study presented to the project's Steering Committee in Cambridge, October 1986. A much extended final version of the study will be published elsewhere.

- richness and diversity of the target language lexicon, measured as the number of TL word types in lemmatised samples selected to approximate as closely as possible a length of 200 words (described below);
- degree of reliance on source language, measured as number of occurrences of SL words within otherwise exclusively TL utterances;
- degree of automaticity or idiomaticity in use of the target language, measured as (a) the number of target language expressives (TLXK) and (b) number of target language formulas or collocational expressions (TLFK);
- level of syntactic complexity in use of the target language, measured as the number of uses of target language conjunctions, that is, conventional target language means for marking explicitly the relevance of a particular clause to that which preceded it. This measure includes both 'semantic connectives', that is, the marking of relations between successive parts of an utterance, and 'pragmatic connectives', that is, the contextualising of an utterance with respect to the preceding contributions by other speakers (Gallagher and Craig 1987). The expectation is that more advanced learners will tend toward more frequent use of conventional target language means for marking such interconnections explicitly, whereas earlier learner varieties will rely more on the operation of co-operative implicatures and discourse rules such as those discussed for temporality by von Stutterheim (1986) and in Volume II:I.3, and for such relational predicates as 'cause', 'justification', and 'solutionhood', discussed by Mann and Thompson (1986).

In addition to the measures of linguistic repertoire, the study included several 'nonlinguistic' measures:

- silent pausing
- vocalised pausing
- self-editing
- unelaborated 'yes'/'no' responses

which were included as indirect measures of the amount of effort invested in task completion by the two informant groups. The amount of effort invested on a task can differ between informants for either of two reasons: (a) if the task is easier for one of them than the other (that is, repertoire limitations), or (b) if one of them is trying harder to perform well than the other (that is, motivational pressure).

Considering motivation first, the Longitudinals would generally be expected to try harder than the Controls since their level of personal commitment to the project was considerably greater – they had, unlike the Controls, committed themselves in advance to a two and a half-year series of encounters. So far as level of difficulty is concerned, in the absence of a directly 'pedagogical' facilitation from project participation, level of difficulty in performing the tasks should start at the same level for the two groups and decrease commensurately over time.

Joint interpretation of these non-linguistic measures with the linguistic measures noted above, allows a determination of whether the production of the two groups differ. Four outcomes are possible:

(i)   there are no significant differences between the groups;
(ii) there are significant differences for both sets of measures;
(iii) there are significant differences for the linguistic measures only;
(iv) there are significant differences for the motivational measures only.

The preferred pattern of results would be an observed difference between the two groups on the non-linguistic measures, with Longitudinals scoring higher than Controls, but no difference between the groups on (equally reliable) linguistic variables. This would indicate that the groups differed, but only with respect to their motivation to perform on the tasks, and not in terms of their actual linguistic repertoires.

(iii), and hence (ii) are less desirable outcomes, since the presence of a factor 'participation in the ESF project' (whether facilitative, with the Longitudinals scoring higher than the Controls, or detrimental, vice versa!) intervening in the linguistic development of the Longitudinals would make it more difficult to interpret other, shared determining factors. Outcome (i) would cast some doubt on the validity of the measures selected, as it seems unlikely that project participation had no effect whatsoever on the Longitudinals' TL performances.

The data
The Control group consisted of four informants each from the following six SL-TL pairs: Moroccan-French, Spanish-French, Moroccan-Dutch, Turkish-Dutch, Finnish-Swedish, Spanish-Swedish, selected for reasons of similarity to the Longitudinals on several socio-biographical dimensions: sex, age, source country area, source country

schooling, marital status, length of stay in the target country at the time of the first interview, target language proficiency at that time, amount of contact with target language speakers. Details are given in Appendix B.

Data were gathered from Control informants roughly once every cycle, on a sub-set of the activities used with Longitudinal informants. This sub-set included conversation in all cases. In addition, for target languages French and Swedish, the sub-set included a second task: picture description/comparison. Picture description and conversation may be characterised as opposing poles on a continuum ranging from less open-ended, stimulus-oriented interaction to more open-ended, socially-relevant interaction. These differences will be seen to be important for the analyses below.

The study was limited by the amount and comparability of the data available on the deadline for the start of analysis. The Swedish team had supplied conversation and picture descriptions for eight longitudinal/control pairings from the initial study (Time 1) and from the end of the longitudinal study (Time 3); the Dutch team had comparable conversations from Time 1, Time 3 and from a point mid-way through the longitudinal study (Time 2), for eight longitudinal/control pairings; the Aix-en-Provence team had available conversations from Time 1 and Time 3, for two longitudinal/control pairings. Hence, it was impossible to achieve a fully balanced design involving all informants simultaneously. In place of this, several sub-analyses were performed. To minimise possible artifacts due to individual differences, the informants included in a particular comparison are only those from whom data were available for both of the conditions being compared (Times and Tasks; see below).

This methodological (design) necessity of strictly repeated measures plus the need to include as many data points as possible (for increased power in the statistical tests) from as many different TL-SL pairs as possible (for greater external validity of results) dictated the selection of the following comparisons:

- Both tasks at two points in time: eight pairs from Göteborg; total of sixty-four observations;
- Conversation at two points in time: eight pairs each from Tilburg and Göteborg, two pairs from Aix; total of thirty-six observations;
- Conversation at three points in time: eight pairs from Tilburg; total of forty-eight observations.

Data preparation
In order to maximise comparability of data across tasks, groups, time periods, and SL-TL pairs, a specialised computer programme was used for selecting a sub-set of 200 words from the available data for each task for each informant. The programme scanned the text for learner utterances, and for each utterance, gave half a page of context above and below, while querying the user as to whether that utterance should or should not be included in the sample to be analysed. Excluded from the sample were:

- opening or closing greeting sequences;
- segments of the text which were concerned with task instructions;
- utterances spoken totally in the source language;
- utterances which were totally unintelligible or uninterpretable;
- uninterpretable portions within otherwise fully interpretable utterances.

Everything else was included in the sample. In the event that the number of informant words meeting these conditions fell short of the criterion of 200 words, segments of informant utterances from equivalent other encounters were included in the sample until either the criterion was reached or the supply of appropriate data was exhausted.

A concordance listing (exhaustive listing of items in a file, with one-sentence context for each), and a type-token frequency listing (exhaustive listing of different items in a file and their frequencies of occurrence) were generated separately for each sample file. A modified lemmatisation programme (see 8.2) used the type-token frequency listing as input, and, for each word type, prompted the user for responses concerning:

- language identification of the word type (TL, SL, mixed, or other);
- syntactic category of the word type (noun, conjunction, etc.);
- verification of the frequency (in case of polysemy).

In addition to word types, the programme presented frequences for silent pauses, vocalised pauses, repeated words or sentence fragments, and unelaborated 'yes'/'no' responses to be verified and categorised during the course of lemmatisation.

Results
As noted above, it was not possible to achieve the criterion of 200 language tokens per sample for all the comparison conditions (that is,

conversation and picture description at one to three points in time). Since total sample length in some sense places an upper limit on the possible values of the other measures, it was incorporated into the design as an additional measure, computed as the total number of target and source language tokens, excluding expressives and formulaic utterances.

Given that the potential for silent pauses, vocalised pauses, self-corrections, and unelaborated 'yes'/'no' responses depends in a roughly linear way on the length of the encounter, the raw scores for these variables were adjusted simply by multiplying the raw values by a constant equal to the ratio of 200 to the total lemmatised tokens in a given language sample (excluding expressives and formulaic utterances).

The function relating total sample length to total number of word types is not a linear function and is furthermore known to vary as a function of other variables, such as register, content, and conversational style. For this reason, no clearly sound adjustment of score could be made for the number of target language types, or the number of target language conjunctions, so they were used in their raw forms in the analyses.

Whether total sample length should be grouped with the linguistic or with the motivational variables, is not decidable on the basis of theoretical considerations alone. In fact, this variable tended to correlate more strongly with the study's linguistic variables (.76 with total target language types, .55 with total target language conjunction tokens) than with the motivation or effort variables ($-.51$ with adjusted vocalised pauses, $-.29$ with adjusted silent pauses, $-.25$ with adjusted self-repetitions, $-.48$ with adjusted unelaborated 'yes'/'no' responses). This is all the more surprising given that total sample length was part of the ratio used in adjusting the raw non-linguistic values, and could therefore have been expected to be actually more closely related (via redundant variance) to the non-linguistic variables. It indeed seems (see 8.2) that increase in text length ties in with progress in acquisition. The correlation between total sample length and total number of source language tokens was only $-.11$, but this is probably due to the small number of these in the samples, and therefore a highly restricted variance.

The most critical analytic task of these analyses was to determine whether the Control informants could be differentiated from Longitudinal informants on the basis of any multivariate function of any combination of linguistic and motivation variables. For this purpose, the most appropriate type of statistical analysis is discriminant analysis. Three separate discriminant analyses were performed, one for each of the three comparisons noted in the preceding section.

Discriminant analysis proceeds in three steps:

(a) testing 'whether or not groups of previously classified cases differ significantly on one or more linear combinations' of the available variables (McLaughlin 1980: 176);
(b) determining which of the variables are the best discriminating variables; and
(c) as a sort of double check, using in turn the sub-set suggested by (b) to classify individuals into groups, in order to determine the percentage of cases classified correctly.

While the main discrimination to be made in this study was that between Controls and Longitudinals, two additional discriminations were: (a) between successive time points during the acquisition process and (b) between the two task activities. Given the carry-over of task performance strategies, response biases, and other factors, it is usually easier to discriminate between scores from different individuals under equivalent circumstances than between scores from the same individual under different circumstances. For this reason, the finding of discriminable differences due to time or task (that is, intra-individual differences) in the absence of discriminable differences due to group membership (that is, inter-individual differences) would constitute especially strong evidence against the presence of large differences between Controls and Longitudinals along the constructs being measured. Prior to interpreting the absence of a significant discriminant, however, two additional conditions must be met: (a) the groups for which discrimination failed must be known to have comparable variances on the measures (as may be determined with Box's M test), and (b) the measures employed must be precise enough that the researcher can be confident that the null result is not due simply to error variation.

One final constraint on the analysis concerns the total number of variables used in the discrimination. There is a limit to the allowable number of variables, and this limit is determined by the number of observations. Where the groups are known to be very different, a ratio of ten observations per variable is recommended; otherwise, a ratio of twenty to one (McLaughlin 1980: 188). The danger in entering too many variables is that the discriminant functions become overly affected by chance variation and the classifications are then noticeably less accurate. For the present analysis, in order to give the 'null hypothesis' (of no difference between Control and Longitudinals) the fairest chance of being rejected, it was decided to include only the most precise measures of each of the dimensions of interest – the linguistic and the motivational – and as few measures of each as possible.

To determine the most reliable sub-set of measures of each dimension, the two groups of measures, linguistic and motivational, were subjected separately to reliability analyses, using first the full data set (Dutch, Swedish, and the French from Aix) and then, in separate analyses, the Dutch and Swedish data. From these analyses, it became apparent that the following measures were much less reliable than the others, and they were therefore excluded from further analyses: expressives, formulas, and source language tokens, self-repetitions, and self-standing 'yes'/'no' responses. Their unreliability is partly due to the relatively low number of occurrences of each of these types of phenomena in the lemmatised samples.

In contrast to these, the following measures were found to be highly reliable, and were included in the discriminant analyses: total number of target language types, total number of target language conjunctions, and total sample length, as the linguistic measures (with Cronbach standardised item alpha coefficients of between .71 and .88 for the three data sets); the adjusted silent pauses and adjusted vocalised pauses as the effort or motivational variables (with Cronbach standardised item alphas of between .77 and .83 for the three data sets). It is important to note that the reliabilities of these measures were equally high for all three data sets and for both measured dimensions, since this suggests that the discriminant analyses based on them had roughly the same potential for precision.

The individual discriminant analyses will be summarised separately for each of the three comparison modes. The first analysis below is presented in greater detail than the others. All other analyses proceeded in the same way.

Both tasks at two points in time: The Swedish data alone were used for this first analysis. These data consisted of four observations each from sixteen informants (eight Controls, eight Longitudinals), for a total of sixty-four observations. These data enabled a test in microcosm (that is, with a small data set) of all three of the types of discriminations to be made here (that is, time, task, and group), and, indirectly, the relative independence of these variables.

(1) TIME. The following sub-set of measures was entered 'directly' (that is, simultaneously): group, task, sample length, TL types, TL

conjunction tokens, adjusted silent pauses, and adjusted vocalised pauses. The resultant discriminant function was statistically significant, so these same variables were next entered on a step-wise basis. Only three of the entered variables were used in the resulting function: TL types, conjunctions, and adjusted silent pauses, of which the third variable loaded negatively on the factor. This three-variable function was found to have an accuracy rate of 81 per cent in classifying the observations into time groups. This analysis shows a statistically significant difference between scores during the first and third cycles of data collection, with the best discriminators being the main linguistic variables, followed by one of the motivation or effort measures (adjusted silent pauses). The polarity of the factor loadings (and the group means) indicate an increase over time in the number of TL word types and occurrences of conjunctions, and a decrease in the amount of silent pauses.

(2) TASK. The variables entered in this analysis were the same as in (1) except that 'task' was substituted for 'time'. With direct entry, the function was found to be statistically significant, so step-wise entry was used in order to determine the relative importance of the various measures in making the discrimination. Five of the seven variables (that is, all except 'time' and 'group') were entered into the function. The variables were ordered as follows: TL types, TL conjunctions tokens, sample size, adjusted silent pauses, and adjusted vocalised pauses. An examination of factor loadings and sample means indicates that there were more TL types and more vocalised pauses, but fewer silent pauses and conjunctions for conversation than for the picture description task. Of these variables, TL types was clearly the best discriminator. The accuracy rate in classification based on this five-variable function was 78 per cent. These findings suggest that the two tasks differ with respect to both the nature of the linguistic demands (with picture description being associated with a wider range of TL types and more conjunctions than conversation) and the overall level of effort required to perform the task (with picture description being associated with more silent pauses and vocalised pauses than conversation).

(3) GROUP. The variables entered were the same as in (1) except that 'group' was substituted for 'time'. With direct entry, the function discriminating Controls from Longitudinals was found to be statistically significant. From the step-wise analysis the most important variables discriminating the groups were found to be: adjusted silent

pauses, adjusted vocalised pauses, and total sample length, and then, followed after a noticeable drop in the size of the factor loadings, the linguistic variable: TL types. The accuracy of the classification function composed of loadings on these five factors was 73 per cent. This result indicates that the two groups are best discriminated on the basis of the effort or motivational variables, and only to a much lesser degree on the basis of linguistic variables. This finding suggests a motivational rather than repertoire difference between the two groups.

Conversation at two points in time: The data for this analysis came from three of the teams: eight pairs each from Tilburg and Göteborg, two pairs from Aix, for a total of thirty-six observations.

(4) TIME. The same variables were entered as in (1), except for the elimination of the 'task' variable, since only one task is represented in these data. The discriminant function resulting from direct entry, was statistically significant. With step-wise entry, the variables found to contribute most to the discriminant function were, in order: TL types, TL conjunction tokens, and adjusted silent pauses. This function had a classification accuracy of 77 per cent. These results are conceptually identical to those of the Time analysis reported in (1), even though the data base used here only partially overlaps with the other data base, including fewer informants and only one task. Both this and the preceding time analysis indicate a strong developmental influence on both linguistic variables, combined with an influence on one of the effort variables, in a direction suggesting less effort at the later point in time. These results also provide good evidence for the validity of the so-called 'linguistic' variables as measures of repertoire characteristics.

(5) GROUP. The same variables were entered as in (4), except for substituting 'time' for 'group'. The discriminant function resulting from direct entry of the variables was statistically non-significant. The fact that Box's M test for non-equivalence of variance was also non-significant, is evidence that the failure of the discriminant function to reach significance was not due to low power in the test. Though it is not technically necessary to examine the results of a step-wise procedure when the direct procedure yields non-significant functions, when this was examined in the present case, it was found that the discriminant function generated by the step-wise procedure consisted of only two variables: adjusted silent pauses, and sample length, that

is, one effort measure and the ambivalent measure of sample length. Together these two variables had a classification success rate of only 62 per cent, which is the lowest rate of any of the other analyses for the data set, and not so far from a chance rate of 50 per cent accuracy. From these results it seems reasonable to return to the null result of the 'direct' method, and to conclude that there was in fact no evidence of a discriminant function capable of separating the two groups in this analysis, and that this lack of significance is not due to low power but rather to high similarity of the two groups.

Conversation at three points in time: The data for this analysis came from the eight pairs from Tilburg, for a total of forty-eight observations.

(6) TIME. The same variables were used as were entered in (4). The discriminant function resulting from direct entry of the variables was statistically significant. The discriminant function resulting from step-wise entry contained only two variables: TL types, and sample length, which together had a classification accuracy rate of 58 per cent. While these results differ somewhat from those of the other two Time analyses, this difference may be partly attributable to the much reduced number of observations in this data set (that is, forty-eight in comparison with sixty-four). One is reminded of McLaughlin's warning to include at most only one variable for each ten observations. While these results may be based to a larger degree on the effects of random variation, it is nevertheless interesting to note that even under these conditions (that is, of lower power due to fewer total observations), the highest loading discriminant variable here, as in the two prior analyses, was the number of TL types.

(7) GROUP. The same variables were used as were entered in (5). The discriminant function resulting from direct entry of the variables was non-significant, but the presence of a significant result for Box's M test of non-equivalence of variance across the groups, raises doubts concerning the potential power of the test in this particular case. For this reason, the step-wise method was used next. The resulting function, which was significant, contained only three variables, in this order: adjusted silent pauses, adjusted vocalised pauses, and time. The classification accuracy rate of this function was 68 per cent, which is quite good considering the very small number of observations. This result replicates the finding from the Group analysis in (3), that effort or motivational variables serve as the best em-

pirical basis for discriminating between Controls and Longitudinals. The large contribution also of Time in the discriminant function suggested a statistical interaction between Time and the Group variable, as might arise, for example, if the groups differed substantially with respect to the rate at which their value on the effort variables declined over time. In fact, an examination of the means suggested a definite trend of this type in the data. For both measures (that is, silent pauses and vocalised pauses) and for both groups there is a large decrease in values from Time 1 to Time 2, having roughly the same slope and partly overlapping. But the actual values at Time 2 are higher for Longitudinals on both measures than they are for the Controls, and this is true also at Time 3. It would be possible to interpret this interaction as revealing both the effort aspects (Time 1 to Time 2) and the motivation aspects (Time 2 to Time 3) of these measures. That is, from Time 1 to Time 2 the curves for the two groups overlap because they are experiencing similar levels of difficulty with the task. From Time 2 to Time 3, the task is no longer so difficult, but the Longitudinals, being more highly motivated, are trying harder.

Conclusions
Concerning the discrimination of major importance to the generalisability of results from other parts of the ESF project, that is, the discriminations between Control and Longitudinal informants, the three relevant analyses were encouraging. Where the discriminant functions were statistically significant, the variables included in them were effort or motivation variables rather than the 'pure' linguistic measures, TL types or TL conjunction tokens. This suggests that the differences between the groups, are more due to effort or familiarity than to actual differences in repertoire.

Concerning the discriminations based on Time, these analyses provide evidence of a systematic effect on the linguistic variables, together with a milder effect on the effort or motivation variables. This finding serves the joint purpose of (a) showing TL types and TL conjunction tokens to be valid measures of learner repertoire, and (b) actually providing statistical evidence of an acquisition effect.

Concerning the discriminations based on Task, these analyses provide evidence that the demands of the tasks were in fact quite different, which is also important methodologically, in that it ensures that the Control versus Longitudinal comparisons were not non-significant due to a restriction in variance due to stimulus condition.

There always remain two questions in work such as this: (a) were those aspects of learner repertoire included here really the most important ones with reference to questions of generalisability, and (b) were those aspects which were included here measured to an adequately sensitive degree? As was noted above, the findings from the Time discriminations provide some evidence that the measures used were valid measure of some aspects of repertoire, but there are obviously others which could be measured in addition. As regards the question of measurement sensitivity, the number of TL types is certainly a very global measure; the actual degree of overlap of individual types in the repertoires, at least for those categories seen as least sensitive to conversation topic and most enlightening concerning syntactic complexity (that is, conjunctions and adverbs), could also be assessed in future work of this kind.

In conclusion, the relevance of the present results for the generalisability of the ESF findings as a whole can be tersely summarised as follows: the effect of participation in the project and intensive interaction with project researchers is small, and where it does exist, it is of a clearly effort-related or motivational nature and does not show any substantial influence on the structure of the acquisition process.

Appendix A:
Steering Committee and researchers

A. The following scholars served as members of the project's Steering Committee:

> Professor A. Aksu, Turkey
> Professor D. Coste, France
> Professor N. Dittmar, Germany
> Professor W. Levelt, the Netherlands
> Professor B. Norberg, Sweden
> Professor R. Lo Schiavo, Italy
> Professor D. Slobin, U.S.A.

The Steering Committee was chaired by Sir John Lyons, Great Britain, from 1981 until 1985; he was succeeded by Professor Georges Lüdi, Switzerland.

Monique Flasaquier, Jostein Mykletun and John Smith served successively as Secretaries of the Steering Committee.

B. Six research teams were engaged in the project (including two in France). They were:

> 1. Ealing College of Higher Education
>   School of Languages
>   Grove House,
>   The Grove, Ealing,
>   London W5, Great Britain
>
>   Team leaders: Celia Roberts and Margaret Simonot
>
>   Researchers: Mangat Bhardwaj, Netta Biggs, Eliza
>   Sponza

2. Universiteit Brabant
   Subfaculteit Letteren
   Hogeschoollaan 225
   5000 LE Tilburg, The Netherlands

   Team leader: Guus Extra

   Researchers: Peter Broeder, Josée Coenen, Korrie van
   Helvert, Roeland van Hout, Rachid Zerrouk

3. Universität Heidelberg
   Institut für Deutsch als Fremdsprachenphilologie
   Plöck 55
   6900 Heidelberg, FRG

   Team leader: Rainer Dietrich

   Researchers: Angelika Becker, Katharina Bremer, Mary
   Carroll, Ann Kelly, Maren Kogelheide
   Enrica Pedotti

4. Göteborgs Universitet
   Institutionen för Lingvistik
   Renströmsparken
   41298 Götenborg, Sweden

   Team leader: Jens Allwood

   Researchers: Yanhia Abelar, Elisabeth Ahlsén, Paula
   Andersson, Beatriz Dorrioz, Sören
   Sjöström, Sven Strömqvist, Kaarlo
   Voionmaa

5. Groupement de Recherches sur l'Acquisition des Langues (GdR
   0113, CNRS)
   Université Paris VIII
   2, rue de la Liberté
   93526 Saint Denis Cédex 02, France

Team leader: Colette Noyau (Paris X)

Researchers: Maria-Angela Cammarota, Jorge Giacobbe
(Lyon II), Christine de Hérédia (Paris V),
Françoise Hickel, Michèle Mittner, Rémy
Porquier (Paris X), Anne Trévise (Paris X),
Marie-Thérèse Vasseur (Paris V)

6. Groupement de Recherches sur l'Acquisition des Langues (GdR
0113, CNRS)
Université de Provence
29, avenue Robert Schumann
13100 Aix-en-Provence, France

Team leader: Daniel Véronique

Researchers: Christine Coupier, José Deulofeu, Alain
Giacomi, Et-Tayeb Houdaïfa, Robert Vion

C. Central co-ordination:

Max-Planck-Institut für Psycholinguistik, PB 310, NL-6500 AH Nijmegen.

Jane Edwards, Helmut Feldweg, Heather Holmback, Wolfgang Klein,
Clive Perdue.

Appendix B:
The learners

In this appendix, we give a short biography of the learners introduced in chapter 3, followed by the characteristics of each pairing of longitudinal/control informants analysed in the control group study (chapter 8.4).

1. Abdelmalek

Socio-biographical information
Abdelmalek arrived in France from a town in Morocco in the autumn of 1981, at the age of twenty. In Morocco he had had only elementary education and had not been employed. He had picked up a little Spanish before arrival.

In France he became a fisherman but suffered a very bad accident in 1984 after which he attempted to get the compensation owed to him. As a single man, he lived in rented accommodation for workers.

General progress in the target language
At the start of data collection, Abdelmalek produced only one-word utterances. He was an active participant in the data collection and used sessions to extend his skills as a communicator. By the end of the project, his vocabulary was quite well developed, noun and verb forms had emerged and overall he had become a competent communicator.

2. Alfonso

Socio-biographical information
Alfonso was recorded from ten months after his arrival, while he was attending a full time French course for refugees. He was a very social and talkative person. However, the course was seemingly too difficult for him,

and he did not get much benefit out of it for his TL acquisition. In France, he worked in industry and hotel cleaning. He already had relatives in Paris when he arrived, and lived with his family, rather than in a refugee centre like the other Paris-based informants. Most of his acquaintances were Colombian, but he enjoyed getting acquainted with people at work and in a cycling club. He liked listening to the news on TV, and reading French newspapers.

General progress in the target language
Alfonso already had a fairly rich although idiosyncratic communicative potential at the time of the first recording, and continued developing.

3. Andrea

Socio-biographical information
Andrea is an Italian in his mid-thirties. He finished the *scuola media* (receiving some tuition in French), then obtained a professional qualification as a technician. He came to England for personal reasons, having separated from his wife, leaving her and their son behind in Italy.

He was employed in Central London successively as a waiter and barman, working long hours on shift with mainly Italian colleagues. With the exception of one English person, his friends are also Italian. He eventually found a better job in a bakery.

When first interviewed he had been sporadically attending language classes three times a week, but pressures of work (split shift at that time) soon put an end to this and he attended no more classes in English. His wife and son joined him in London towards the end of the data-collection period.

His few contacts with TLS were mainly with institutions: companies where he applied for jobs, the administration that goes with being a car owner, estate agents and travel agents. After the arrival of his wife and son he had contact with schools, doctors, dentists etc.

General progress in the target language
Andrea was still a beginner in English when he started the project, despite taking some part-time classes. Throughout the period of the project, he remained a reserved and cautious learner but he made considerable progress over the three cycles.

He used the conversations with researchers as a pedagogic opportunity, particularly to develop his lexicon. However, in both internal and external encounters he remains quite non-assertive. The overall impression, by cycle 3, is of a learner with adequate syntax and quite a good lexicon, but far from native-speaker competence.

4. Angelina

Socio-biographical information
Angelina was in her early twenties when she married and moved to Germany in 1981. She comes from a town near Naples, where she attended primary school and three years of secondary school. Before her marriage, she helped out in her father's ironmonger's shop. She had virtually no German at the start of the project and very few opportunities to acquire it during the data collection period. She worked at home as a housewife, looking after two small children. Her Italian husband spoke better German than she did and he did the shopping and dealt with all official contacts. Their leisure time was spent exclusively with Italians – relatives and friends.

Apart from watching German TV, helped by her husband, and rare chats with the woman next door, project sessions were Angelina's main opportunity to use the TL. Project sessions were very important to her as a possibility of getting out of the house and, in a small way, having some kind of independent area of her life.

General progress in the target language
It was difficult to assess Angelina's general motivation. She was dissatisfied with her progress, but never tried very seriously to attend a language course. She always did her very best in the data collection sessions. She enjoyed her successes and was very disappointed or embarrassed when she felt she had 'failed'.

She preferred conversations and role plays to more experimental tasks. Given her extremely restricted means she was successful in understanding and making herself understood, but needed a friendly relationship with her interlocutors. Once she told us that she felt she was making 'brutta figura' when having to communicate in German. In other words, she was acutely aware of the impression she gave when trying to speak German and was aware of a loss of face.

At the outset of the data collection, Angelina knew about 'five words' of German. In the middle of the project it was possible to have a small conversation on simple, everyday subjects, but even in the last session some interpreting by the SL researcher was still necessary.

5. Ayshe

The informant

Ayshe was born in 1966 in Bafra (Trabzon). She attended primary and secondary school for five and a half years. She went to Germany to join her father and her two brothers. From autumn 1982 to summer 1983, she attended an MBSE course (*Maßnahmen zur beruflichen und sozialen Eingliederung*: the vocational training that Çevdet and Ilhami also followed). She then worked in a laundry. It was during the MBSE course that she was contacted by the project.

General progress in the target language

Ayshe was a very talkative and eloquent person and – according to her MBSE teacher – an attentive and keen pupil. She was very outgoing and, thus, had many social contacts. In short, she had a good deal of the properties of a good language learner. At the time when we first met her, she had already acquired some verb inflection, and had a rich lexical repertoire. She continued to make good progress in German over the whole period of the data collection.

6. Berta

Socio-biographical information

Berta came to France from Chile as a political refugee one month before the project started. She had had six years of primary and two years of secondary education in Chile where she worked as a shopkeeper. She had no knowledge of French on arrival and started a course in French for refugees. She is married to a compatriot and they have three children (then aged seven to fourteen) who started French school on arrival. For the first six months the family lived in a refugee centre and then moved to a flat of their own.

Initially (until April 1984) Berta worked as a kitchen assistant and in June 1984 she started a four-month course in French, followed by an intensive course of 'préformation professionelle'. By the end of 1984 she was watching television quite often and had the opportunity to talk French with her sister-in-law's husband. The children talked French fluently, but Spanish was used in the home. Throughout the data collection Berta was very co-operative and eager to understand and be understood.

General progress in the target language

Berta was lively and friendly. In her contacts with French natives and re-searchers she was very co-operative and willing to learn. Her understanding and speaking competence continually improved.

In the first stages, she relied a lot on her first language, but very quickly, made clear efforts to express herself in a more TL-like way. In conversations she added comments and initiated topics, while in argumentative role plays she was able to take up the native speaker's words and elaborate on them.

7. Çevdet

Socio-biographical information

Çevdet decided, on his own initiative, to emigrate to Germany in 1981, when he was fifteen years old and had had eight and a half years' schooling.

He first lived in a hostel with his father and received a little German tuition from a social worker. Soon after data collection began, he started an MBSE (vocational) course – about ten hours per week German and skills training in metalwork. After the course, he worked in a paint-removing plant, where he learnt more German. The workers had a good relationship with the German supervisors and the Turkish workers would talk to the German gaffers at break times. But the work was hard and the pay low.

Soon after, he got a job with a construction team and in September 1984 he started work with a roof-insulating firm. He also belonged to a mixed Turkish-German sports team, so his linguistic contacts were comparatively intensive. When his elder brother and mother arrived in Germany, his parents, his brother and himself rented a flat together.

General progress in the target language

Çevdet was already well beyond beginner level at the beginning of the project. By cycle 2 an external interviewer stated that he already spoke 'very good' German. He was able to describe his job using specialised vocabulary and would readily talk about events and difficulties in his life.

By cycle 3 he was very fluent. He was still a little shy and occasionally searched for the right word, but had nonetheless achieved near native-speaker competence.

8. Ergün

Socio-biographical information

After five years of primary school, Ergün started work as a motor-mechanic in Turkey. He came to Holland to join his family in October 1981 when he was seventeen. He joined the project eleven months after his arrival. He was still very much a teenager at this stage.

He first lived with his parents. He played in a Turkish football club and regularly went to discos and dances, where he had brief contacts with Dutch girls. He also had occasional contacts with TL speakers at the unemployment agency.

He was in and out of work until the last months of the project, when he got a job in a textile factory. He worked with TL-speakers and with immigrants of other nationalities. He then moved to a city in the North of Holland where he spoke more Dutch than before because there were few Turkish people living in the city. He played in a Dutch football team. He also had a Dutch girlfriend.

General progress in the target language

Over time, Ergün developed the capacity to communicate well, even with limited TL syntax and lexicon. He was willing to indicate understanding difficulties so that they could be surfaced and repaired. In this way, he created more learning opportunities for himself than Mahmut, Fatima or Mohamed, the other learners of Dutch.

From the beginning, Ergün was very aware of his own level of proficiency:

TLS: What do you think about your Dutch?
E: Bad. I cannot construct sentences.
TLS: Did you understand his questions?
E: Yes, but I cannot give adequate answers.

He frequently mentioned that he got irritated if he could not understand:

'As soon as I do not understand something I get irritated and then I cannot talk any more.'

Throughout all three cycles, he maintained that he was not too preoccupied with the grammar of Dutch:

'to be honest, I don't see any difference between 'ik ben' (I am) and 'ik heb' (I have). I do not care about this. It is only confusing.'

However, Ergün's comments on his use of the TL underestimate his own competence and ability to manage talk in Dutch.

9. Fatima

Socio-biographical information
Fatima came to Holland from Morocco, when she was twenty-five, to join her husband. She had left primary school after two years and for some years she was a successful needlewoman in Morocco. She had a little shop and taught other needlewomen.

When she joined the project, ten months after arrival, her TL proficiency was almost zero. She was working in the kitchen of a motel with other Moroccan and Turkish women and she had also started a course in Dutch at the Community Centre. (This was a very basic course and had, primarily, a social function.) Her contacts with TLS were very limited except for a period at the end of cycle 1 when her husband was abroad. Apart from this period, she relied on him in all encounters with officials.

During cycle 2 she had a baby and, therefore, contacts with TL health workers and with other Dutch women with babies. In the third cycle she started work again at the motel. At the end of the cycle she joined a knitting club with nine Dutch women.

General progress in the target language
Fatima's communicative competence remained low throughout the project. In self-confrontations with the SL researcher she explained that she understood very little in all the encounters.

In those sessions at which her husband was present, she remained a very low participator – a role appropriate to an Arabic woman in public. Here she relied for her few contributions on assumptions based on the limited words she knew. When her husband was unable to accompany her she was much more outgoing. Although she learnt little Dutch over the three cycles, she had positive attitudes towards learning Dutch and – when circumstances permitted – she participated in the data collection sessions with enthusiasm. Perhaps her knitting club provided her with the opportunity to make real progress. We will never know.

10. Fernando

Socio-biographical information
Fernando was thirty-four years old when he arrived in Sweden as a political refugee from Argentina in January 1982. There he had had seven years' primary and two years' secondary schooling and had worked as an electrical worker. He participated in two courses for immigrants after arrival

and later attended a technical course. Nonetheless, the work he found in Sweden was less qualified than his job in Latin America. As a mature adult he was used to engaging in discussions about politics and issues that went beyond his immediate vocational sphere.

During the project he made little contact socially with Swedes and was thinking of returning to Latin America.

General progress in the target language

His progress was very even, systematic and goal-oriented but he did not achieve as much as could have been expected given the amount of formal tuition he received.

11. Gina

Socio-biographical information

Gina came to live in Germany in 1982 at the age of eighteen. Her parents had emigrated to Mannheim in 1972. Not being married, Gina had no choice but to join them on finishing her schooling, even though she had found secretarial work in Italy and would have liked to stay there. Her hopes of using her secretarial skills in Germany diminished as time went on.

Data collection began in October 1982, one month after her arrival. At the beginning, Gina was attending a language course provided by the Centro Italiano in Mannheim (two hours per week). On her own account, this mainly gave her the opportunity of meeting other Italians without having to be in the company of her parents.

Contact with Germans was not encouraged at home, and her engagement in 1983 to an Italian living in Italy did little to help her progress in German.

In 1983 Gina found work as a cleaner. Practically all her colleagues were Italians so that the opportunities for learning German were relatively limited. After her engagement, her interests centred on the prospect of setting up a home and future in Italy.

General progress in the target language

Although Gina attended a language course for a while, she showed little active interest in extending her knowledge of the language in exchanges with native speakers. If problems arose either in making herself understood, or understanding the interlocutor, these were generally glossed over. Requests for information on the language were rarely made, Gina was quite content to 'manage' with the means available, and where these were insufficient, either to drop or avoid the message.

12. Ilhami

Socio-biographical information
Ilhami was born in 1965. After seven years' schooling he worked for a glazier for a year then returned to school for a year before emigrating to Germany in 1981.

His first two years in Germany were very similar to Çevdet's. After the MBSE vocational course, he moved out into a private hostel because he did not get on with his father.

He worked as an occasional labourer in a refrigerating firm until 1984 when he was taken on permanently there. His contacts with German speakers at work were limited. He only used German when being instructed by German supervisors or in disputes. The working conditions were bad but he was even more embittered by his experiences of racial discrimination. He considered returning to Turkey during a period of unemployment and although his circumstances became less stressful, he consciously kept at a distance from life in Germany, and the Germans: 'The Germans don't want to talk to us' and 'people don't say Gastarbeiter they say Ausländer (foreigners/aliens)' were typical of his remarks.

General progress in the target language
In the early stages, Ilhami had a better competence than Çevdet. He appeared more self-confident and his responses were more extensive. However, by cycle 2, an external interviewer considered he only had 'fairly good' German, compared with Çevdet's 'very good' German. Ilhami conversed less readily than Çevdet. He remained more aloof and less willing to show politeness. By the final phase of the project, the contrast with Çevdet was very apparent.

There are several factors which may account for Ilhami's much less rapid progress than Çevdet. Differences started to emerge six months after the MBSE course when their personal circumstances began to diverge.

Çevdet had more opportunity to use German at work than Ilhami, whose motivation appeared to have been severely impaired by his long search for work and his experience of discrimination. Çevdet saw some good things about life in Germany and recognised there were also problems in Turkey. By contrast, Ilhami's rejection was generalised. Finally, Çevdet's family situation was much more supportive than Ilhami's.

Their contrastive experiences show the interrelationship between social circumstances and individual/psychological factors. These produced in Çevdet a fairly positive attitude and in Ilhami a degree of distancing which was both expressed and created in interaction.

13. Lavinia

Socio-biographical information

Lavinia came to England from Trieste in her early twenties with her Italian husband and a small child. In Italy she had not worked. In England she first worked as a waitress, but after data collection had started she attended English language courses.

She progressed very quickly from ESL classes to pre-vocational classes and finally to a clerical/English language skills course. In-between courses she had two separate jobs as an unskilled worker in the rag trade.

Her main contacts with the TL outside these courses were through the children (she had a second child at the end of the project), that is health care, child care, schooling. However, despite being a very outgoing person she found it extremely difficult to make friends and felt very isolated.

Although she had welcomed the chance that the move to the UK had given her to play a role outside the home, the difficulty both she and her husband had in finding appropriate employment, plus housing difficulties, forced them to return to Italy.

General progress in the target language

Although Lavinia only had a limited command of English when she arrived, her acquisition of the TL was very fast. She was obviously very motivated to learn and made full use of the language courses she attended. By the end of the data collection she was very fluent indeed.

14. Leo

Socio-biographical information

Leo came to Sweden as a young man immediately after completing vocational schooling in Finland. He learned Swedish for three years in his comprehensive school before coming to Sweden and received a further twenty weeks of formal instruction on arrival. He also learned English for six years.

He worked in a factory where he communicated mainly with other Finns.

General progress in the target language

Leo's Swedish, although quite limited, was better than that of the other learners of Swedish by the end of the project. However, he lacked the confidence of the Spanish informants and their willingness to take risks. He conscientiously undertook the tasks given to him in data collection encounters, but did them without getting very involved. He talked less than the Spanish informants, but he showed his willingness to collaborate in other quiet ways and the level of misunderstandings was lower than with the Spanish informants. This can be largely attributed to the cultural closeness of Finland and Sweden. He is open to making contacts with Swedish people but the fact he had a Swedish girlfriend apparently did not affect the development of his Swedish.

15. Madan

Socio-biographical information

Madan arrived in England in February 1981 at the age of twenty-five, for his arranged marriage to a Punjabi woman of British citizenship who had lived in that country for eighteen years.

Madan was born in India and grew up speaking the Mawlai dialect of Punjabi. He completed six years of primary school in his native village and then worked on the family farm there. He had studied English as a foreign language for one year and Hindi for three.

Before arriving in England, Madan had spent varying lengths of time in Afghanistan, Jordan, and Syria as a labourer but claims to have learned no other language during those periods. At the time of the study, which began twenty months after his arrival in England, he was working as a press operator in a factory where he used both English and Punjabi, although his meal breaks at the job were spent with his Punjabi work mates. He lived in a private house shared with his wife's sister's family. Although his wife speaks English quite well, he reports having very little exposure to English: mostly through work, in the evenings at his brother's shop, and on television. His wife and sister-in-law used English to talk to each other, but Madan was obviously inhibited by this display of proficiency and would only talk Punjabi in their presence.

General progress in the target language

Given that Madan had painfully little free time as a result of work pressures, he was extremely co-operative towards the project and seemed to enjoy data collection sessions.

At the outset of the project, his competence was very limited but he made attempts at interactional harmony, which created an impression of co-operation. With researchers he was quite capable of pursuing his own track to the extent of overriding the other, until the meaning was clarified for him in the TL.

By the end of cycle 3, his confidence in using the TL, specifically with researchers, had improved considerably. For example, he was able to challenge TLS comments but remain a co-operative interactant. His competence in syntax and lexicon was still somewhat limited.

16. Mahmut

Socio-biographical information
Mahmut was born in a small town in Turkey. He attended primary school and after that he worked as a car mechanic. At the age of nineteen he went to the Netherlands, joining his wife, who had been living in the Netherlands for about four years. He joined the project nine months after his arrival. After a year of unemployment, Mahmut found a job in a meat factory on a ten months' contract. This contract was renewed. His contacts with native speakers were restricted to Dutch colleagues; authorities, hospital staff (during the data collection period he had an operation) and people in second-hand car markets. As a former mechanic he war very interested in cars. Mahmut often reflected on his linguistic proficiency. He was fully aware of his shortcomings in Dutch but also knew that owing to his family responsibilities (during the data collection period his daughter was born) he was unable to attend a language course. He mostly spent his spare time with Turkish friends and relatives. Compared to the other Dutch informants, Mahmut ended up quite well in the Dutch community. In 1992 he has a permanent job, promoted to chief of the packing department of a factory. He owned a home of his own, had just bought a new car, etc.

General progress in the target language
Even by cycle 2, Mahmut's linguistic repertoire was quite limited, with few traces of morphology. He used a severely reduced pronominal system. However, he made progress in his ability to understand, as demonstrated by the fact that whereas in the early stages he merely repeated the TLS words, he later used these utterances as a springboard for his own production, signalling clearly what was and was not understood.

17. Marcello

Socio-biographical information
Marcello came to Heidelberg from Italy in 1981 to live with the Italian family of his girl-friend. She was born and grew up in Heidelberg and spoke German like a native speaker.

The language spoken in the family was Italian, but nevertheless the 'standard' of acquisition was set for him, and in later stages he would readily ask for words, grammatical rules etc. The family's attitude towards living in Germany was quite positive and they expected Marcello to learn. Marcello hoped to find employment in his profession as a cutter (instead of his current work as a waiter in an Italian café) if he improved his German.

Marcello would have liked to attend a language course but the working hours in his job did not allow it. (His colleagues there were Italians, but of course he still had much more contact with Germans than other Italian informants.) Project sessions were a good opportunity for him to have something like a language course. He tried to take advantage of all the contacts he had with Germans as he was aware of the importance of 'practice' in language learning.

General progress in the target language
Given the above information, it is not difficult to account for Marcello's strong motivation to make good progress.

In the first session, Marcello's proficiency in German was very limited (he joined the project after nine months in Germany). During the first cycle he made very fast progress, and in cycle 3, he was an advanced learner.

He took an active part in project encounters. Indeed, in some of the first sessions, Marcello gave an impression of being somewhat over-enthusiastic because he used 'too many' repetitions to indicate understanding, but he soon developed a broad repertoire of appropriate feedback.

As with most of the Italian informants learning German, establishing a good relationship with his interlocutor was really important to him and normally he succeeded in creating a relaxed, harmonious climate in interactions.

18. Mari

Socio-biographical information
Mari emigrated to Sweden in 1982, at the age of twenty-two, from a town in Finland. She had had an elementary education which included some

tuition in English, and had worked in textiles. Once in Sweden, she had no social contacts with Swedes despite having had two courses in Swedish. She worked as a cleaner in an adult education centre. She married a Finnish man and moved outside Göteborg where she got a job as a textile worker again.

General progress in the target language
Despite being willing to talk a lot, and despite evidence of metalinguistic awareness, Mari did not make as much progress as one might have expected from the courses she followed. However, by the end of the project she had achieved an adequate command of Swedish.

19. Mohamed

Socio-biographical information
Mohamed was born in Casablanca, Morocco. After primary school he attended secondary school for two years. Afterwards he was trained to be a car mechanic but this did not lead to a diploma. At the age of nineteen he and most of his family left Morocco to join his father, who had been living in the Netherlands for almost fourteen years.

Soon after his arrival, he found a job as a factory worker, which he retained throughout the data collection period – only temporarily interrupted by short period of unemployment. At the time of the first recording Mohamed had been living near Tilburg for eight months. As a young man living in a small town with relatively few immigrants, he soon had lots of contacts with native speakers – from authorities to discotheques and bars. After a year and a half he moved in with his Dutch girlfriend in her parents' house. At the end of the data collection he was living with another Dutch girl. He took no language courses.

General progress in the target language
Presumably as a result of his high level of contact with target language speakers, Mohamed quickly became an accomplished speaker of Dutch. By the second cycle, his linguistic repertoire was elaborate and he had acquired some morphology. His pronominal system was extensively developed to include anaphoric forms and he had command of many prepositions. However, he was a low contributor and during the third cycle of data collection became less and less motivated to participate.

20. Nora

Socio-biographical information
Nora came to Sweden from Uruguay where she had been a qualified worker.
She had no formal second language instruction before coming to Sweden.
She was married with three children, and was forced to take a job as a
cleaner on arrival, which severely limited the benefit of the refugee language
courses. Later she got a job delivering newspapers. Although she was over-
qualified for these jobs, she was a woman with pride who preferred a poor
job to being dependent on social security. However, having such a low-
status job depressed her.

She divorced in January 1984 and after the divorce her Swedish rapidly
improved.

General progress in the target language
Nora's knowledge of Swedish was extremely limited at the beginning of the
project. Like Fernando, with whom she shared many characteristics, she
had no formal TL instruction before arriving in Sweden.

Both Nora and Fernando had experience of political activities and an
interest in the arts. As political refugees, they had already had a wide
experience of life. As a result, they had more confidence and were more
willing to take risks than the younger, more inexperienced Finnish informants.

Although Nora did not have any opportunity at work to speak Swedish
regularly, when she did use Swedish, she talked more than the Finnish
informants.

After her divorce, her learning of Swedish developed rapidly and she
was able to communicate quite well by the end of the project. However, as
with Fernando, there were more misunderstandings than with the Finnish
informants.

21. Paula

Socio-biographical information
Paula was thirty-two and came from Chile, where she attended school until
the age of fifteen, that is she followed elementary school and two years of
secondary school. She then got married at the age of seventeen. She
worked as a dental surgery assistant for three months.

Paula arrived in France in January 1983 as a political refugee, with her
Chilean husband (who had been imprisoned and tortured before being able

to leave Chile), and their two children (a fifteen-year-old girl and a twelve-year-old boy). Both her husband and daughter were seriously affected by their previous experience in Chile. The husband spent some time in hospital and the daughter had frequent problems at school.

Paula too had had problems, and felt very lonely and anxious with her husband in hospital. She had had no contact whatsoever with French people and only very few with Latin Americans. She dared not go out in the streets alone and always came to project encounters accompanied by her son.

In later encounters Paula's anxiety took the form of terrible headaches. She would not go out on guided tours because they put too much stress on her, she said. Her feeling of insecurity was very clearly transmitted through her soliciting, hesitating, SL-linked strategies.

General progress in the target language

Generally speaking and due to extralinguistic factors, Paula was a very insecure learner and acquisition and progress in her case were often blurred by the high number of insecurity markers such as hesitations and solicitations.

In the first stages she used her SL a lot, not only lexical items but whole utterances. She encountered a lot of understanding problems and most of the interviews were composed of strictly linear phases initiated by the TLS who did a lot of scaffolding, but still could not avoid numerous misunderstandings.

Progressively, though, Paula's utterances grew longer, and her understanding progressed, which was clearly demonstrated by the number of her coherent answers.

Until the end she kept hesitating and using her SL but she had gained a little self-confidence and was expressing herself adequately in French.

22. Rauni

Socio-biographical information

Rauni was born in Finland, and grew up in the countryside, in a gipsy family. She did not learn any Romany, except for a few formulae. She attended the elementary school (six years), then a public citizen school (one year) and a Christian folk college (one year). She came to Sweden at the age of twenty-nine, and she started working as a baby sitter for Finnish relatives. She attended a course of Swedish (300 hours) at the beginning, but did not complete it. It seems that she got too much theoretical input in relation to her needs. All her friends in Sweden were Finnish, members of the Pentecostal sect, which was her most important social connection. She experienced cultural conflicts, between her gipsy background, her religious involvement and her affective relationship with a Swede whom she finally married. Her husband talked to her in 'foreigner talk', he also tried to learn words in Finnish when she needed a word in Swedish. He accompanied her when she had to face situations of high TL communicative demand.

General progress in the target language
Rauni had a positive attitude towards the learning of Swedish, and monitored herself while speaking (slow and hesitant delivery, some self-editing). She made some progress in Swedish over the course of the data collection.

23. Ravinder

Socio-biographical information
Ravinder came to the UK at the age of twenty, from a small village in the Punjab where he had received basic schooling. Shortly after arrival he was married to a girl who had grown up and been educated in the UK and who therefore spoke native-speaker English. However, she and Ravinder communicated mainly in Punjabi.

Initially, Ravinder's brother-in-law supported the idea that he should attend language classes, but this motivation very soon dwindled as it became clear that Ravinder could make himself very useful in the family fish and chip business and builder's merchant business with or without knowledge of English.

Thus, Ravinder's main contact with the TL was through customers in both shops. It was further supplemented by social visits to pubs, although several pubs in the area he lived in were run by Punjabi-speaking landlords.

General progress in the target language
He was shy and at times highly embarrassed in data collection sessions by his low competence in English, although he clearly stated at one stage that he wanted to learn English and liked the language.

By the end of the project, his minimal contact with the TL had given him sufficient confidence to enable him to have passed the driving test and to deliver goods for his brother-in-law and he seemed to feel that his knowledge of English was now adequate for his purposes.

24. Santo

The Informant

Santo was in his mid-twenties at the time of data collection. Born in the province of Naples, his first language is the Neapolitan dialect of Italian spoken in his home town. He completed eight years of schooling there.

He came to England in January 1983 for work and personal reasons, expecting to stay indefinitely. His first project interview was conducted seven months later. At that time, he was renting a room in a house shared by people of various nationalities, he was working in an Italian restaurant, and he had an Italian-speaking girlfriend. He reported using Italian at work and with his girlfriend and family. Nonetheless, at the beginning of the study, his speaking and listening skills in English were judged to be 'quite good.' His reading skills in English, by contrast, were judged to be poor and he claimed no ability to write in that language.

General progress in the target language

In cycle I, Santo's repertoire showed many similarities with that of Andrea conducted at more or less the same period. But in strong contrast to Andrea, it scarcely changed over the period of observation. Santo became more proficient at using the same repertoire.

25. Tino

The informant

Tino was born in Southern Italy in 1963. He went to an elementary school for five years and to the *scuola media* for a further three years. He had no professional training and was unemployed until, at the suggestion of a friend, he first came to Germany in 1982, where he worked in a pizzeria. After a few months, he returned to Italy, but came back to Heidelberg in February 1983, where he then worked as a kitchen hand and, at the end of the observation period, as a waiter in an Italian restaurant. He had regular and frequent contacts with Germans, including a German partner, with whom he lived for a while.

General progress in the target language

At the time of the first encounter, his knowledge of German was very elementary, but due to his relatively intensive contacts, he made rapid progress, and by the end of the observation period was speaking fluently.

26. Zahra

Socio-biographical information
Zahra came to Marseilles from Morocco in 1981 to join her husband. She was thirty-two years old. In Morocco, she received no formal education but in France she attended a French course twice a week for a short period. She is married and has four children who settled reasonably well into the education system. In France she worked as a kitchen assistant, then as a cleaning lady, then as a seamstress in the clothing workshop where her husband worked.

General progress in the target language
Zahra started out with only isolated words in the TL. Despite being a low participator, she made slow but steady progress in the TL. By the end of the data collection period she was able to use the TL to build up sentence structure, although on the whole, she still only had limited fluency in French.

27. Matching longitudinal and control group informants

The following table gives the characteristics of the longitudinal group/ control group pairings, and the extent to which they match. The control group study may be found in chapter 8.4. Abbreviations used in the table are given below.

The line following each pair of informants indicates the number of characteristics believed to match (+) or not match (−). The number at the end of the line is the number of matching characteristics. Ages are considered to match if they are within five years of each other. Stays are considered to match if they are within six months of each other. Schooling is considered to match if they are within one year of each other. Status is considered to match if both informants are married regardless of differing numbers of children.

Grp	Name	Sex	Age	Area	School	Status	Stay	Level	Contact	Totals
	Netherlands – Tilburg: Moroccan Informants									
L	Fatima	F	26	U	P2	M	10	L	L	
C	Zeyneb	F	22	U	S4	M	12	L	L	
		+	+	+	–	+	+	+	+	7
L	Mohamed	M	19	U	S2	S	8	L	L	
C	El Mofadal	M	22	R	PX	S	15	L	L	
		+	+	–	–	+	–	+	+	5
L	Hassan K	M	18	U	S3	S	7	L	L	
C	El Yazid	M	20	R	PX	S	14	L	L	
		+	+	–	–	+	–	+	+	5
L	Hassan M	M	25	U	S4	M	14	L	L	
C	Abdeslam	M	20	U	S1	M	2	L	L	
		+	+	+	–	+	–	+	+	6
	Netherlands – Tilburg: Turkish Informants									
L	Mahmut	M	20	R	P5	M	9	L	L	
C	Haydar	M	22	R	P5	M:1	10	L	L	
		+	+	+	+	+	+	+	+	8
L	Osman	M	17	R	P5	S	12	L	L	
C	Hikmet	M	18	R	S4	S	12	L	L	
		+	+	+	–	+	+	+	+	7
L	Ergün	M	18	U	P5	S	11	L	L	
C	Miyese	F	19	R	S3	M	16	L	L	
		–	+	–	–	–	+	+	+	4
L	Abdullah	M	18	U	S3	S	12	L	L	
C	Erdal	M	18	R	S3	S	13	L	L	
		+	+	–	+	+	+	+	+	7
	France – Aix: Moroccan Informants									
L	Abdelmalek	M	20	R	P1	S	13	L	L	
C	Mohamed B	M	32	R	none	M:4	3	L	L	
		+	–	+	+	–	–	+	–	4
L	Abdessamad	M	24	U	P2	M	13	M	M	
C	Mohamed R	M	30	U	P3	M:4	24	M	M	
		+	–	+	+	+	–	+	+	6
L	Zahra K	F	34	U	none	M:4	13	M	L	
C	Zahra L	F	32	U	P5	M	22	L	L	
		+	+	+	–	+	–	–	+	5
L	Malika H	F	20	U	none	M	12	L	M	
C	Rquia	F	28	U	P5	M:2	17	L	M	
		+	–	+	–	+	+	+	+	6

Grp	Name	Sex	Age	Area	School	Status	Stay	Level	Contact	Totals
					Sweden: Finnish Informants					
L	Leo	M	18	R	P:H	S	4	M	M	
C	Volmari	M	24	U	P:M	M	14	M	M	
		+	+	−	−	−	−	+	+	4
L	Mari	F	22	U	P:M	S	10	L	L	
C	Ismo	M	28	U	P:M	S	9	L	L	
		−	−	+	+	+	+	+	+	6
L	Rauni	F	29	R	P:M	M	7	L	H	
C	Raisa	F	30	U	P:L	M	18	L	M	
		+	+	−	−	+	−	+	−	4
L	Neiti	F	22	U	P:M	S	6	M	H	
C	Tarja	F	18	R		P:M	M	3	M	M
		+	+	−	+	−	+	+	−	5
					Sweden: Spanish Informants					
L	Nora	F	39	U	P:M	M:3	10	L	M	
C	Raquel	F	52	U	None	M	8	L	M	
		+	−	+	−	+	+	+	+	6
L	Luisa	F	30	U	P:L	M	18	L	M	
C	Camila	F	31	U	P:L	M	18	L	M	
		+	+	+	+	+	+	+	+	8
L	Leandro	M	31	U	P:L	M	17	L	M	
C	Carlos	M	35	U	P:M	M	11	L	M	
		+	+	+	−	+	+	+	+	7
L	Fernando	M	34	U	P:H	M	15	L	M	
C	Magela	F	30	U	P:M	M	18	L	M	
		−	+	+	−	+	−	+	+	6

*Abbreviations used in the foregoing table:

GRP:	Control (C) or Longitudinal (L)
AREA:	R = rural
	U = urban
	S = suburban
	Region name is given when R/U/S is not certain.
SCHOOL:	Amount of schooling in source country.
	P2 = two years of primary schooling
	S2 = two years of secondary schooling
	PR = professional training
	P:M = moderate amount of primary schooling
	P:L = low amount of primary schooling
	P:H = high amount of primary schooling
	None = no schooling of any type
STATUS:	S = single
	M = married
	M:2 = married with two children
STAY:	Length of stay in host country at the time of the first interview (given in number of months)
LEVEL:	Target language proficiency at the time of the first interview
	L = little or no knowledge of target language
	M = enough target language to get along but not highly proficient
	G = good target language knowledge
CONTACT:	Amount of contact with the target language
	L = little or no contact
	M = sporadic contact
	H = frequent contact

Appendix C:
Sample transcripts

This appendix provides a sample transcription for each of the target languages studied in the project. The samples are taken from the film-retelling of *Modern Times* described in chapter 6.3. The plot of the whole *montage* is as follows:

Episode 1:
Subtitle: America 1930 – poverty, hunger, unemployment.

Charlie gets into a demonstration against unemployment, is taken for the leader and put into prison. At dinner one of his fellow-prisoners hides heroin in the salt-cellar, and Charlie helps himself by mistake. With the drug he gains a heroical force: he foils an escape attempt and frees the governor, who, in gratitude, releases him with a letter of recommendation for a job. Charlie is not too enthusiastic about this because he feels he is better off in prison than at liberty.

Parallel with this we see a second story: a young girl (whose father is a widower, unemployed and without the means to feed his three children) steals food for her family. Her father is shot in a demonstration, and the children are sent to an orphanage. The girl manages to escape at the last moment.

Episode 2
Subtitle: Determined to return to prison.

Charlie finds work in a shipyard. Clumsily, he causes the launching of a ship that was not finished. He is immediately fired and all the more determined to return to prison. Meanwhile the girl, alone and hungry, sees a bakery van unloading bread at a bakery. As she steals a loaf of bread, a woman comes round the corner, sees her, tells the baker, who in turn calls the police. In flight, the girl bumps into Charlie, and when the policemen arrives, he admits to the theft in order to return to jail. As the policeman is preparing to take him away, the woman arrives to say that in fact the girl stole the bread. The policeman arrests the girl and releases Charlie. Still determined to return to jail, Charlie goes into a restaurant, eats, and as he is standing at the cash desk, sees a policeman outside the window. He calls the policeman in and tells him that he has no money. Again, Charlie is arrested. While the policeman is calling a police van from a phone next to a kiosk, Charlie orders a cigar and generously gives chocolate to two boys who happen to stop there. Again, he cannot pay. The police van arrives, and Charlie enters to find it crowded with other unfortunates. Eventually the van stops and the girl gets in. There is a struggle and Charlie, the girl and the policeman fall out. The policeman is unconscious; Charlie and the girl escape. As they are walking through a residential area, they see an idyllic, middle-class family scene: a couple come out of the front door, the husband kisses the apron-clad wife, he goes off to work, she re-enters the house. Ten days later, the girl announces to Charlie that she has found a house and takes him to see it. It is a dilapidated shed. Inside, beams fall, tables collapse, and floors give way as the two protagonists try to make it habitable. Eventually they succeed and walk blissfully off into the sunset.

The following samples all describe the girl stealing a loaf of bread. The final sample (6) is the reformatted version of the Swedish raw file (5) immediately preceding it.

1. Arabic–Dutch

```
LADFC29I.1TR      INT: j,z        INF: f              Header information¹
FILENAME: ladfc29i.1tr
EPISODE: 05 Film scene Charlie Chaplin 'Modern Times';
         film retelling
SUBJECTS:      F= FC= Fatima
INTERVIEWERS: J= JC= Josee
               Z= RZ= Rachid
DATE:          20-APR-1984
REGISTRATION: audio + video
#                                                            #²
                                                             @³
f @die uh meisje honger@
#
j ja
#
f @uh + <*comme si comme ca*>                            <>⁴, *⁵
- <=f, i=expression which means to steal something;      =f⁶, i=⁷
- expression which is used in tilburg area>
f die brood/[stuk brood]@                                /⁸, []⁹
j [<> <*comme si comme ca*>]                             <>¹⁰
- <laughs> <=f, expression>
f @[ja ?of niet]?@                                        ?¹¹
j [<>]
- <laughs>
j ja dat zeg je niet in ut nederlands maar stelen
#
f @<stelen>@
- <imitates; echoes>
#
j ja
#
f @<stelen>@
```

---

¹Transcripts start with a header providing global information about the episode transcribed. The first line serves for computer programmes getting ready access to the codes used for the informants and interviewers in the transcript. The following lines are given in the format: KEYWORD: text, where KEYWORD is taken from a set of labels and text is any free-text entry for the label. Whenever practicable, the text is in a standardised format, such as for dates, participants etc.

More detailed information of this type is provided in a protocol file which is available for every encounter.

²Lines with *sharp signs* in the first column function as speaker's turn markers.

³Sense-units (or T-units) may be enclosed in pairs of @–characters.

⁴Angle brackets are used to mark scope for various phenomena. The nature of the phenomena are explained in the comment line(s) following.

⁵Non-TL words and sequences in non–TL languages (excluding loan words) are enclosed in asterisks.

⁶Non-TL language material is marked by an equal sign followed by a one letter code indicating the non-TL spoken. Here, f stands for French.

⁷The symbol i= indicates innovative non-L2/non-L1 use in the corresponding string in the speech part.

⁸Self-interruption is indicated by a slash. Speaker shift with interruption is marked by a backslash.

⁹Overlapping utterances are signalled by enclosing the simultaneous parts of the speakers utterances in brackets.

¹⁰A pair of empty angle brackets is used to allow references in the comment line to material that does not have a representation in the speech line.

¹¹Sequences interpreted as questions by the transcriber are enclosed in a pair of question-marks.

```
-   <imitates; echoes>
#
j   ja <>
-   <tries to write it down>
#
j   doen we straks wel
#
f   Qstelen die stuk broodQ
#
j   ja
#
f   Qdie ander vrouw kijkQ
#
j   ja
#
f   Qpraat met uh bakkermanQ
#
j   heel goed ja bakker ja
#
f   QbakkerQ Qdie + (daar) die meisje ++Q              +12, ()13
#
j   laat maar ?wat doet ze?
#
f   Qdie +/die man pakt [+]                            [+]14
j   [ja]
f   die meisjeQ
#
j   ja
#
f   Qpolitie komtQ
#
f   Qdie vrouw zeg met uh bakkermanQ [+]
j   [ja]
f   Qdie bakkerman loop [+]
j   [ja]
f   met die meisjeQ
#
j   ja achterna ja
#
f   QjaQ
#
j   ?en dan?
#
f   Q+Q Qpakt die meisjeQ
#
j   ja ja dat meisje en charlie
#
f   Quh jaQ
#
j   +
#
f   Q<bos>
-   <nonsense word, meaning botsen>
f   + [+]
j   [ik zeg niks]
f   <(teen)>Q
-   <nonsense word>
#
j   <>
-   <laughs>
#
f   Q<bos>Q
-   <nonsense word>
#
j   <botsen>
```

---

[12]Unfilled pauses are indicated in the text by plusses. One + corresponds to one speaker subjective time unit.

[13]Inaudible stretches of speech are indicated between parentheses. Attempted reconstructions of what has been said may be given between parentheses.

[14][+] with the simultaneous [ja] is to be interpreted as a hesitation pause.

```
- <completes>
#
f @<botsen>@
- <echoes; imitates>
#
j ja
#
f @<botsen> met uh <charlo>@
- <imitates> <=f=m=eigennaam carlie chaplin>              =f=m¹⁵
#
j ja ?en dan?
#
f @die + <charlo> zeg <ik doen>@
- <=f=m=cc> <ds>                                          cc¹⁶, ds¹⁷
#
j ja ja ?en dan? dan komt de politie
#
f @++@ @pakt die meisje@ @die <charlo> zeg <ik doen>@
- <=f=m=cc> <ds>
#
j ja
#
f @maar die vrouw zeg <niet>@
- <ds>
f @<die meisje + zelf doen>@
- <ds>
```

---

[15]Cognates are traced by replication of non-TL indicators.
[16]cc is an abbreviation for *Charlie Chaplin*.
[17]ds is an abbreviation for *direct speech*.

2. Spanish–French

```
LSFPA24I.1TR           INT: C          INF: a
FILENAME         : LSFPA24I.RAW
CASSETTE: LSFPA14       SIDE B (001-275)
INFORMANT: a = paula
INTERVIEWERS: C = cecile poussard
SOURCE LANGUAGE: Spanish
TARGET LANGUAGE: French
DATE:30-06-84
EPISODE: les temps modernes
TRANSCRIBER: clive perdue
TYPING: ina stroscio
REVISED: ina stroscio
#
```

a eh un madame <# :le le vyu le vyu ke vole #> le pain $:^{18}$

- <= la voir Qù voler > Q^{19}
#
a eh madame <# le di a #> monsieur de la boulangerie / :eh +
- <= lui dire au >
a <# :ke #> un <# fiZ fiZ le vole #> le pain Z^{20}
- <= Qù > <= fille lui voler >
#
C hm hm
#
a :eh la / la fille :eh <* como se *> <# di la fil #> :eh
- <=s= comment on > <= dire la fille >
a <* al *> <# sortir #> rapidement :eh :se <* no se *>

- <=s= en > <= sortir > <=s= je ne sais pas > $=s=^{21}$
a <# :se + tromp #> <* con *> monsieur <* con *> chaplin
- <= se heurter =s= tropezar > <=s= avec > <=s= avec >
a chaplin   <* con *> [monsieur]
- <=s= avec >
#
C [? (elle sort) ?]
#
a <* como se *> <# di #> :eh + :la fille <# :se #> +
- <=s= comment on > <= dire > <= se >
a <* como se *> <# di #> :eh ++ :eh + la fille et un monsieur
- <=s= comment on > <= dire >
a <# se #> <* como se *> <# di #> + <* se cruz/ no *> ^{22}
- <= se > <=s= comment on > <= dire > <=s= se croisent non >
#
C ? se croisent ? chaplin et la fille se croisent ?
#
a oui
#
C c est ça ? se rencontrent ?
#
a <# se rekontren #> :eh <# sE tũmb se tũmb #> $E^{23}\ ^{24}$
- <=s= se rencontrer > <= tomber tomber >
#
C ah oui d accord oui hm hm hm hm
#
a :eh le police :eh eh <# ariv #> <* al *> à côté <# de lo du #>
- <= arriver > <=s= à > <=s= des deux, d eux >
#
C hm hm
#
a <* por *> le le pain <# ke le vole #> la la fille
- <=s= pour > <= Qù voler >

---

[18] syllable lengthening
[19] Q is used to mark *Qu*–subordinators.
[20] Z is an ASCII representation of the phonetic symbol 'ʒ', *yogh*.
[21] Indicates translation of non-TL expression, s is *Spanish*.
[22] Rising intonation on following syllable
[23] E is an ASCII representation of of the phonetic symbol 'ə', *schwa*.
[24] Diacritic tilde is used for nasalisation.

```
#
C oui
#
a <* y *> <# arest arest #> :à chaplin à monsieur
- <=s= et > <= arrêter >
```
                              ...

```
#
a eh madame <# di ke #> monsieur <# il ne vol/ vole #> le pain
- <= dire Qù > <= il ne pas voler >
#
C hm hm
#
a eh <# di ke la fil le vole #> le pain
- <= dire Qù la fille lui voler >
#
C hm hm
#
a eh + <# marS #> :eh monsieur de la boulangerie <* y *>
madame
- <= marcher > <=s= et >
a <* tra/ *> eh <* como se / *> ar/ derrière de mons/ de la police
- <=s= derrière > <=s= comment on >
a <* con *> chaplin + :eh <* y *> <# le di ke #> monsieur <# ne #>
- <=s= avec > <=s= et > <= lui dire Qù > <= ne >
a monsieur <# ne pa de kulp kulpab/ #>
- <= ne pas être coupable >
#
C hm hm
#
a <* es la joven *> <# fil #>
- <=s= c est la jeune > <= fille >
#
C ? la ?
#
a la <# Zõn fil #>
- <= jeune fille >
#
```

S[25]

---

[25]S is an ASCII representation of the phonetic symbol 'ʃ', *esh*.

3. Punjabi–English

```
LPERA24I.1TR        INT: m, b        INF: r
FILENAME         :  LPERA24I.RAW
INTERVIEWERS     :  m = margaret simonot
                    b = mangat bhardwaj
SUBJECT          :  r = ravinder
SOURCE LANGUAGE  :  P
TARGET LANGUAGE  :  E
DATE             :  14-FEB-1984
COMMENTS         :  Broken off film (Modern Times)
EPISODE 1 as in PRT
#
r + its/ another one girl + its name + girl er s <    >
- <laughs>
#
m yeah
#
r its pinch + its er +++ pinch some bread + and van
#
m mhm
#
r and <+++>
- <longish pause>
#
r after <its> coming man + m er +++ girl is push like man is drop it
r then floor
- <it is unclear here and in the following whether r says 'its' or 'is' or
- he's' with this word>
#
m mhm
#
r its bread + its +++ <cant explain proper>
- <laughs>

                                          ...

#
r man is er + coming in + its it erm pinching bread
#
m mhm
#
r and its/ plan is go to back to jail
#
m right
#
r and ++ shop man its coming its lady looking said not pinching it its this
r man
#
m uhuh
#
```

″26

```
r its "she pinching
#
m good
#
r <     >
- <coughs>
r and + police ++ shop man and lady police m tell him er not this man
r pinching its er [girl]
m [(xxx)]
r pinching
#
m uhuh good
#
r <     >
- <coughs>
r and mh ++ charlie <     >
- <coughs>
r its police +++ girl arresting
```

4. Italian–German

```
LIGMO25I.1TR        INT: b        INF: o
FILENAME:           LIGMO25I.RAW
INTERVIEWER:        b
SUBJECT:            o = MARCELLO (MO)
SOURCE LANGUAGE:    I
TARGET LANGUAGE:    G
DATE:               12-DEC-1983
CASSETTE:           11
                    UHER counter 0-226 7 pages
EPISODE:            CHARLIE CHAPLIN SECOND CYCLE FREE RECALL
#
```

o in di ßtat/ in däc ßtat :dii: meetßän   Alphabet[27]
o dii rroibin E äa E/ ;zii at gäzeeä dii E prroot ßtük

prroot   ,28
                                                             ,29
o in,E ;vaagän   ,
#
b mhm
#
o un _zii hoolän ainc ßtük ^brroot und,E E ;väk

und,äc,ist,^;väk   30
o aba ainä _;frrau at E at zoo zo,ainc ßläßtä aktsjoon gczeän ‾
#
b mhm
#
+ 69   counter[31]
#
o un rruufä :dii:/ däc ^ßäf + zou und,E kOmä aux di pOlitsa/
o ain ^pOlitsist
#
b mhm
#
o dii ;meetßän un ;ßä/ und,E ;tßäplin <*si scontrano* E> u tßäplin
o E E <*si scontrano*> E ßäplin,unt _;määtßän E + zoo + :ainä:
o < > ;unfal
- <softly>
- <softly>
- <laughs a little>
#
b ja
#

───

[27]The Heidelberg team used a phonemic transcription system with the following alphabet:
```

| | | | | | | |
|---|---|---|---|---|---|---|
| a | *A*nanas | ä | *S*enf | e | *E*sel | |
| c | Aff*e* | E | filled pause (eh) | i | *I*gnoranz | |
| o | *o*hnehin | u | hallel*u*ja | ai | *E*i | |
| au | *au*a! | oi | Fr*eu*de | oo | d*oo*f | |
| 0 | M*o*nster | ö | bl*ö*d | ü | D*ü*nkel | |
| b | *b*lablabla | p | *P*usteblume | d | *D*epp | |
| t | *T*atze | g | *G*esetz | k | *k*iss | |
| v | oh *w*eh! | f | *f*ootball | z | *S*ignale | |
| x | a*ch* nee! | G | i*ch* | j | *J*esus Maria Josef! | |
| h | *H*ilfe! | t | *t*rallala | m | *M*umie | |
| n | *n*ein | q | Si*ng*er | r | radikal, wi*r* | |
| rr | *r*amazan | s | Ma*ss*enblatt | Z | *G*enie | |
| ß | *Sch*warzenberg | | | | | |

[28]Word stress is marked by a semi-colon in front of the stressed word.

[29]A comma may be used to indicate 'non-normal' liason between two words.

[30]falling intonation of the next syllable is indicated by an underscore in front of the syllable.

[31]References to tape counters are given in lines starting with a *plus*.
```

```
o  vi,ain ^;unfal ^dzuzaamän <  > unt ^rruunta/ ^uunta + dzuzamän,E
o  vii _unfal
-  <laughs>
#
b  ja
#
o  zo [und,E (uunda)]
b  [ja ja ja ich verstehe]
b  <;so>
-  <demonstrates the collision with glasses>
+  89
#
o  ^;ja ^zo kOm,di _pOlitsistän unt,_ßäf aba iZ/ E tßäplin brriqs
o  ;heea dii,E däc brrot
#
b  mhm
#
o  und,E zaakt pOlitsai iß haabä dääc brrootc ^hoolän o ^gähoolän
o  zo di _;pOlitsai/ di pOlitsisdä E + (cbrriq) ;brriq E ßaar/ E
o  tßäplin in ^gäfäqgnis
#
b  + aha
#
o  zo E un/ in ain ^vaagän nee nee + mOmäntc nain _;äcstmaal
#
b  ja
#
o  di bOlidistc brriqä ßaplin füüa/ in,E ;vaagän
#
b  ja
#
o  E ^gäoolän + aba :dii: di _;frrau zaag,di/ däc ßäfc dii
o  _;määtßän istc dii ^rroibin
#
b  aha
+  112
#
o  (neea) dea ^man neec ^ßäplin ;zo und,E ßOn viida däc ßäfc
o  E rruufä di ^pOlitsai füa määtßän E hoolcn
#
b  mhm mhm
#
o  E däc _;pOlitsiistc E <(x) E däc pOlitsiistc> brriqst dii
o  määtßän
-  <softly,searching>
#
b  mhm
#
o  in ^gäfäqnis
```

5. Spanish–Swedish

```
LSSFE29I.1TR        INT: s, b        INF: f
FILENAME: LSSB07A2.
Interviewers: Sören = s,  Beatriz = b
Subject: Fernando = f
Source language: Spanish
Target language: Swedish
Date: 22-MAR-1984
Recording: A 29 18
Transcriber: Beatriz
Checked by: Joakim Nivre
EPISODE: broken-off film experiment Modern times
Comments: f tells s the end of Modern Times by Chaplin
Episode: B 108-
#
s ?va den bra?
#
f (xx) + bra + en flicka eh + stjäla bröd
#
s mm
#
f å kommer en + kvinna + å titta på + å säljare gå + inne
f restaurangen tror ja
#
s mm
#
f eh:: + säljare tittade inte + på:: flicka + men kvinna
f att kommer + titta på flicka
#
s mm
#
f å säjer <a> säljare + henne + ta en bröd +++ å + sen eh::
- <möjl. *a* = till>                                              möjl.³²
f springa + <springa> flicka
- <svårtolkat; möjl. springer>
#
s aa
#
f å ++ (å se/) nej säljare + tror ja + springe(r)
#
s ?springer han efter?
#
f ja efter ++ å sen eh:: ++ *como es* (...) ++
f eh:: eh på andra sida kommer eh + chap'lin                        ,³³
#
s mm
#
f å + träffa:: med flicka
#
s ha ?kä/ känner han henne?
#
f nej
#
s (xxx)
#
f nej eh:: +
#
s < > +
- <harklar sig>
#
f *no se como se dice eh:: chocar* +
#
s ?vadå att? + ?#to'kar#?
#
f eh:: + till exempel eh:: + eh flicka eh springer
#
s mm
#
f å chaplin kom/ komme(r)
```

---

³²möjl. Swedish for possibly.

³³Syllable stress is marked by a single quote in cases where it corresponds to places where the speaker wrongly assigns stress within a word.

```
#
s ?å dom springer mot va[rann]? < >
- <någon slår ihop händerna>
f [ja]
#
s <jaha> + mm
- <lågmält>
#
f sen + kastade dom på + golv
#
s mm
#
f å:: ++ eh säljare + hinner dom + å polisen <trodde> eh:: +
- <svårtolkat; möjl. tror eh>
f chaplin eh::
```

6. Sample output of reformatting programme

Output from the programme REFFORM when run with the file LSSFE29I.1TR as input, see chapter 7.3.

```
= FILENAME: LSSB07A2.
= LSSB07A2
= Interviewers: Sören = s,  Beatriz = b
= Subject: Fernando = f
= Source language: Spanish
= Target language: Swedish
= Date: 22-MAR-1984
= Recording: A 29 18
= Transcriber: Beatriz
= Checked by: Joakim Nivre
= EPISODE: broken-off film experiment Modern times
= Comments: f tells s the end of Modern Times by Chaplin
= Episode: B 108-
=
001 s: 01 ?va den bra?
002 f: 01                          f: (xx) + bra + en
002 f: 02                          f: flicka eh + stjäla
002 f: 03                          f: bröd
003 s: 01 mm
004 f: 01                          f: å kommer en + kvinna
004 f: 02                          f: + å titta på + å
004 f: 03                          f: säljare gå + inne
004 f: 04                          f: restaurangen tror ja
005 s: 01 mm
006 f: 01                          f: eh:: + säljare
006 f: 02                          f: tittade inte + på::
006 f: 03                          f: flicka + men kvinna
006 f: 04                          f: att kommer + titta på
006 f: 05                          f: flicka
007 s: 01 mm
008 f: 01                          f: å säjer <1 a>
008 f: 02                          f: säljare + henne + ta
008 f: 03                          f: en bröd +++ å + sen
008 f: 04                          f: eh::
008 -: --                                      - <1 möjl. *a* = till>
008 f: 05                          f: springa + <2 springa>
008 f: 06                          f: flicka
008 -: --                                      - <2 svårtolkat; möjl.
008 -: --                                      - springer>
009 s: 01 aa
010 f: 01                          f: å ++ (å se/ ) nej
010 f: 02                          f: säljare + tror ja +
010 f: 03                          f: springe(r)
011 s: 01 ?springer han efter?
012 f: 01                          f: ja efter ++ å sen
012 f: 02                          f: eh:: ++ *como es*
012 f: 03                          f: (...) ++ eh:: eh på
012 f: 04                          f: andra sida kommer eh
012 f: 05                          f: + chap'lin
013 s: 01 mm
014 f: 01                          f: å + träffa:: med
014 f: 02                          f: flicka
015 s: 01 ha ?kä/ känner han
015 s: 02 henne?
016 f: 01                          f: nej
017 s: 01 (xxx)
018 f: 01                          f: nej eh:: +
019 s: 01 <1 > +
019 -: --                                      - <1 harklar sig>
020 f: 01                          f: *no se como se dice
020 f: 02                          f: eh:: chocar* +
021 s: 01 ?vadå att? +
021 s: 02 ?#to'kar#?
022 f: 01                          f: eh:: + till exempel
022 f: 02                          f: eh:: + eh flicka eh
022 f: 03                          f: springer
023 s: 01 mm
024 f: 01                          f: å chaplin kom/
```

```
024 f: 02                         f: komme(r)
025 s: 01 ?å dom springer mot
025 s: 02 va[1 rann] ? <1   >
025 -: --                                - <1 någon slår ihop
025 -: --                                - händerna>
025 f: 01                         f: [1 ja]
026 s: 01 <1 jaha> + mm
026 -: --                                - <1 lågmält>
027 f: 01                         f: sen + kastade dom på
027 f: 02                         f: + golv
028 s: 01 mm
029 f: 01                         f: å:: ++ eh säljare +
029 f: 02                         f: hinner dom + å
029 f: 03                         f: polisen <1 trodde>
029 f: 04                         f: eh:: +
029 -: --                                - <1 svårtolkat; möjl.
029 -: --                                - tror eh>
029 f: 05                         f: chaplin eh::
```

References

Allwood, J. 1988. Om det svenska systemet för språklig återkoppling. In Linell (ed.) *Svenskans Beskrivning* 16. University of Linköping.

Andersen, R. 1984. The one-to-one principle of interlanguage construction. *Language Learning*, 34:77-95.

Arnaud, P. 1984. The lexical richness of L2 written productions and the validity of vocabulary tests. In T. Culhane et al. (eds.) *Practice and problems in language testing*, 14-28. Essex: University of Essex.

Belder, S., Hulshof, H., Visser, B. and de Vries, J. 1980. Een probabilistische grammatica voor Nederlandse nominale groepen van enkele Turken. *GLOT*, 3:99-116.

Benveniste, E. 1966. *Problèmes de linguistique générale*. Paris: Gallimard.

Bernini, G. and Giacalone-Ramat, A. (eds.). 1990. *La Temporalità Nell'Acquisitione di Lingue Seconde*. Milano: Franco Angeli.

Bley-Vroman, R. 1983. The comparative fallacy in interlanguage studies: the case of systematicity. *Language Learning*, 33:1-17.

1986. Hypothesis testing in second-language acquisition theory. *Language Learning*, 36:353-76.

Bloom, L. 1981. The importance of language for language development: linguistic determinism in the 80s. In H. Winitz (ed.) *Native language and foreign language acquisition*, 172-189. New York: New York Academy of Sciences.

Brown, R. 1973. *A first language: The early stages*. Cambridge, Mass.: Harvard University Press.

Bühler, K. 1934. *Sprachtheorie: die Darstellungsfunktion der Sprache*. Jena: Fischer. Reprinted in 1965 by Gustav Fischer Verlag, Stuttgart.

Carey, S. 1982. Semantic development: the state of the art. In E. Wanner and L. Gleitman (eds.) *Language acquisition: The state of the art*, 347-398. Cambridge: Cambridge University Press.

Carroll, J. 1964. *Language and thought*. Englewood Cliffs, New Jersey: Prentice Hall.

Cazden, C., Cancino, H., Rosansky, E., and Schumann, J. 1975. *Second language acquisition sequences in children, adolescents, and adults*. Final Report, Dept. of Health, Education and Welfare.

Chomsky, N. 1981. *Lectures on government and binding*. Dordrecht: Foris.

Clahsen, H. 1984. The acquisition of German word order: a test case for cognitive approaches to L2 development. In R. Andersen (ed.) *Second Languages: A Cross-Linguistic Perspective*, 219-242. Rowley, Mass.: Newbury House.

1987. Connecting theories of language processing and (second) language acquisition. In C. Pfaff (ed.) *First and Second Language Acquisition Processes*, 103-116. Rowley, Mass.: Newbury House.

Clahsen, H., Meisel, J., and Pienemann, M. 1983. *Deutsch als Zweitsprache: der Spracherwerb ausländischer Arbeiter*. Tübingen: Gunter Narr.

Clyne, M. 1984. *Language and Society in the German-speaking Countries*. Cambridge: Cambridge University Press.

Coppetiers, R. 1987. Competence differences between native and near-native speakers. *Language*, 63:544-73.

Corder, S. P. 1967. The significance of learners' errors. *International Review of Applied Linguistics*, 5:161-170.

1971. Idiosyncratic dialects and error analysis. *International Review of Applied Linguistics*, 9:147-160.

1973. The elicitation of interlanguage. In *Errata: Papers in Error Analysis*, 36-47. Lund: C.W.K.Gleerup.

Dittmar, N. 1981. On the verbal organization of L2 tense marking in an elicited translation task by Spanish immigrants in Germany. *Studies in Second Language Acquisition*, 3:136-164.

1984. Semantic features of pidginized learners of German. In R. Andersen (ed.) *Second languages: A cross-linguistic perspective*, 243-270. Rowley, Mass.: Newbury House.

1991. Berliner Längsschnittstudie zum Deutscherwerb. *Linguistische Berichte*, 131:37-46.

Ehlich, K. and Rehbein, J. 1976. Halbinterpretative Arbeitstranskriptionen (HIAT). *Linguistische Berichte*, 45:21-41.

Ehlich, K., Tebel, C., Flickermann, I., and Becker-Mrotzek, M. 1991. Handbuch zur Erstellung von Transkripten nach dem Verfahren HIAT-DOS 2.0. Dortmund.

Ellis, R. 1985. *Understanding second language acquisition*. Oxford: Oxford University Press.

Erickson, F. 1976. Gate-keeping encounters: a social selection process. In P. Sanday (ed.) *Anthropology and the public interest*. New York:

Academic Press.

Fechner, G. 1860. *Elemente der Psychophysik.* Leipzig: Breithopf und Härtel.

Gallagher, T. M. and Craig, H. K. 1987. An investigation of pragmatic connectives within preschool peer interactions. *Journal of Pragmatics,* 11:27-37.

Garret, M. 1982. Production of speech: observations from normal and pathological language use. In A. Ellis (ed.) *Normality and pathology in cognitive functions,* 19-76. London: Academic Press.

Gentner, D. 1982. Why nouns are learned before verbs: linguistic relativity versus natural partitioning. In S. Kuczaj (ed.) *Language development: Language, cognition and culture,* 301-344. New Jersey: Hillsdale.

Giacobbe, J. and Lucas, M. 1980. Quelques hypothèses sur le rapport langue maternelle-systhmes intermidiaires. *Encrages,* (No. Spécial):25-36.

Givón, T. 1979. From discourse to syntax: grammar as a processing strategy. In T. Givon (ed.) *Syntax and Semantics 12. Discourse and Syntax,* 81-111. New York: Academic Press.

Grießhaber, W. 1991. syncWRITER, Kongreßdokumentation CIP Kongreß Berlin.

Grillo, R. 1989. *Dominant languages: language and hierarchy in Britain and France.* Cambridge: Cambridge University Press.

Hakuta, K. and Cancino, H. 1977. Trends in second language acquisition research. *Harvard Educational Review, 47:294-313.*

Hatch, E. 1980. Conversational analysis: an alternative methodology for second language acquisition studies. In R. Shuy and A. Shnukal (eds.) *Language use and the uses of language,* 182-96. Washington DC: Georgetown University Press.

    1983. *Psycholinguistics. A second language perspective.* Rowley, Mass.: Newbury House.

Herdan, G. 1966. *The advanced theory of language as choice and chance.* Berlin: Springer Verlag.

Hickmann, M. 1991. The development of discourse cohesion: some functional and cross-linguistic issues. In G. Piéraut-Le Bonniec and M. Dolitsky (eds.) *Language bases...Discourse bases,* 157-185. Amsterdam: Benjamins.

Hilles, S. 1986. Interlanguage and the pro-drop parameter. *Second Language Research,* 2:33-52.

    1991. Access to universal grammar in second language acquisition. In L. Eubank (ed.) *Point counterpoint: Universal grammar in the second language,* 305-338. Amsterdam/Philadelphia: Benjamins.

Horn, L. 1986. Presupposition, theme and variations. Paper presented at the twenty-second meeting of the Chicago Linguistic Society.

Huebner, T. 1983. *The acquisition of English.* Ann Arbor: Karoma.

Jansen, B. and Lalleman, J. 1980a. Interferentie en woordvolgorde: het Nederlands van buitenlandse arbeiders. Publ. Instituut Algemene Taalwetenschap Amsterdam, 27:1-48.

1980b. De invloed van de moedertaal op de zinsbouw van het Nederlands van Turkse en Marokkaanse arbeiders. In R. Appel *et al.* (eds.) *Taalproblemen van buitenlandse arbeiders en hun kinderen*, 137-150. Muiderberg: Coutinho.

Jansen, B., Lalleman, J., and Muysken, P. 1981. The alternation hypothesis: acquisition of Dutch word order by Turkish and Moroccan foreign workers. *Language Learning*, 31:315-336.

Jordens, P. 1988. The acquisition of word order in L2 Dutch and German. In P. Jordens and J. Lalleman (eds.) *Language Development*, 149-180. Dordrecht: Foris.

Kellerman, E. 1987. Aspects of transferability in second language acquisition. Unpublished doctoral dissertation, Nijmegen University.

1991. Compensatory strategies in second language research: a critique, a revision, and some (non-)implications for the classroom. In R. Phillipson, E. Kellerman, L. Selinker, M. Sharwood-Smith and M. Swain (eds.) *Foreign/second language pedagogy research*, 142-161. Clevedon: Multilingual Matters.

Kellerman, E. and Sharwood-Smith, M. (eds.). 1986. *Crosslinguistic influence in second language acquisition.* New York/Oxford: Pergamon Press.

Kessler, C. and Idar, I. 1979. The acquisition of English by a Vietnamese mother and child. *Working Papers on Bilingualism*, 18:65-77.

Klein, W. 1981. Knowing a language and knowing to communicate. In A. Vermeer (ed.) *Language problems of minority groups*, 75-95. (= *Tilburg Studies in Language and Literature*, 1)

1984/6/9. *Zweitspracherwerb: eine Einführung.* Athenäum Verlag 1984. English version: *Second language acquisition.* Cambridge: Cambridge University Press 1986. French version: *L'acquisition de langue seconde.* Paris: Colin 1989.

Klein, W. and Dittmar, N. 1979. *Developing Grammars.* Berlin: Springer.

Klein, W. and Rieck, B.-O. 1982. Der Erwerb der Personalpronomina im ungesteuerten Spracherwerb. *Zeitschrift für Literaturwissenschaft und Linguistik*, 45:35-71.

Lalleman, J. 1983. The principle of elimination: establishing word order regularities in the Dutch of foreign workers. *Linguistische Berichte*, 87:40-63.

Labov, W. 1972. *Language in the inner city.* Philadelphia: University of Pennsylvania Press.

Larsen-Freeman, D. and Long, M. 1991. *An introduction to second language acquisition research.* London: Longman.

Levelt, W. 1982. Linearization in describing spatial networks. In S. Peters and E. Saarinen (eds.) *Processes, beliefs and questions*, 199-220. Dordrecht: Reidel.

Li, C. and Thompson, S. 1976. In C. Li (ed.) *Subject and topic: a new typology*, 457-490. New York: Academic Press.

Long, M. 1983. Linguistic and conversational adjustments to non-native speakers. *Studies in Second Language Acquisition*, 5:177-193.

1990. Maturational constraints on language development. *Studies in Second Language Acquisition*, 12:251-268.

MacWhinney, B. 1991. The CHILDES project: tools for analyzing talk. Hillsdale: Lawrence Erlbaum.

Mann, W. C. and Thompson, S. A. 1986. Relational propositions in discourse. *Discourse processes*, 9:57-90.

Maratsos, M. 1982. The child's construction of grammatical categories. In E. Wanner and L. Gleitman (eds.) *Language acquisition: The state of the art*, 240-266. Cambridge: Cambridge University Press.

McLaughlin, B. 1987. *Theories of second-language learning.* London: Edward Arnold.

McLaughlin, M. L. 1980. Discriminant analysis in communication research. In P. R. Monge and J. N. Cappella (eds.) *Multivariate techniques in human communication research* 175-204. New York: Academic Press.

Meara, P. 1983. *Vocabulary in a second language.* London: Centre for Information on Language Teaching and Research.

Meisel, J. 1980. Linguistic simplification: a study of immigrant workers' speech and foreigner talk. In S. Felix (ed.) *Second language development. Trends and issues*, 13-40. Tübingen: Gunter Narr.

1987. Reference to past events and actions in the development of natural second language acquisition. In C. Pfaff (ed.) *First and second language acquisition processes*, 206-224. Rowley, Mass.: Newbury House.

1991. Principles of universal grammar and strategies of language learning: some similarities and differences between first and second language acquisition. In L. Eubank (ed.) *Point counterpoint: Universal grammar in the second language*, 231-276. Amsterdam/Philadelphia: Benjamins.

Meisel, J., Clahsen, H. and Pienemann, M. 1981. On determining developmental stages in natural second language acquisition. *Studies in Second Language Acquisition*, 3:109-135.

Menard, N. 1983. *Mesure de la richesse lexicale*. Paris: Slatkine.

Nicholas, H. 1984. 'To be' or not 'to be': is that really the question? Developmental sequences and the role of the copula in the acquisition of German as a second language. In R. Andersen (ed.) *Second languages: a cross-Linguistic perspective*, 299-317. Rowley, Mass.: Newbury House.

1987. Contextually defined queries: Evidence for variation in orientations to second language acquisition processes? In C. Pfaff (ed.) *First and second language acquisition processes*, 117-142. Rowley, Mass.: Newbury House.

Noyau, C. 1986. *L'acquisition du français dans le milieu social par des adultes hispanophones: la temporalité*. Unpublished doctoral dissertation, Université Paris-Sorbonne, Paris.

Pienemann, M. 1984. Psychological constraints on the teachability of languages. *Studies in Second Language Acquisition*, 6:186-214.

Pienemann, M., Johnston, M. and Brindley, G. 1988. Constructing an acquisition-based procedure for second language assessment. *Studies in Second Language Acquisition*, 10:217-243.

Py, B. 1982. Propositions épistémologiques pour une étude du bilinguisme. *Travaux Neuchâtelois de Linguistique*, 4:9-19.

1990. Les stratégies d'acquisition en situation d'interaction. In D. Gaonac'h (ed.) *Acquisition et utilisation d'une langue étrangère. L'approche cognitive*. Paris: Hachette (special number of *Le Français dans le Monde*).

Reinhart, T. 1984. Principles of gestalt perception in the temporal organization of narrative texts. *Linguistics*, 22:779-809.

Richards, B. 1987. Type/token ratios: What do they really tell us? *Journal of Child Language*, 11:689-695.

Rizzi, L. 1982. *Issues in Italian syntax*. Dordrecht: Foris.

Roche, J. 1989. *Xenolekte: Struktur und Variation im Deutsch gegenüber Ausländern*. Berlin: de Gruyter.

Rutherford, W. 1989. Preemption and the learning of L2 grammars. *Studies in Second Language Acquisition*, 11:441-458.

Sato, C. 1990. *The Syntax of Conversation in Interlanguage Development*. Tübingen: Gunter Narr.

Schumann, J. 1978. *The pidginization process: a model for second language acquisition*. Rowley: Newbury House.

1987. Utterance structure in basilang speech. In G. Gilbert (ed.) *Pidgin and Creole languages*, 139-160. Honolulu: University of Hawaii Press.

Selinker, L. 1972. Interlanguage. *International Review of Applied Linguistics*, 10:209-231.

1985. Attempting comprehensive and comparative empirical research in second language acquisition: I. *Language Learning*, 35:567-584.

Selinker, L. and Lamendella, J. 1979. The role of extrinsic feedback in interlanguage fossilization. *Language Learning*, 29:363-375.

Skehan, P. 1989. *Individual differences in second language learning.* London: Edward Arnold.

Slobin, D. 1979. A case study of early language awareness, In A. Sinclair, R. Jarvella and W. Levelt (eds.) *The child's conception of language*, 45-54. Springer: Berlin.

Smith, D. 1972. Some implications for the social status of pidgin languages. In D. Smith and R. Shuy (eds.) *Sociolinguistics in cross-cultural analysis*, 47-56. Washington DC: Georgetown University Press.

Sperberg-McQueen, C. M. and Burnard, L. (eds.). 1990. Guidelines for the encoding and interchange of machine-readable texts. Chicago and Oxford: ACH, ACL, ALLC.

Stallman, R. M. 1985. The GNU Manifesto. Electronic text, available at internet node prep.ai.mit.edu.

Stutterheim, Ch. von. 1986. *Temporalität in der Zweitsprache: Eine Untersuchung zum Erwerb des Deutschen durch Türkische Gastarbeiter.* Berlin: De Gruyter.

Stutterheim, Ch. von. and Klein, W. 1987. A concept oriented approach to second language studies. In C. Pfaff (ed.) *First and second language acquisition processes*, 191-205. Rowley, Mass.: Newbury House.

Swain, M. 1985. Communicative competence: some roles of comprehensible input and comprehensible output in it development. In S. Gass and C. Madden (eds.) *Input in second language acquisition*, 235-253. Rowley, Mass.: Newbury House.

Talmy, L. 1985. Lexicalization patterns: semantic structure in lexical form. In T. Shopen (ed.) *Language typology and syntactic descriptions.* Cambridge: Cambridge University Press.

Tarone, E. 1979. Interlanguage as chameleon. *Language Learning*, 29:189-191.

1984. On the variability of interlanguage systems. In F. Eckman, L. Bell and D. Nelson (eds.) *Universals of second language acquisition*, 3-23. Rowley, Mass.: Newbury House.

Tuthill, W. 1981. Hum – A concordance and text analysis package. Berkeley: Universtity of California, Computing Services.

Vermeer, A. 1986. *Tempo en struktuur van tweede-taalverwerving bij Turkse en Marokkaanse kinderen.* Unpublished doctoral dissertation, University of Tilburg.

Wells, G. 1985. *Language development in the pre-school years.* Cambridge: Cambridge University Press.

The ESF–SLDB bibliography

This bibliography lists all published work using data collected during the ESF project, and available in the Second Language Data Bank (see chapter 7). It also includes references to the project's six Final Reports, and to a handful of unpublished working papers and theses which are cited in the text of Volume I.

Allwood, J. (ed.) 1988. *Feedback in adult language acquisition*, (= *Final Report to the European Science Foundation*, II). Strasbourg, Göteborg.

Allwood, J. and Abelar, Y. 1984. Lack of understanding, misunderstanding, and adult language acquisition. In G. Extra and M. Mittner (eds.) *Studies in second language acquisition by adult immigrants*, 27–55. Tilburg: Tilburg University.

Allwood, J. and Ahlsén, E. 1986. Lexical convergence and language acquisition. In Ö. Dahl (ed.) *Papers from the Ninth Scandinavian Conference of Linguistics*, 27–55. University of Stockholm: Dept. of Linguistics.

Andersson, A.-B. and Strömqvist, S. 1990. Adult L2 acquisition of gender. A cross-linguistic and cross-learner types perspective. *Göteborg Papers in Theoretical Linguistics*, 61:1–23.

Becker, A. 1986. Référence spatiale chez les apprenants italiens: une analyse préliminaire. In A. Giacomi and D. Véronique (eds.) *Acquisition d'une langue étrangère: Perspectives et Recherches*, 419–446. Aix-en-Provence: Université de Provence.

Becker, A., Carroll, M., and Kelly, A. (eds.) 1988. *Reference to space*, (= *Final Report to the European Science Foundation*, IV). Strasbourg, Heidelberg.

Becker, A. and Perdue, C. 1984. Just one misunderstanding: a story of miscommunication. In G. Extra and M. Mittner (eds.) *Studies in second language acquisition by adult immigrants*, 57–82. Tilburg: Tilburg University.

Bhardwaj, M., Dietrich, R., and Noyau, C. (eds.) 1988. *Temporality*,

(= *Final Report to the European Science Foundation*, V). Strasbourg, London, Heidelberg.

Bremer, K., Broeder, P., Roberts, C., Simonot, M., and Vasseur, M.-Th. (eds.) 1988. *Ways of achieving understanding: communicating to learn in a second language*, (= *Final Report to the European Science Foundation*, I). Strasbourg, London.

Broeder, P. 1987. Learning to repeat to interact. Learner's repetitions in the language acquisition process of adults. *Tilburg papers in Language and Literature*, 114.

1989a. Learning to talk about people: Towards a FL syllabus for adult learners. *Language culture and curriculum*, 2.1:31–41.

1989b. Praten over mannen en vrouwen: Pronominale referentie in tweede-taalverwerving door volwassenen. *Tijdschrift voor taal- en tekstwetenschap*, 9:51–75.

1990. Reference to people in adult language acquisition. *ITL Review of Applied Linguistics*, 87/88:23–43.

1991. *Talking about people. A multiple case study on adult language acquisition*, (= *European studies on multilingualism*, 1). Amsterdam: Swets & Zeitlinger.

Broeder, P., Coenen, J., Extra, G., Hout, R. van, and Zerrouk, R. 1984. Spatial reference by Turkish and Moroccan adult learners of Dutch: the initial stages. In G. Extra and M. Mittner (eds.) *Studies in second language acquisition by adult immigrants*, 147–184. Tilburg: Tilburg University.

1986. Ontwikkelingen in het nederlandstalig lexicon bij anderstalige volwassenen. Een macro- en micro-perspectief. In J. Creten, G. Geerts, and K. Jaspaert (eds.) *Werk-in-uitvoering. Momentopnamen van de sociolinguïstiek in België en Nederland*, 39–57. Leuven/Amersfoort: Acco.

Broeder, P., Coenen, J., Extra, G., Helvert, K. van, and Hout, R. van to appear. *A multiple case study on Turkish and Moroccan learners of Dutch*.

Broeder, P. and Extra, G. 1988. Woordvormingsprocédé's bij verwijzing naar objecten in tweede-taalverwervingsprocessen van volwassenen. *Toegepaste Taalwetenschap in Artikelen*, 1.30:105–117.

1991. Acquisition of kinship reference: A study on word-formation processes of adult language learners. *International Journal of Applied Linguistics*, 1.2:209–227.

Broeder, P., Extra, G., and Hout, R. van 1986. Acquiring the linguistic devices for pronominal reference to persons: A crosslinguistic perspective on complex tasks with small words. In F. Beukema and A. Hulk (eds.) *Linguistics in the Netherlands*, 27–40. Dordrecht: Foris.

1987. Measuring lexical richness and variety in second language use. *Polyglot*, 8:1–16. Special issue on lexicon, edited by Paul Meara.

1989. Processes in the developing lexicon of adult immigrant learners. *AILA Review*, 6:86–109.

Broeder, P., Extra, G., Hout, R. van, Strömqvist, S., and Voionmaa, K. (eds.) 1988. *Processes in the developing lexicon*, (= *Final Report to the European Science Foundation*, III). Strasbourg, Tilburg, Göteborg.

Broeder, P. and Voionmaa, K. 1986. Establishing word-class distinctions in the vocabulary of adult language learners – a crosslinguistic perspective. In Ö. Dahl (ed.) *Papers from the Ninth Scandinavian Conference of Linguistics*, 74–85. University of Stockholm: Dept. of Linguistics.

Broeder, P. et al. 1985. Spatial reference in L2 Dutch of Turkish and Moroccan adult learners; the initial stages. In G. Extra and T. Vallen (eds.) *Ethnic minorities and Dutch as a second language*, 209–252. Dordrecht/Cinnaminson: Foris.

Cammarota, M.-A. 1986. Des difficultés dans l'acquisition de langue étrangère par des réfugiés politiques latino-américains. *Langue Française*, 71:101–116.

Cammarota, M.-A. and Giacobbe, J. 1986. L'acquisition du lexique en français par des adultes hispanophones. *Langages*, 84:65–78.

Cammarota, M.-A. and Porquier, R. 1984. Acquisition de la référence spatiale en français chez des adultes hispanophones: localisation et mouvement directionnel. In G. Extra and M. Mittner (eds.) *Studies in second language acquisition by adult immigrants*, 185–210. Tilburg: Tilburg University.

Carroll, M. 1990. Word order in instructions in learner languages of English and German. *Linguistics*, 5.28:1011–1037.

Carroll, M. and Dietrich, R. 1985. Observations on object reference in learner languages. *Linguistische Berichte*, 98:310–337.

Chaudenson, R., Valli, A., and Véronique, D. 1986. The dynamics of linguistic systems and the acquisition of French as second language. *Studies in Second Language Acquisition*, 8.3:277–292.

Chevalier, J.-C. 1986. Structuration d'un discours français par un migrant, apprenant en milieu naturel. *Langue Française*, 71:17–31.

Chur, J. and Dietrich, R. 1990. The structure of elementary learner language: A semantic approach to its description. *Linguistics*, 28:417–452.

Coenen, J. and Hout, R. van 1987. Word order phenomena in second language acquisition of Dutch. In F. Beukema and P. Coopmans (eds.) *Linguistics in the Netherlands*, 41-51. Dordrecht/Cinnaminson: Foris.

Coupier, C. 1983. L'emploi des pronoms personnels chez R'quia D. et Zahra

K. In D. Véronique (ed.) *G.R.A.L./Papiers de travail*, 39–59. Aix-en-Provence: Université de Provence.

1985. Tentative descriptive du verbal et du gestuel en interaction au cours d'une tâche spatiale. In D. Véronique (ed.) *G.R.A.L./Papiers de travail*, 19–36. Aix-en-Provence.

1986. Or les mots manquent toujours. *Langue Française*, 71:70–86.

Coupier, C., Dalmas, P., and Véronique, D. 1984. La specificité de la communication dans l'enquête linguistique. In C. Noyau and R. Porquier (eds.) *Communiquer dans la langue de l'autre*, 37–59. Paris: Presses Universitaires de Vincennes.

Coupier, C., Houdaïfa, T., and Véronique, D. 1983. Insertion sociale des informateurs et enquête linguistique. In D. Véronique (ed.) *G.R.A.L./Papiers de travail*, 17–24. Aix-en-Provence: Université de Provence.

Coupier, C. and Taranger, M.-C. 1986. L'utilisation de la vidéo dans la recherche sur l'acquisition des langues secondes: approches du gestuel. In A. Giacomi and D. Véronique (eds.) *Acquisition d'une langue étrangère: Perspectives et recherches*, 167–184. Aix-en-Provence: Université de Provence.

Dalmas, P. 1983. Sociabilité diffuse et implication de terrain (sur Marseille et la Porte d'Aix). In D. Véronique (ed.) *G.R.A.L./Papiers de travail*, 25–38. Aix-en-Provence: Université de Provence.

Deulofeu, J. 1983. Premières remarques sur la constitution de la grammaire dans l'interlangue d'un informateur. In D. Véronique (ed.) *G.R.A.L./Papiers de travail*, 61–80. Aix-en-Provence: Université de Provence.

1986. Sur quelques procedes de hiérarchisation de l'information dans les récits d'apprenants marocains en milieu naturel: pour une conception souple des rapports entre phénomènes de micro et de macro thématisation. In A. Giacomi and D. Véronique (eds.) *Acquisition d'une langue étrangère: Perspectives et Recherches*, 263–284. Aix-en-Provence: Université de Provence.

Deulofeu, J. and Noyau, C. 1986. L'étude de l'acquisition spontané d'une langue étrangère: méthodes de recherche/méthodes en linguistique/apports. *Langue Française*, 71:3–16.

Deulofeu, J. and Taranger, M.-C. 1984. Relations entre le linguistique et le culturel: microscopie de quelques malentendus et incompréhensions. In C. Noyau and R. Porquier (eds.) *Communiquer dans la langue de l'autre*, 99–129. Paris: Presses Universitaires de Vincennes.

Dietrich, R. 1982. Bestimmtheit und Unbestimmtheit im Deutschen eines türkischen Arbeiters. Eine Hypothese. In H. Fix, A. Rothkegel, and E. Stegentritt (eds.) *Sprachen und Computer*, 81–94. Beim Weisenstein: AQ-Verlag.

1989a. Communicating with few words. An empirical account of the second language speaker's lexicon. In R. Dietrich and C. Graumann (eds.) *Language processing in social context*, 233–276. Amsterdam: North-Holland.

1989b. Nouns and verbs in the learner's lexicon. In H. Dechert (ed.) *Current trends in European second language acquisition research*, 13–22. Clevedon and Philadelphia: Multilingual Matters.

Dorriots, B. 1986. How to succeed with only fifty words – analysis of a role-play in the frame of adult language acquisition. *Göteborg Papers in Theoretical Linguistics*, 52:1–80.

Extra, G. and Helvert, K. van 1987a. Référence temporelle dans l'acquisition d'une seconde langue par des adultes. In H. Blanc, M. Le Douaron, and D. Véronique (eds.) *S'approprier une langue étrangère... Actes du VIe colloque international 'Acquisition d'une langue étrangère: perspectives et recherches'*, 143–154. Paris: Didier-Erudition.

1987b. Verwijzing naar tijd in tweede-taalverwervingsprocessen van volwassenen. In G. Extra, R. van Hout, and T. Vallen (eds.) *Etnische minderheden. Taalverwerving, taalonderwijs, taalbeleid*, 117–138. Dordrecht: Foris.

Extra, G. and Mittner, M. 1984. (Mis)understanding and spatial reference: two topics in studying adult language acquisition. In G. Extra and M. Mittner (eds.) *Studies in second language acquisition by adult immigrants*, 9–16. Tilburg: Tilburg University.

Extra, G. and Vallen, T. 1988. Language and ethnic minorities in the Netherlands. *International Journal of the Sociology of Language*, 73:85–110.

Extra, G. et al. 1985. Tweede-taalverwerving door volwassen immigranten in Europa: een internationaal onderzoekproject (Deel 1). *Info-minderheden*, 4:22–27.

Feldweg, H. 1991. *The European Science Foundation Second Language Databank*. Nijmegen: Max-Planck-Institut für Psycholinguistik.

Garmiryan, A. 1984. Les formules rituelles dans l'allemand des travailleurs turcs. In C. Noyau and R. Porquier (eds.) *Communiquer dans la langue de l'autre*, 173–190. Paris: Presses Universitaires de Vincennes.

Giacobbe, J. 1986. Le pronom 'on' dans l'interlangue française des adultes hispanophones. In *Actes du Colloque de Linguistique Hispanique. Cahiers du CRIAR*, 19–24. Rouen: Faculté des Lettres et Sciences Humaines.

1989. *Construction des mots et construction du sens: cognition et interaction dans l'acquisition du Français par des adultes His-*

panophones. Université Paris VII. Unpublished doctoral dissertation.

Giacobbe, J. and Cammarota, M.-A. 1986a. L'acquisition du lexique en français par des adultes hispanophones. *Langages*, 84:65–78.

1986b. Learner's hypotheses for the acquisition of lexis. *Studies in Second Language Acquisition*, 8.3:327–342.

1986c. Un modèle du rapport langue source/langue cible dans la construction du lexique. In A. Giacomi and D. Véronique (eds.) *Acquisition d'une Langue Etrangère. Perspectives et Recherches*, 193–210. Aix-en-Provence: Université de Provence.

1986d. Un modello del rapporto L1/L2 nella costruzione del lessico. In A. Giacalone Ramat (ed.) *L'apprendimento spontaneo di una seconda lingua*, 254–263. Bologna: Il Mulino.

Giacomi, A. 1983. Une analyse de l'interaction en langue seconde: le jeu des questions/reponses. In D. Véronique (ed.) *G.R.A.L./Papiers de travail*, 81–94. Aix-en-Provence: Université de Provence.

1985. Feedback, interlangue, communication interculturelle. In D. Véronique (ed.) *G.R.A.L./Papiers de travail*, 51–65. Aix-en-Provence: Université de Provence.

1986. Processus de structuration de l'énoncé en acquisition et interaction. In A. Giacomi and D. Véronique (eds.) *Acquisition d'une langue étrangère: Perspectives et Recherches. Actes du V Colloque International*, 285–304., Aix-en-Provence: Université de Provence.

Giacomi, A. and Hérédia, C. de 1986. Réussites et échecs dans la communication linguistique entre locuteurs francophones et locuteurs immigrés. *Langages*, 84:9–24.

Giacomi, A., Houdaïfa, E.-T., and Vion, R. 1984. Malentendus et/ou incomprehensions dans le dialogue interculturel: à bon entendeur salut! In C. Noyau and R. Porquier (eds.) *Communiquer dans la langue de l'autre*, 79–98. Paris: Presses Universitaires de Vincennes.

Giacomi, A. and Véronique, D. 1985a. L'analyse des échanges interculturels et l'observation des processus d'acquisition d'une langue étrangère. In D. Véronique (ed.) *G.R.A.L./Papiers de travail*, 37–50. Aix-en-Provence: Université de Provence.

1985b. Situations interculturelles et apprentissage du français par des travailleurs marocains arabophones. In C. Clanet (ed.) *L'interculturel en éducation et en sciences humaines*, 269–276. Toulouse: Université de Toulouse-Le Mirail.

Giacomi, A. and Vion, R. 1986a. La conduite du récit dans l'acquisition d'une langue seconde. *Langue Française*, 71:32–47.

1986b. Metadiscursive processes in the acquisition of a second language. *Studies in Second Language Acquisition*, 8.3:355–368.

Gray, D. 1986. *Interaction and acquisition in context: Making some connexions*. University of Lancaster. Unpublished doctoral dissertation.

Gumperz, J. 1984. Miscommunication as a resource in the study of second language acquisition: a discourse analysis approach. In G. Extra and M. Mittner (eds.) *Studies in second language acquisition by adult immigrants*, 139–144. Tilburg: Tilburg University.

Hérédia, C. de 1986a. Asymmetric communication in bilingual exchanges. *Studies in Second Language Acquisition*, 8:127–147.

1986b. Intercompréhension et malentendus. Etude d'interactions entre étrangers et autochtones. *Langue Française*, 71:48–69.

1987. Tuteurs et cache-pots ou le maître quincailler: étude sur les malentendus en situation exolingue. In H. Blanc, M. le Douaron, and D. Véronique (eds.) *S'approprier une langue étrangère*, 23–31. Paris: Didier-Erudition.

Hérédia, C. de and Noyau, C. 1986. Communicazione esolingue estrema: strategie di communicazione tra autoctoni e immigranti principianti nella lengua. In A. Giacalone-Ramat (ed.) *L'apprendimento spontaneo di une seconda lingua*, 221–244. Bologna: Il Molino.

Hickel, F. 1991. Stratégiés argumentatives et fonction contrastive dans l'interlangue d'apprenants hispanophones en situation de resolution de conflit: Une etude longitudinale. In C. Russier, H. Stoffel, and D. Véronique (eds.) *Modalisations en langue étrangère*, 133–142. Aix-en-Provence: Université de Provence.

Houdaïfa, E.-T. 1983a. La référence personnelle et temporelle dans le récit d'un apprenant en milieu naturel. In D. Véronique (ed.) *G.R.A.L./Papiers de travail*, 125–140. Aix-en-Provence: Université de Provence.

1983b. L'organisation de la référence temporelle dans une interlangue. In D. Véronique (ed.) *G.R.A.L./Papiers de travail*, 95–114. Aix-en-Provence: Université de Provence.

1983c. Syntaxe et lexique des verbes de mouvement dans une interlangue. In D. Véronique (ed.) *G.R.A.L./Papiers de travail*, 115–124. Aix-en-Provence: Université de Provence.

1985. L'acte de dénomination dans le corpus d'un apprenant migrant. In D. Véronique (ed.) *G.R.A.L./Papiers de travail*, 169–183. Aix-en-Provence: Université de Provence.

1986. Quelques aspects de la grammaire des verbes et, en particulier, des verbes de mouvement dans un corpus de migrant. In A. Giacomi and D. Véronique (eds.) *Acquisition d'une langue étrangère: Perspectives et Recherches*, 447–474. Aix-en-Provence: Université de Provence.

Houdaïfa, E.-T. and Véronique, D. 1984. La référence spatiale dans le français parlé par des Marocains à Marseille. In G. Extra and M. Mittner (eds.) *Studies in second language acquisition by adult immigrants*, 211–261. Tilburg: Tilburg University.

Huebner, Th. 1989. Establishing point of view: the development of coding mechanisms in a second language for the expression of cognitive and perceptual organization. *Linguistics*, 27:111–143.

Klein, W. 1982. Second language acquisition by adult immigrants: A European Science Foundation project. In R. Stuip and W. Zwanenburg (eds.) *Handelingen van het Zevenendertigste Nederlands Philologencongres, Utrecht 82*, 127–136. Amsterdam: Het Nederlands Philologencongres.

Klein, W. and Perdue, C. 1986. Comment résoudre une tâche verbale complexe avec peu de moyens linguistiques? In A. Giacomi and D. Véronique (eds.) *Acquisition d'une langue étrangère: Perspectives et Recherches*, 305–330. Aix-en-Provence: Université de Provence.

(eds.) 1988. *Utterance Structure*, (= *Final Report to the European Science Foundation*, VI). Strasbourg, Nijmegen.

1989. The learner's problem of arranging words. In B. MacWhinney and E. Bates (eds.) *The cross-linguistic study of sentence processing*, 292–337. Cambridge: Cambridge University Press.

(eds.) 1992. *Utterance structure. Developing grammars again.*. Amsterdam: Benjamins.

Kogelheide, M. 1987. *Repeating the interlocutor's words in second language acquisition. A comparative study of how often and for what purpose two learners of German use native speakers' words.* Heidelberg: Institut für Deutsch als Fremdsprachenphilologie.

Lüdi, G. 1984. Réponse à Clive Perdue. L'acquisition d'une langue seconde par des migrants: naissance d'un bilinguisme. In B. Py (ed.) *Acquisition d'une langue étrangère, III. Actes du Colloque de Neuchâtel 82*, 275–281. Paris: Presses Universitaires de Vincennes.

Mittner, M. 1984. Stratégies discursives, variabilité et situations de communication. In G. Extra and M. Mittner (eds.) *Studies in second language acquisition by adult immigrants*, 83–112. Tilburg: Tilburg University.

1987. Répétitions et réformulations chez un apprenant: aspects metalinguistiques et metadiscursifs. *Encrages*, 18/19:135–151.

Noyau, C. 1984a. Communiquer quand on ignore la langue de l'autre. In C. Noyau and R. Porquier (eds.) *Communiquer dans la langue de l'autre*, 8–36. Paris: Presses Universitaires de Vincennes.

1984b. The development of means for temporality in French by adult Spanish-speakers: linguistic devices and communicative capacities. In

G. Extra and M. Mittner (eds.) *Studies in second language acquisi-tion by adult immigrants*, 113–137. Tilburg: Tilburg University.

1984c. Recherches sur l'acquisition spontanée d'une langue étrangère par des adultes dans le milieu social. *Dialogues et cultures*, 31:208–218.

1986a. Aspects de la communication exolingue: interactions entre au-tochtones et immigrés debutants dans la langue. In D. Kremer (ed.) *Actes du XVIIIe Congrès international de linguistique et philolo-gie romanes*, 425–438. Tübingen: Niemeyer.

1986b. Le développement de la temporalité dans l'acquisition en milieu naturel du français par des hispanophones. In *Actes du 2e Colloque de linguistique hispanique. Cahiers du CRIAR*, 25–44. Rouen: Uni-versité de Haute-Normandie.

1987a. La catégorie verbale dans la construction du français par des hispanophones. In *Mélanges offerts à Maurice Molho*, 261–273. Paris: Les Cahiers de Fontenay.

1987b. L'acquisition des moyens de la référence temporelle en langue étrangère chez des adultes: perspectives translinguistiques. In H. Blanc, M. Le Douaron, and D. Véronique (eds.) *S'approprier d'une langue étrangère*. Paris: Didier-Erudition.

1987c. Le développement du lexique en langue étrangère: lemmatisa-tion de données orales d'acquisition. In *Actes du 2eme Colloque de Linguistique Hispanique*, 199–216. Brest: Université de Bretagne Occidentale.

1988. Recherches sur l'acquisition spontanée d'une langue étrangère par des adultes dans le milieu social. *Dialogue et Cultures*, 31:208–218.

1989a. The development of means for temporality in the unguided acqui-sition of L2: cross-linguistic perspectives. In H. Dechert (ed.) *Current trends in European second language acquisition research*, 143–170. Clevedon and Philadelphia: Multilingual Matters.

1989b. Présentation. In J. Canavaggio and B. Darbord (eds.) *La tra-duction*, 251–256. Caen: Presses de l'Université de Caen.

1989c. Traduction interne et construction de la langue étrangère (his-panophones apprenant le Français). In J. Canavaggio and B. Darbord (eds.) *La traduction*, 261–267. Caen: Presses de l'Université de Caen.

1990a. Le développement de la temporalité dans l'acquisition ini-tiale d'une langue étrangère: apports d'une recherche translinguis-tique. In G. Bernine and A. Giacalone Ramat (eds.) *La temporalità nell'acquisizione di lingue seconde*, 219–238. Milano: Franco Angeli.

1990b. Structure conceptuelle, mise en texte et acquisition d'une langue étrangère. *Langages*, 25:101–114.

1991. Comunicarse en un país extranjero: aspectos lingüísticos de las comunidades hispánicas. In C. Strosetzki, J.-F. Botrel, and

M. Tietz (eds.) *Actas del I Encuentro Franco-Alemán de His-panistas*, 134–143. Frankfurt am Main: Vervuert Verlag.

Noyau, C. and Porquier, R. 1984. Présentation. In C. Noyau and R. Porquier (eds.) *Communiquer dans la langue de l'autre*, 1–7. Paris: Presses Universitaires de Vincennes.

Noyau, C. and Vasseur, M.-Th. 1986. L'acquisition des moyens de la référence temporelle en français langue étrangère chez des adultes his-panophones. *Langages*, 84:105–117.

Noyau, C. and Véronique, D. 1986. Survey article: Second language acqui-sition research in France and French-speaking Switzerland. *Studies in second language acquisition*, 8:245–263.

Perdue, C. 1982. L'acquisition d'une deuxième langue par des adultes im-migrés. *Travaux Neuchâtellois de Linguistique*, 4:57–85.

1984a. Aims and goals of the ESF project on adult language acquisi-tion. In G. Extra and M. Mittner (eds.) *Studies in second language acquisition by adult immigrants*, 17–23. Tilburg: Tilburg University.

1984b. Recueil de données: les enseignements d'une année pilote (pro-jet ESF: Second language acquisition by adult immigrants). In B. Py (ed.) *Acquisition d'une langue étrangère. III*, 239–274. Paris: Presses Universitaires de Vincennes.

(ed.) 1984c. *Second Language Acquisition by Adult Immigrants. A field manual*. Rowley: Newbury House.

1986. Présentation. *Langages*, 84:5–8.

1987a. Real beginners. real questions. In H. Blanc, M. le Douaron, and D. Véronique (eds.) *S'approprier une langue étrangère*, 196–210. Paris: Didier-Erudition.

1987b. Structure thématique des énoncés dans le français d'une adulte hispanophone (traduit et adapté par Mireille Prodeau). *Encrages*, 18/19:153–168.

1987c. Understanding and misunderstanding in adult language acquisi-tion: Recent work in the ESF project. In G. Lüdi (ed.) *Devenir bilingue – parler bilingue*, 171–189. Tübingen: Niemeyer.

1990. Complexification of the simple clause in the narrative discourse of adult language learners. *Linguistics*, 5.28:983–1009.

1991. Les pronoms chez Paula. In C. Russier, H. Stoffel, and D. Véronique (eds.) *Interaction en langue étrangère*, 141–151. Aix-en-Provence: Université de Provence.

Perdue, C. and Becker, A. 1984. Données authentiques: l'enjeu réel d'une 'simple' incomprehension entre un avocat allemand et son client turc. In C. Noyau and R. Porquier (eds.) *Communiquer dans la langue de l'autre*, 60–78. Paris: Presses Universitaires de Vincennes.

Perdue, C. and Deulofeu, J. 1986. La structuration de l'énoncé: étude longitudinale. *Langages*, 84:43–64.

Perdue, C. and Klein, W. 1992. Why does the production of some learners not grammaticalize? *Studies in Second Language Acquisition*, 14:259–272.

Roberts, C. and Simonot, M. 1987. 'This is my life': how language acquisition is interactionally accomplished. In R. Ellis (ed.) *Second language acquisition in context*, 133–148. New York: Prentice Hall International.

Simonot, M. 1984. Compétence et situation: des Pendjabis en Grande-Bretagne. In C. Noyau and R. Porquier (eds.) *Communiquer dans la langue de l'autre*, 153–172. Paris: Presses Universitaires de Vincennes.

Strömqvist, S. 1983. Lexical search games in adult second language acquisition. A model and some results. *Göteborg papers in Theoretical linguistics*, 44:2–25.

1984. Gaze aversion, code-switching, and search activities in route descriptions by six adult language learners. In *Proceedings from the Fourth Scandinavian Conference on Bilingualism, Uppsala*.

1989a. Chaotic phases in adult second language acquisition – evidence from speech planning and monitoring phenomena. *Göteborg Papers in Theoretical Linguistics*, 57:1–18.

1989b. Perspectives on second language acquisition in Scandinavia – with special reference to Sweden. *Göteborg Papers in Theoretical Linguistics*, 55:1–40.

Strömqvist, S. and Day, D. 1989. The development of discourse cohesion – an asymmetry between child L1 and adult L2 acquisition. *Göteborg Papers in Theoretical Linguistics*, 56:1–24.

Taranger, M.-C. 1983. A propos de l'utilisation de la vidéo dans la recherche sur l'apprentissage des langues secondes: réactions, choix et stratégies. In D. Véronique (ed.) *G.R.A.L./Papiers de travail*, 141–154. Aix-en-Provence: Université de Provence.

1986. Ratons-laveurs et 'nouvelles' techniques. L'utilisation de la vidéo dans une enquête linguistique. *Langue Française*, 71:87–100.

Taranger, M.-C. and Coupier, C. 1986. Recherche sur l'acquisition des langues secondes: approche du gestuel. In A. Giacomi and D. Véronique (eds.) *Acquisition d'une langue étrangère: Perspectives et Recherches*, 167–184. Aix-en-Provence: Université de Provence.

Trévise, A. 1984. Les malentendus: effets de loupe sur certains phénomènes d'acquisition d'une langue étrangère. In C. Noyau and R. Porquier (eds.) *Communiquer dans la langue de l'autre*, 130–152. Paris: Presses Universitaires de Vincennes.

1986. L'émergence et la spécification des marqueurs de prédication en langue 2. In A. Giacomi and D. Véronique (eds.) *Acquisition d'une langue étrangère: Perspectives et Recherches*, 365–382. Aix-en-Provence: Université de Provence.

1987. Toward an analysis of the (inter)language activity of referring to time in narratives. In C. Pfaff (ed.) *First and second language acquisition processes*, 225–251. Cambridge, Mass.: Newbury House Publishers.

Trévise, A., Perdue, C., and Deulofeu, J. 1991. Word order and discursive coherence in L2. In G. Appel and H.W. Dechert (eds.) *A case for psycholinguistic cases*, 163–176. Amsterdam: John Benjamins.

Trévise, A. and Porquier, R. 1986. Second language acquisition by adult immigrants: exemplified methodology. *Studies in Second Language Acquisition*, 8:265–275.

Vasseur, M.-T. 1987. La collaboration entre les partenaires dans les échanges entre locuteurs natifs et apprenants étrangers: formes, développement, variations. In H. Blanc, M. le Douaron, and D. Véronique (eds.) *S'approprier une langue étrangère*. Paris: Didier-Erudition.

1989a. La gestion de l'intercomprehension dans les échanges entre natifs et étrangers. In Association des Sciences du Langage (ed.) *L'interaction*, 36–55. Paris: Buscila.

1989b. Observables et réalité de l'acquisition d'une langue étrangère. *Langage et société*, 50/51:67–85.

1990a. Dialogue et acquisition des moyens d'expression de la temporalité. In G. Bernine and A. Giacalone Ramat (eds.) *La temporalità nell'acquisizione di lingue seconde*, 239–268. Milano: Franco Angeli.

1990b. Interaction et acquisition d'une langue étrangère en milieu social. *Le Français dans le Monde, recherches et applications*, 89/100. (Numeró spécial acquisition et utilisation d'une langue étrangère: L'approche cognitive.)

1990c. La communication entre étrangers et autochtones: stratégies pour se comprendre, stratégies pour apprendre. In F. François (ed.) *La communication inégale, heurs et malheurs de la communication*, 239–260. Genève: Delachaux et Niestlé.

Vasseur, M.-T. and Noyau, C. 1986. L'acquisition d'une langue étrangère par des adultes immigrés: un an d'analyses longitudinales. *Bulletin de la Fondation Maison des Sciences de l'Homme. MSH Informations*, 52:29–36.

Véronique, D. 1983a. Observations préliminaires sur 'li' dans l'interlangue d'Abdelmalek. In D. Véronique (ed.) *G.R.A.L./Papiers de travail*, 155–180. Aix-en-Provence: Université de Provence.

1983b. Présentation du projet européen. In D. Véronique (ed.) *G.R.A.L./Papiers de travail*, 1–15. Aix-en-Provence: Université de Provence.

1985a. Acquisition de la référence spatiale en français par des adultes marocains: observations à partir d'une enquête longitudinale. In D. Véronique (ed.) *G.R.A.L./Papiers de travail*, 135–167. Aix-en-Provence: Université de Provence.

1985b. De quelques aspects de l'apprentissage de la référence nominale en français. In D. Véronique (ed.) *G.R.A.L./Papiers de travail*, 97–134. Aix-en-Provence: Université de Provence.

1985c. Présentation. In D. Véronique (ed.) *G.R.A.L./Papiers de travail*, 7–18. Aix-en-Provence: Université de Provence.

1986. L'apprentissage du français par des travailleurs marocains et le processus de pidginisation et de créolisation. In A. Giacomi and D. Véronique (eds.) *Acquisition d'une langue étrangère: Perspectives et Recherches*, 559–584. Aix-en-Provence: Université de Provence.

1988. Des régularités linguistiques dans l'apprentissage d'une langue étrangère: Réflexions sur la règle d'"interlangue'. *Travaux du Cercle Linguistique D'Aix-en-Provence*, 6:163–180.

1989. Reference and discourse structure in the learning of French by adult Moroccans. In H. Dechert (ed.) *Current trends in European second language acquisition research*, 171–201. Clevedon and Philadelphia: Multilingual Matters.

1990a. Étude longitudinale de la construction d'un système d'expression de la temporalité en français par des apprenants arabophones. In G. Bernine and A. Giacalone Ramat (eds.) *La temporalità nell'acquisizione di lingue seconde*, 269–291. Milano: Franco Angeli.

1990b. L'apprentisage du français par des travailleurs arabophones et la genèse des créoles 'Français'. *Langage et Société*, 50/51:9–37.

Véronique, D. and Porquier, R. 1986. Acquisition de la référence spatiale en français par des adultes arabophones et hispanophones. *Langages*, 84:79–103.

Vion, R. 1985. Compréhension et comportement communicatif. In D. Véronique (ed.) *G.R.A.L./Papiers de travail*, 67–95. Aix-en-Provence: Université de Provence.

1986. L'acitivité de réformulation dans les échanges entre linguistes et apprenants non guidés (migrants marocains). In A. Giacomi and D. Véronique (eds.) *Acquisition d'une langue étrangère: Perspectives et Recherches*, 231–248. Aix-en-Provence: Université de Provence.

Vion, R. and Giacomi, A. 1987. Opérations métadiscursives et conduite du récit. La conduite du récit chez un migrant et un natif. *Encrages*, 18/19:169–180.

Vion, R. and Mittner, M. 1986. Activité de reprise et gestion des interactions en communication exolingue. *Langages*, 84:25–42.

Voionmaa, K. 1982. Aikuinen, uusi maa ja uusi kieli. In K. Sajavaara et al. (ed.) *Psycholinguistic papers III, 34*, 147–156. Jyväskylä.

1983a. Collecting and dealing with data in second language acquisition. In K. Häkkinen (ed.) *Publications of the Linguistic Association of Finland*, 59–77. Turku.

1983b. On interpersonal power and its relation to second language acquisition. In F. Karlsson (ed.) *Papers from the Seventh Scandinavian conference of linguistics*, 556–567. University of Helsinki, Helsinki.

1984. Lexical överföring och rationalitet. Paper presented to the 4th Scandinavian Conference on Bilingualism.

1986. Learning to express processes. A study on Aktionsarten in adult language learners. In P. Lilius and M. Saari (eds.) *Proceedings from the Sixth International Conference of Nordic and General Linguistics, Helsinki 86*, 459–470. Helsinki: Helsinki University Press.

1987. En studie av lexikal överföring hos vuxna spraakinlärare. In E. Wande et al. (ed.) *Aspects of bilingualism*, 313–324. Uppsala.

Weissenborn, J. 1984. La genèse de la référence spatiale en langue maternelle et en langue seconde: similarités et différences. In G. Extra and M. Mittner (eds.) *Studies in second language acquisition by adult immigrants*, 262–271. Tilburg: Tilburg University.

Author index

Subject index

.